The Thunder of Angels

The Montgomery Bus Boycott and the People Who Broke the Back of Jim Crow

DONNIE WILLIAMS with WAYNE GREENHAW

Lawrence Hill Books

Library of Congress Cataloging-in-Publication Data

Williams, Donnie, 1953–

The thunder of angels : the Montgomery bus boycott and the people who broke the back of Jim Crow / Donnie Williams with Wayne Greenhaw.—1st ed.

p. cm.

Includes bibliographical references and index.

ISBN 1-55652-590-7

1. African Americans—Civil rights—Alabama—Montgomery—History—20th century. 2. Civil rights movements—Alabama—Montgomery—History—20th century. 3. African American civil rights workers—Alabama—Montgomery—Biography. 4. Boycotts—Alabama—Montgomery—History—20th century. 5. Segregation in transportation—Alabama—Montgomery—History—20th century. 6. Montgomery (Ala.)—Race relations. 7. Montgomery (Ala.)—Biography. I. Greenhaw, Wayne, 1940- II. Title.

F334.M79N476 2006

323'.09761'4709045—dc22

2005008397

Cover design: Joan Sommers Design
Interior design: Monica Baziuk

Published by Lawrence Hill Books
An imprint of Chicago Review Press, Incorporated
814 North Franklin Street
Chicago, Illinois 60610
ISBN 1-55652-590-7
Printed in the United States of America

5   4   3   2   1

For Vivian Summerford Williams
and Shane, Wes, and Hayley Williams;
in memory of Hubert Summerford;
and for Sally Maddox Greenhaw

"And there appeared in the sky a multitude of angels, and the music they made was roaring thunder, and the righteous among them roared, and their lightning struck down the evil."

—an elderly black Montgomery minister describing the results of the bus boycott

Contents

Author's Note

I WROTE *The Thunder of Angels* because I believe that the full
story of what happened in the days and years building up to
Rosa Parks's refusal to give up her seat on a city bus on December 1, 1955, and of what happened during the turbulent year that
followed, has not been fully told. In particular, the role of Edgar
Daniel (E. D.) Nixon, an uneducated Pullman porter who organized the NAACP in Alabama while Martin Luther King, Jr.,
was still a child, has not been given its due.

After numerous deplorable incidents built up to Mrs. Parks's
action, the black men and women of Montgomery became so
infuriated that they stood up against the white power structure.
The bus boycott that ensued precipitated the founding of the
Montgomery Improvement Association (MIA)—the birth of
the civil rights movement.

My father-in-law saved the bus on which Parks took her his-
toric stand, inspiring me to delve into the history of the bus and
the boycott. My coauthor already knew most of the participants
as a reporter. Together, we hope we have illuminated a turning
point in our nation's history.

—DONNIE WILLIAMS

Preface

America's Bus

MY FATHER-IN-LAW, Roy Hubert Summerford, was a man's man, but he loved his daughter as much as any man could love a child. In my eyes, he was a gentle giant. Brought up in the blue-collar community of Chisholm in north Montgomery, Alabama, he was surrounded by racism most of his life. But, as far as I know, he never displayed a racist trait. Neither did he simply look the other way. On the other hand, he did not try to change that world. However, he did pass along something to his daughter Vivian, me, and his grandchildren that changed us all.

In the early 1970s Hubert read in the *Montgomery Advertiser* that the city bus company would soon scrap several buses that were no longer used to transport riders. From the gossip among the mechanics at the Montgomery bus station, he discovered that one of the buses was the vehicle on which Rosa Parks had been riding when she was arrested on December 1, 1955. As far as the other mechanics were concerned, it was good riddance to that bus; they were glad to know that it would soon be junked and forgotten forever.

Hubert Summerford had other ideas. Without saying a word to anyone, he went to the offices of the bus company, inquired about the buses, and told officials there that he needed some discarded equipment to use in his own private automotive shop. The officials at the bus company quoted him a price that he thought was fair. He paid for and took possession of his property. He dismantled the rollers that held the fabric signs drivers displayed as they headed toward different neighborhoods, announcing to the waiting riders where they would be going next. Hubert stored the fabric and rollers of bus 2857 in a box, which he put high up in a closet in his Garden Street house.

As far as a passerby could discern, the two old buses, which now served as tool sheds or storage rooms, were nothing out of the ordinary.

But Hubert Summerford knew the difference. Many times he took Vivian, me, and our boys, Shane and Wesley, out to the field and told us about bus 2857 and its importance to the history of Montgomery, Alabama, the South, the nation, and the world. Once when we were out there, Hubert ran his rough, gnarled fingers gently over the old, cracked cushions of the vehicle. He looked me in the eye and said, "Donnie, always take care of this bus."

On a number of occasions, he warned us against making the bus's true history known too soon. He knew that if people discovered that bus 2857, which had been carrying Rosa Parks on the day she was arrested, was sitting in a field in rural north Montgomery County, some would become so inflamed that they would want to destroy it. The time was still too close to the days of church bombings and daily demonstrations, when Jim Crow ruled the courts, the schools, and everyday social life. "You will know when the time is right," he said. Later, after

Hubert died and my wife inherited the bus, I decided to prepare for that day, and I began to research the history of the bus
and the Montgomery bus boycott.

I became a regular in the first-floor reference room of the
Alabama Department of Archives and History. The librarians
there grew accustomed to my dogged investigations. I dug out
articles, diaries, photographs, and even transcripts of the Montgomery Circuit Court trial of Martin Luther King, Jr. In my
own quiet, offhanded way, always trying to be polite and understanding, I hounded the keepers of records outside the confines
of libraries. I tracked down bus drivers, policemen, bus riders,
black people, and white people who had been involved in the
events that took place in the mid-1950s.

More than ten years after the death of my father-in-law,
Vivian and I, along with our children, decided the time was
right to sell the bus. In September 2001 an article in the *Wall
Street Journal* announced that the original Rosa Parks bus
would be available in an Internet auction in October. Curators
from the Henry Ford Museum and Greenfield Village in Dearborn, Michigan, expressed interest and began detailed exami-
nations of the bus to ensure its authenticity. At the end of the
auction, the museum owned the bus.

As soon as the purchase was made, a team of restorers went
to work. They carefully swept out the dust and pine needles
that had settled on the floor of the old bus. They vacuumed the
rusty interior. With dry brushes, they extracted every speck of
dust from the crevices. The vintage diesel engine that Hubert
had meticulously taken from the chassis was once again
installed. The wheel wells and threads of the original tires were
filled with the red clay that is so distinctively Montgomery and
central Alabama. Then the bus was lifted gingerly and placed
with great care onto a truck that would carry it north.

When it arrived in Dearborn, bus 2857 was proudly displayed. Like a prideful old warrior, it stood aloof, head held

high, untouchable. Among those who walked around the relic and gazed at it from behind the red velvet rope that separated it from the onlookers was sixty-three-year-old, Georgia-born James Phelps, a Detroit resident who brought seven members of his family to the reception. "You got to know where you came from in order to know where you are going," he said. "I used to ride segregated streetcars in Georgia. And now, to sit here and see this, well—" His voice broke and he shook his head.

For the most part, people looked at the bus with quiet reverence. Few spoke. Hundreds walked slowly in single file around the bus. Flashbulbs flickered, recording the busted-out taillights, the flabby old tires, the scratches and nicks—all scars of time.

Renovation continued until the bus was once again in the same condition as it was that night of December 1, 1955, when Rosa Parks stepped aboard, sat down, and, two blocks later, refused to give up her seat. Finally, after it was totally revitalized, the bus was declared a national treasure, putting it in the same category as the Liberty Bell and the Declaration of Independence. As such, it has been viewed by hundreds of thousands of people every year—people who gaze at it and relive that moment in time when precious freedom began its march across America in the form of the civil rights movement. It has become known to many as America's bus, and my family and I are proud to have been a part of making it a symbol of real freedom.

This book tells the story not just of bus 2857, but of the people in Montgomery, Alabama, who rode the city buses when Jim Crow ruled; and of how, when they stopped riding them, they changed the world.

—DONNIE WILLIAMS

Preface

A Personal History

WHEN ROSA PARKS was arrested in Montgomery, I was fifteen years old and living in Tuscaloosa, ninety miles northwest of Alabama's capital city. During the previous year, Autherine Lucy had attempted to enroll as the first black student at the University of Alabama in my hometown. When she actually enrolled, three months after Rosa Parks's arrest, white people took to the streets. Mobs rioted on University Avenue and around the flagpole downtown. Photographs of angry white students shaking their fists covered page one of the *Tuscaloosa News*, where I worked as a part-time sports reporter, putting together Friday-night three-paragraph stories about area high school football games. Also on page one, in a black-bordered box, was *Tuscaloosa News* publisher Buford Boone's editorial, in which he begged local citizens to remain calm and to avoid violence. Today it seems mild. But in those days, the clearheaded thinking and bravery of the editorial made the blood of white Tuscaloosa boil—and brought home a Pulitzer Prize.

It was not until nine years later that I actually witnessed history in the making at the end of the Selma-to-Montgomery march. On the night before the final day, the marchers were met by demonstrators from around the world in the broad field beyond St. Jude Catholic Church, where the Mobile highway met West Fairview Avenue. As I traversed the crowd, weaving in and out of tents, blankets spread on the ground, and people sitting in clusters, Peter, Paul and Mary, the long-standing anthem singers of protesters in the 1960s, lifted most to their feet with "If I Had a Hammer," "Blowin' in the Wind," and "Tell It on the Mountain." Sammy Davis, Jr., sang "What Kind of Fool Am I?" Pete Seeger tore up a flat-top banjo while singing "This Land Is Your Land." Joan Baez sang "Joe Hill," the haunting ballad about the death of a labor union organizer. And Harry Belafonte did several of his all-time favorite hymns, then called all the performers on to the stage to join hands and sing "We Shall Overcome." As the song's crescendo rang through the night air, the entire crowd rocked back and forth. We were all brothers and sisters that night, swaying together to that rousing spiritual of togetherness.

Out of the crowd I heard a voice say, "Let's go to the Durrs." I had no idea what it meant, but I followed. At an old frame house that had been divided into apartments, I followed a new friend from Brown University inside. As we moved down the hall, I began spotting people whose faces I recognized from magazines or television shows: the historian C. Vann Wood-ward; *New Yorker* columnist and jazz writer Nat Hentoff; and Pete Seeger himself, a tall, skinny guy with a long face and flam-ing red hair, talking animatedly with a movie star whose name I couldn't recall but whose films I'd seen. The entire place was a sea of noise, out of which I heard phrases like "but all people have rights" and "it's been a long, hard fight, but the battle is yet to be won" and "in the end, we will overcome."

The kitchen was as crowded as the rest of the house. There, a woman who seemed a head taller than others barked orders. Those around her did as she wished. It was obvious that she was the leader. It was not until later that I was introduced to Virginia Durr, who, in the midst of all the chaos asked, "Now, honey, where'd your people come from?"

I was swept by the flow of the crowd into a living room where a dozen people sat on the floor. Sitting in a straw-backed rocking chair was a slender man in gold-rimmed glasses, smoking an unfiltered cigarette and speaking in a soft Southern twang. He spoke about his own problems of coming to terms with his strong Southern roots and of making friends with his conscience over the black-white issue. As he spoke, those gathered around him leaned in to hear every single syllable of his voice. I soon learned that Clifford Durr was that kind of man; he didn't speak unless he had something to say, and when he said it, you wanted to hear the precise words. It was the first of many evenings in the Durr household when Cliff would talk and I would listen.

Later that summer, after I became a reporter for the *Alabama Journal*, Montgomery's afternoon daily, I drove fourteen miles northwest to the Durrs' country home in Elmore County for Sunday dinner. The place they called the Pea Level sat on a knoll beyond an orchard. Here Cliff Durr had built room after room with his own hands, adding to the original cabin he had inherited along with several acres that bordered a small, rocky creek. The house was plain and a bit odd-shaped, following Cliff's own creative design as he extemporaneously planned each next phase of construction. I sat in the shade of a scuppernong arbor, sipped red wine, and listened to the conversation. I learned that spirited conversation filled any visit to the

Durrs—especially those that occurred on Pea Level Sundays—
and I always felt especially privileged to be asked to join them
here.

As the fragrant smells of a pot of spaghetti sauce wafted
from the kitchen window through the heavy afternoon air, a
white-haired man with coal-black skin sat at the end of the rus-
tic table. I had met E. D. Nixon before but had never heard him
say much. Answering a question, he now said, "We had to stay
with 'em to keep the whole community focused. All of us did
it together: Reverend King, Coach Lewis, Mrs. Parks and Mrs.
Robinson, Reverend Abernathy. I could go on and on. Folks had
to *believe* to make it work, Lord knows." His big head was held
high, his features strong in the dappled sunlight blinking
through scuppernong leaves.

Out here in the country, folks talked slowly and deliber-
ately. Out here, people listened. In the years to follow, I would
listen to many tales told by Edgar Daniel Nixon, whom I
learned to respect with solemn appreciation. Like his friend
Cliff Durr, he was a man who did not speak unless he had something to say. For me, he would come to represent the quiet dignity, the burning drive, and the powerful force that embodied
the civil rights movement. On that afternoon, sitting outdoors
under the arbor, I listened, enjoying the words.

Nearby, stretching his long legs out from his lean body,
Frank Minis Johnson, Jr., the federal district judge who first
ruled, in 1956, on Alabama laws requiring segregation of races
on public transportation, said, "To me, it was a matter of the
U.S. Constitution. I believed then, and I believe now: the local
laws requiring segregation of races on *any* public conveyance
were unconstitutional." Johnson carved off a slice of Red Man
tobacco, placed it between his teeth, and began to chew in slow
motion, then spat into a nearby flower bed. He added, deliber-
ately, "The U.S. Constitution is very clear on that," as if to dot
an exclamation mark. Johnson's flat, hill-country twang was a

sound akin to what I imagined Abraham Lincoln would sound
like, and his words were always chosen with great care. On his
desk in the federal courthouse in downtown Montgomery he
kept a Lincoln quote: "I'll do the very best I know how—the
very best I can; and I mean to keep doing so until the end. If
the end brings me out all right, what is said against me won't
amount to anything. If the end brings me out wrong, ten angels
swearing I was right would make no difference."

From the kitchen, carrying a large wooden bowl filled with
tossed salad, stepped the large woman with the large voice, Virginia Durr. Her voice a bit screechy and loud, she said, "But
Frank, if it was so clear, why did so many people interpret it so
differently for so long?"

"Well, Virginia," Judge Johnson said, bending slightly to
spit. "They either chose not to read the text or to look in
another direction. They didn't attack it straight on."

"Nobody cared," E. D. Nixon growled in his guttural
baritone.

"What'd you say, Mr. Nixon?" Virginia asked, plopping the
salad onto the table.

"I said, 'Nobody cared.' They didn't want to care, until we
made 'em. We pushed their face into the slop jar, and only then
did they see that it was sour and rancid and ought to be
emptied."

Several people gazed questioningly into Nixon's face.

In his old gravel-rumbling voice, he said, "Folks will take
what's given to 'em, even if it's slop-jar food, until they have to
face the fact that they're eatin' feces. When they become aware
of that fact, they're alarmed—even shocked. And when you tell
'em, 'If you don't throw it away and demand something good
and nourishing and wholesome, you ain't ever gonna get it,'
then—sometimes—they act. That's what happened to the black
folks through the years. They'd been treated like dirt so long
they got to thinking it was all right. You've got to *feel* the hurt

deep down before you respond. You've got to see the light at
the end of the tunnel. If you don't, you'll turn around and run
away from the struggle. But if you see the light and it gets
brighter and brighter—and you know that pretty soon you
might come out in Jericho, or some place just as fine—then
you'll keep on trudging toward that goal. All we did was open
their eyes where they could see the light. Then we kept tellin'
'em over and over, it's right out there—just over yonder hill.
Just keep on climbin' and pretty soon you'll get there."

When he finished speaking, everybody at the table was star-
ing into his big chiseled face with its broad grin. He'd been in
the front lines of the battle for civil rights. He'd fought the
fight and was still fighting it. He felt deeply the strong emotions he expressed in his dirt-poor, bone-deep language. It was
not until many years later, after listening to hour after hour of
his talk and after hearing others who had been there, that I
learned the true depth of his world-class leadership in the early
days of the struggle.

Sometime in the mid-1970s my wife Sally and I picked up Mr.
Nixon at his house and carried him out to the Pea Level. We
listened to his deep gravel voice all the way out to the country
place, where we were met by Chicago journalist and oral historian Studs Terkel, who was staying with the Durrs. As it
turned out, Terkel was interviewing Cliff, Virginia, and Mr.
Nixon for his radio program and an upcoming book. Sally and
I sat back in a corner and observed, and later we told each other
how privileged we had been to witness such a quiet event as
that night of talk.

In the 1980s I had lunch at a posh restaurant in Washington, D.C., with my friend Howell Raines, who was then bureau
chief of the *New York Times*. Howell and I had been friends
since he was a graduate student at the University of Alabama

and I was a young reporter. To our table stepped a tall, almost regal black man. I recognized him immediately as Vernon Jordan, president of the National Urban League. He and Howell exchanged pleasantries, and Howell introduced me as a writer from Montgomery. Jordan spoke fondly of my town and his friends there, then asked if I knew E. D. Nixon. I told him briefly about my acquaintance with Mr. Nixon. He smiled and said, "You ought to go home and write the real story of the bus boycott and tell about the great leadership of E. D. Nixon. He's the real hero, and the father of the civil rights movement, but nobody has ever told his story."

Through much of the late 1960s and 1970s I took breakfast almost every morning with Joe Azbell, who in 1968 was George C. Wallace's public relations adviser to his third-party candidacy for the presidency. Azbell came up with the slogans Stand Up for America and Send Them a Message. On the surface it seemed that Azbell, who had become a neighborhood columnist for the weekly *Montgomery Independent*, would have always been on the opposite side of the fence from my other friends. However, like many people in most communities, there were not-so-secret facts in his past that showed a different side of the man and his profession. From many personal encounters with him and with E. D. Nixon through the years, I learned about their friendship, which had started in the Jim Crow days and had grown deeper and deeper through the years.

When Donnie Williams called me at the end of the summer of 2002, telling me with rousing enthusiasm about his selling of the Rosa Parks bus and about his research into the birth of the civil rights movement, I chuckled and thought: *I've heard all this before.* However, Donnie would not be turned away. We met and talked. I sat with him in his tiny, cramped office overlooking his grocery store and meat market in north Montgomery.

I watched as customers—most of them black women—came and went. I saw how they acted toward him, and he toward them: each with a great deal of respect toward the other. When he told me about the people he'd interviewed, explaining how he'd gone back to them time and again to ferret out new facts and bits and pieces of information, I listened with respect.

I was a reporter in Montgomery for a number of years. After I left the *Alabama Journal* in the mid-1970s, I became Jimmy Carter's Alabama press secretary during the 1976 election. Later, with two partners, I bought *Alabama Magazine* and was its editor and publisher for four years. Off and on, I wrote columns for the *Alabama Journal* and the *Montgomery Advertiser* through the late 1980s. In 1993, after he became governor, Jim Folsom appointed me to his cabinet as director of the Alabama Bureau of Tourism and Travel. When Donnie called me, my fifteenth book, *The Long Journey*, a novel set in 1919 north Alabama, was about to be published. I was not interested in writing another long nonfiction book.

But Donnie was very persuasive. He is an interesting young man who has become dedicated to the truth and to the history of his community and its position in the world. He was convinced—and he convinced me—that the true, inside story of the bus boycott had never been told. According to most historians and journalists who had viewed the subject, the civil rights movement leapt full-blown onto the stage in the days after Rosa Parks refused to give up her seat on the Montgomery city bus. They failed to look at the years building up to that fateful night in 1955, and they overlooked the actions of the man who had been setting the stage for years and years, through one small struggle after another, until the right moment was upon him. Too many times before now, E. D. Nixon's role in the birth of the civil rights movement has been ignored or downplayed.

I began putting together a history of people I had known personally since my first days in the town once known as the

Cradle of the Confederacy. I uncovered years-old interviews conducted at Cliff and Virginia Durr's country home in the toe hills of the Appalachians, and I found people I had not spoken with since I was a young reporter covering city court. I remembered old Ku Klux Klan members who had never been discreet about their identities or their overt racism, found them in their current homes, and rode with them through Montgomery's streets while they talked about a time fifty years ago. I remembered Joe Azbell and E. D. Nixon telling me about a young black soldier riding on a bus in August 1950 and the tragic circumstances of that ride.

Listening to all of these voices resonate in my memory, I realized that I had known most of the people who had been responsible for the bus boycott. Not only were they important to the changing of the South, but they were also critical to the formation of the New South of the twenty-first century.

By assisting Donnie in the researching and writing of this book, I felt I had the opportunity to help tell the true, behind-the-scenes story of the birth of the civil rights movement in Montgomery, based on the words of the people who lived it. *The Thunder of Angels* is that story.

—WAYNE GREENHAW

No.		Name								
5	R-R-R	Wesley Tolbert	(P)	21	24	OI	—	CM	co	✓
064	R-R-R	E. H. Ligon	(P)	21	1	aAa	14	CM	co	✓
				BC	25	W MO	18			
7065	R-R-R	Charlie Polk Jr	(P)	21	9	U OO	18	CM	co	✓
				BC		U	15			
7066	R-R	P. M. Blair	(P)	21	17	W I	9	CM	co	✓
7067	R-R	Ida Mae Caldwell	(P)	21	2	U OO	14	CF	co	✓
				BC	1	Ht	16			
7068	R-Rev.	M. C. Cleveland	(P)	21	29	I	14	CM	co	✓
				BC						
7069	R-R	Jimmie L. Lowe	(P)	21	20	OI	17	CF	co	✓
				BC	1	TU	8			
7070	R-R	Eretta F. Adair	(P)	21	1	LU	6	CF	co	✓
				BC	1	IM	9			
7071	R	Frank L. Taylor	(P)	21	20	W M	13	CM	co	✓
				BC	21	W M	14			
7072	R	Tom Parks	(P)	21	11au	I	2	CM	co	✓
				BC	10	U X	10			
7073	R-R	Mathew Kennedy	(P)	21	27	IM	20	CM	co	✓
7074	R-R	B. D. Lambert	(P)	21	11	OI	20	CM	co	✓
				BC	32	IO	16			
7075	R	J. H. Baker	(P)	21	28	OI	—	CM	co	✓
				BC	27	W 8	—			
7076	R	Sam Barnett	(P)	21	6	U O	16	CM	co	✓
				BC	1	R 8	15			
7077	R	John H. Garrison	(P)	21	1	U	7	CM	co	✓
				BC	2	tI	4			
7078	O	J. N. King	(P)	21	17	MO	13	CM	co	✓
7079	R	Henry Williams	(P)	21	11	O	15	CM	co	✓
				BC	31	IM	17			
7080	O	Audrey Belle Langford	(P)	21	28	MM	16	CF	co	✓
7081	R	Lottie Green Varner	(P)	21	5	UA	8	CF	co	✓
				BC	13	R O	8			
7082	R	C. N. French (Rev)	(P)	21	27	W O	9	CM	co	✓
				BC	31	IO	21			
7083	R-R	W. H. Johnson	(P)	21	28	MI	20	CM	co	✓
				BC	9	U OO	—			
7084	R	J. C. Smith	(P)	21	22	U OO	17	CM	co	✓
				BC	25	W I	14			
7085	R+R	George Hill	(P)	21	18	U OO	10	CM	co	✓
7086	R	Arthur Bibbins	(P)	21	1	U II	9	CM	co	✓
				BC	1	TI	11			
7087	R	Eddie Bradford	(P)	21	2	U	11	CM	co	✓
				BC	31	IO	22			
7088	R	P. E. Conley	(P)	21	28	OM	27	CM	co	✓
				BC	3	U OI	7			
7089	R+R	M. L. King Jr	(P)	21	13	U OI	4	CM	co	✓
				BC	2	U OO	15			
7090	R	Rev. H. H. Johnson	(P)	21	1	U II	16	CM	co	✓
				BC	1	U II	9			
7091	R+R	Edward Williams	(P)	21	9	U II	9	CM	co	✓
				BC	1	U OO	16			
7092	R-R-R	Henry G. McClain	(P)	21	31	IO	7	CM	co	✓
7093	R	Louis Christburg	(P)	21	28	OO	15	CM	co	✓
				BC	3	IO	19			
7094	R	Mose W. Richburg	(P)	21	28	O	20	CM	co	✓
				BC	9	R OI	15			
7095	R	Calvin Varner	(P)	21	1	U OO	—	CM	co	✓
7096	R	L. C. Walker	(P)	21	17	W I	12	CM	co	

The Thunder of Angels

No.	Name									
7099	R. B. Binion	P	21	1	R	12	CM	✓		
7100	Fuddie Morris	P	21	5	rAa	7	CM	✓		
7101	George H Jordan	P	21	1	O	15	CO	✓		
7102	J. C. Sanders	P	16	4	II	11	CM	$100 + cost	4-6-56	FB
7103	John Green Hill	P	21	1	aAa	16	CM	✓		
7104	Willie James Kemp	P	21	3	O	11	CM	✓		
7105	Rev R. W. Hilson	P	21	19	O	20	CO	✓		
7106	Jackson Knox	P	21	1	LOI	6	CM	✓		
7107	D C Sanders									
7108	Sellie Bryant	P	16	2	W 80	14	CM	13 months Prob	3-8-56	FB
7109	Edward Jackson	P	6	5	H 00	17	CM	2 years Prob	5-31-56	FB
7110	Richard S. Jordan	P	21	1	aH	13	CM	✓		
7111	Willie Joe Shackleford	P	2	17	W 00	13	CM	Not guilty by jury	6-5-56	FB
7112	Rebecca Tell	P	4	18	H 00	14	CF	Nol Pros		
7113	Walter						14	CO	Nol Pros		
7114	O'Neal Warren		10				WM	Nol Pros		
7115	Floyd Wanner Jr		5	13	R 00	18	CITY	13 months	3-29-56	FB
7116	Frank Hintz		5	1	Rr	5	CITY	13 months	3-29-56	FB
7117	Donald Riley		5	32	IO	—	WM	13 months	3-29-56	FB
7118	Frank Martin		3	9	T	13	CITY	13 months	3-29-56	FB
7119	Henry Albert Goodwin		7+	5	Ha	15	WM	2 years 1st case	7-13-56	FB
7120	Hershel Goodwin	P	7+	1	Tt	5	WM	Released by juvenile		
7121	Henry Holley		10	1	aH2a		CITY	13 months	5-31-56	FB
7122	Richard Pinkston		4	1	H IO	12	CM	6 months 52 da cost		FB
7123	George Giles		4	1	aHa2a		CITY	2 years Prob	5-31-56	FB
7124	Rhondebelle Martin		3	W	O	20	WF	Death	6-6-56	FB
7125	Rev. A. Edward Banks	21	1	R IO	17	CM	Rev. + Reland		
7126	Edward G. Meads	P	60	1	H IO	8	WM	2 years Prob	4-6-56	FB
7127	Clarence Adams	P	16	12	M	12	CM	$100 + cost		FB
7128	Eli Washington	P	16	19	H II	9	CM	Nolle Pros		FB
7129	Mary Ellen Crouse		6	1	OM	12	WF	13 months	4-13-56	
7130	Edward Jackson	P	16	17	R 00	15	CM	$75 + cost	3-30-56	FB
7131	Tom Carr	P	16	1	H 00	8	CM	$100 + cost	2-30-56	FB
7132	Mary L. Carr	P	16	20	M	17	CF	$200 + cost	3-30-56	

Before the Beginning

By August 1950, nothing of any great significance had happened in Montgomery, Alabama, for more than eighty years.

Back in February 1861, white politicians from all over the South had gathered in the small town. They met in the Senate chambers of the state capitol and formed the Confederate States of America. They inaugurated a president and began talking about fighting the United States. Hearing the echoes of such talk, men from all over the South poured into Montgomery, doubling the town's white population of eight thousand within several weeks. It was not long before the politicians declared war against the United States. Four years later, in April 1865, Union troops marched into Montgomery, burned thousands of bales of cotton, bivouacked for a few days, and left. Since then the city had been relatively quiet. Serving as a reminder of its history were two ominous large rocks—one on the eastern edge of town, next to the highway to Atlanta, and another on the southwestern end, next to the road to Selma. On each were the words "Cradle of the Confederacy."

In 1950 suburban streets were slow-moving, lazy places. Especially during the hot, humid, muggy afternoons of summertime. Especially in Old Cloverdale, where streets curled up and down subtly undulating hills without pattern. Unlike the rectangular grids of downtown, streets in Cloverdale followed contours of slight ridges and narrow valleys.

Sounds of children playing in a shaded side yard carried through the half-century-old subdivision. As water from a hose poured over them, the children splashed and giggled, happy to be wet, if not cool. After long naps in the late afternoon, women took lingering third baths. They worked hard to stay cool. They waited quietly for the men to come home from jobs downtown, where they tended darkened shops beneath overhead fans or worked in offices with open windows, trying to catch a breeze from the river. In a little while, Lucy Martin would call her children, who would grumpily comply with her command to come in and get ready for dinner. She would meet them at the back door with towels and guide them toward the bathroom.

The fragrant scent of cooking—fried chicken draining on the morning edition of the *Montgomery Advertiser*, turnip greens and snap beans in pots, potato salad under cellophane wrapping, and corn bread in the oven—wafted through the heavy air of the high-ceilinged, large, dark rooms in the over-sized Tudor-style house where Mattie Johnson had worked as a maid for as long as she could remember. She was forty years old and had been a teenager when she took her mama's place. At first she had worked for Mrs. Martin's mother-in-law, but she came to this house when Lucy married Steven Martin and they moved back from Birmingham, where he had attended business college. Mattie Johnson couldn't remember the exact year she took the job, but it was a job she was glad to have. Sometimes she felt like the Martins were her second family. And sometimes she looked forward to her bus ride back home to Bogge Homa (rhymes with Oklahoma).

It had been a long day. Mattie started early, arriving by bus before seven. She made coffee for Mr. Martin and squeezed fresh orange juice for the children. She cooked eggs, bacon, biscuits, and a pot of grits. By late morning she had dusted and swept and made the beds. After Lucy Martin bathed a second time and went downtown to have lunch with her husband, a little before noon, Mattie put peanut butter and jelly sandwiches together for the kids. And after the children went next door to play with friends, Mattie sat down at the kitchen table and had a dinner of warmed-over roast from last night and a cold biscuit from breakfast. Satisfied that she didn't need to wash and iron until Monday, Mattie began preparing the evening's supper.

In the heat of the kitchen, where a floor fan stirred warm air, Mattie finished cooking shortly after Lucy Martin climbed out of her third tub bath of the day. When she heard Lucy moving about the innards of the house, Mattie slipped into the tiny bathroom beyond the laundry room. She looked at herself in the mirror. The wet half-moons beneath her arms showed the end-of-day toil that she felt deep down in her bones. Slowly she unbuttoned the blouse of her uniform and pulled it off, dropping it into a hamper. She would add it to the wash on Monday. After washing as completely as she could manage, she put on the outfit she'd worn to work: a simple skirt and a short-sleeved print top. She met Lucy Martin in the kitchen, where they said good-bye for the weekend.

Mattie walked out the back door while Lucy called to her children. The black woman, who never entered or exited through the front door of the Martin house unless she was sweeping the stoop, trudged through the hot afternoon toward the corner where she would catch her bus. She walked along the curb looking at the beauty of her surroundings. She could not help but compare it to the small wooden houses of her neighborhood of Bogge Homa. Her house, where she'd raised three children, was about one-fourth the size of the Martin place.

The rooms were small. There was no underpinning. They were lucky; they got indoor plumbing just before World War II. Some of the houses in the low-lying bottom land between Cloverdale and downtown still didn't have indoor facilities. In the 1930s, when the Great Depression was strangling everybody, Mattie Johnson had been proud to have a job, even one that paid just a dollar a day.

The lawns in Old Cloverdale were mostly sloping, broad, green expanses dotted with pine and oak and dogwood and an occasional magnolia. Yards were coiffed with neatly planned circles of azaleas that bloomed bright red and pink in February, clusters of camellias that sported big round red or white flowers in March, and banks of multicolored roses that sparkled at the first hint of summer. In her little yard in Bogge Homa, Mattie kept a small bed of seasonal flowers. Like the house, it was small but well groomed. An old, gnarled crepe myrtle bush in the center of the grassless yard had never bloomed.

Mattie Johnson stood on the corner and waited in the sweltering heat. After a few minutes she saw the yellow and green city bus struggling sluggishly around the curve onto Cloverdale Road.

When bus number 2857 rolled off the General Motors Corporation assembly plant in Pontiac, Michigan, in 1948, no one cheered. There was no celebration. Politicians didn't break champagne bottles at its inauguration. This diesel-powered bus was simply Type TDH 3610-1132, patterned after the 1936-production short model, with seats for only thirty-six people. It was twenty-nine feet long, nine feet high, and eight feet wide.

In Montgomery the bus traveled the Cloverdale route. It followed a circular pattern from Court Square Fountain in the middle of downtown, where the area's original two communities—Alabama Town and New Philadelphia—had grown together at an artesian well in 1819 to form the city named for General Richard Montgomery, a native New Yorker who became a Revolutionary War hero when he was killed in the battle of Quebec. The bus moved west on Montgomery Street, south on Cleveland Avenue through a black residential area to Fairview Avenue, then east toward the country club. At Cloverdale Road it turned north through an upscale white neighborhood to Norman Bridge Road, veered onto Decatur Street, then traveled north through a poor black residential section historically known as Bogge Homa, where, years earlier, cotton-wagon drivers had camped when they brought their harvested crop into town. Then the bus climbed Centennial Hill to South Jackson Street, where more affluent black families lived. It circled the north side of the state capitol, where the government of the Confederate States of America had been organized less than one hundred years earlier. In front of the capitol steps, where Jefferson Davis was inaugurated president of the Confederacy in 1861, the bus turned westward down Goat Hill on Dexter Avenue, toward the fountain where its journey had begun. The regular driver had to shift gears so often on the circuitous Cloverdale Route that he'd complained to the company officials, who ordered that the bus's transmission be changed from straight shift to automatic.

A similar bus on the Cloverdale Route stopped with a jolt a few feet in front of Mattie Johnson. She stepped up the front steps, pulling herself toward the white driver, whom she recognized from her many trips on this line. With a cheerful greeting, Mattie dropped her dime into the coin slot next to the driver's seat.

The driver glanced at her and grumbled something unintelligible.

Then Mattie stepped back down onto the steaming pavement, went to the rear door, pulled herself onto the bus again, and settled into a seat next to an open window in the rear.

As the bus started, its gears catching, the vehicle belched diesel smoke. Fumes drifted up through the window and stung her nostrils.

She sat back and closed her eyes. At least she was off her feet. At least she was sitting on the bus. At least she was going home.

She heard the brakes of the bus and felt the vehicle slowing.

When she opened her eyes, she saw her friend Alma Franklin standing at the corner of Park Avenue and Cloverdale Road, waiting for the bus. At least she would have someone to talk to on the way home.

Alma was loaded down with clean laundry she was taking home to iron for Mrs. Ashcroft and her family. With shoulders stooped and head drooping, Alma pulled herself up into the front of the bus. She lugged the sack of clothes up the two steps. She clutched a dime between thumb and forefinger and dropped it into the slot.

Turning, Alma glimpsed her friend sitting in the rear. Then Alma carried her laundry back down the steps, moved to the rear, where the door opened with a *whish*, and climbed up and found a seat across the aisle from Mattie. She sat next to a window and plopped the sack of clean clothes onto the seat beside her.

After Alma mopped sweat from her high forehead, she caught Mattie's eye again and grinned broadly and shook her head. "It was a long, hard one," she muttered.

It seemed like the bus had no sooner begun its climb up a gentle knoll when its brakes caught and it wheezed to a stop again. Both women reached out automatically to grab hold of the chrome rail in front of them.

They watched as an auburn-haired girl in a fresh yellow dress and white patent-leather slippers danced up the steps, dropped her dime, and slid onto a seat directly behind the driver. To the black women, thirteen-year-old Jane Ann

Thompson appeared to defy nature. Fresh and crisp, she looked as though she'd just stepped out of an icy refrigerator.

The daughter of a vice president at the First National Bank, Jane Ann glanced around and flashed a smile and spoke to the women who worked for her neighbors. She had been in and out of the Martin and Ashcroft houses all of her life. She was sure she had known Mattie and Alma all that time. Today was her day to ride the bus downtown, where she and her father would have a hot dog supper at Chris's and an ice cream soda at Liggett's Drug Store. Both places were Montgomery institutions. Chris Katechis had arrived in Montgomery thirty-some-odd years ago as a little boy from an island off Greece who could speak not a word of English. He worked for his uncle for years then built his own hot dog stand, which featured his own sauce made of chili, onions, sauerkraut, and herbs. Liggett's had an electronic banner around the exterior over its doors on Court and Montgomery streets. It flashed the latest news in the same way that the *New York Times* did in larger lights over Times Square in New York. On election nights, Jane Ann's father brought her to Court Square, and they sat next to the elaborate fountain watching for the latest results in Liggett's moving lights.

On this day, however, after their early evening together, her father would drive them home after twilight. It was a pleasant weekly summer routine that both father and daughter enjoyed. Jane Ann's mother used the opportunity to visit and have supper with her elderly mother before joining her husband and daughter back home after dark.

Jane Ann Thompson was not only pretty, she was a happy, secure girl. She enjoyed the simple, gracious, often glorious life of Old Cloverdale. She was not bothered with problems of growing up. An only child, her father and mother protected her. Nothing was complicated in her world. Several afternoons every week during the summertime, Mama would take her and several friends to the country club about a mile down Fairview Avenue, where they would meet other friends and school chums around the swimming pool.

In the summer of 1950, Jane Ann did not fret about the future. In another month she would start Cloverdale Junior High, and two years down the road she would be a freshman at Sidney Lanier High School with all of the other white students. Her father had already promised that some day she would be presented as a belle at the Blue-Gray Ball, an annual cotillion. She would wear a beautiful full-skirted gown with layer upon layer of petticoats, and she would carry a matching frilly parasol as she sashayed down the aisle while her father and mother's friends delighted in her joy. Her older cousin, Martha Louise, had been presented the year before last. Jane Ann had listened to her mother's description of the splendid evening and dreamed of her own time to glory under the spotlights while the orchestra played "Stars Fell on Alabama" and she would be swept around the dance floor in the arms of a handsome young gentleman.

As the bus made its way along the route, Mattie Johnson told Alma that she was looking forward to seeing her children and being with them over the weekend. Her oldest, Willie James, Jr., was home from Atlanta, where he worked as a mechanic with his uncle, her husband's younger brother. The middle boy, Jasper, was still in high school, and Mattie prayed that he would finish. Unlike his older brother, Jasper seemed to be gifted with book sense; the boy seemed to try hard, and Mattie tried to praise his efforts in the right sort of way, hoping it would take and that he would make a successful life, which she knew was hard at best for a black boy in the South. And her youngest, Tallera, named for Mattie's great-aunt, whom she had adored before the elderly woman died of a heart attack nearly twelve years ago, was the shining light in Mattie's eyes. Tallera was not only pretty, she was also sweet and gentle, and she loved her Mo'dear in the same heartfelt manner that her namesake had loved Mattie when she was a little girl.

"I got a heap of ironing ahead of me when I get home," Alma said wearily. Her children were younger than Mattie's. Like Mattie's, her husband had left some years ago, heading up north when he found life too unbearable in the South. *Life might be hard down here*, Alma often thought, *but it's home.* Like Mattie, she had been born and raised in Montgomery. Her folks all lived here, or near here. Some lived on farms in Lowndes County, about fifteen miles southwest of the Cradle of the Confederacy marker on that side of town. They were share-croppers, and they made gardens behind their little unpainted houses. Sometimes they came into town on weekends. Sometimes she visited them down there. Alma didn't think she'd like farm life. When she was a child, she had spent summers on relatives' farms, but she was always glad to get back to Montgomery. She liked having a job and regular wages, even though the work got her down in the back and she had to tote chores home with her now and then. It wasn't as bad as having to pick cotton all day, every day, not knowing how much the boss would pay for that heavy sack that had to be dragged from row to row until it was filled to the brim. Alma remembered doing that work one summer when she was a girl. She remembered the midday sweat, the strap of the sack cutting into her shoulder, the weight growing heavier and heavier until she could hardly drag it another step. And she remembered the scant wage at the end of a long day, looking down at the meager coins in her brown palm. If it hadn't been so cheaply sad, she would have laughed at the absurdity of the situation. The money she made was barely enough to buy an RC Cola and a MoonPie and have a few cents left over to take home to her Auntie Sue Ellen. No, sir, that life was not for her; she'd take cleaning and cooking, washing and ironing. Mrs. Ashcroft was good to her, for the most part, even if Alma did take ironing home on weekends.

Mrs. Ashcroft smiled at Alma in the mornings. She greeted her with nice words. She asked about the children, although Alma suspected the white woman didn't really listen to her answers.

Mattie was talking about her Tallera's upcoming birthday when the bus stopped at the corner of Cloverdale and Norman Bridge roads. Both women looked up to see a bright-faced young man with dark brown skin, wearing a neatly pressed khaki army uniform, step spryly onto the front of the bus. He dropped his dime into the slot and continued past Jane Ann down the center aisle, looking straight at the older women.

Both Mattie and Alma watched anxiously, knowing the young man was breaking protocol, if not the law, by his actions.

"Hey!" the driver called, his voice splitting the heavy silence in the bus.

The young man stopped before he reached the colored-only line.

"Get off the bus up here and enter through the back doors," the driver barked. "You know the routine."

The soldier, whose face was smooth as that of Mattie's boy Willie James, Jr., smiled, turned, and gazed at the driver, who was now out of his seat and standing between the passengers and the open front door.

"Get off up here, nigger!" the driver ordered. "Then go to the back door!"

"Ain't nobody blocking my way," the young man said, indicating he had clear passage down the aisle between the front door and the back of the bus.

"You don't need to be riding this bus," the driver said. "Git off now!"

The soldier shrugged. "Gimme back my dime."

"I ain't giving you a goddamn thing. Now, git your black ass off, or I'm callin' the cops."

The two black women watched silently. Alma clutched the laundry bag. Mattie wanted to holler for the driver to hush, but she was afraid. All she could do was swallow her words. She'd seen black people get slapped or knocked onto the floor or pushed out the door when they didn't quickly obey the white bus drivers. There was a law, they were told, that black people paid at the front of a bus, got off, entered through the rear door, and sat behind the colored-only line. She had never read such a law, but it was the way things were done in Montgomery, Alabama. It was the way things had been done for as long as Mattie could remember. It was one of the many Jim Crow laws that had been written by the white politicians who were bound and determined to keep Negroes in their place: and their place, they were told, was to do what white folks told them to do and not be smart about doing it.

The driver moved to the open front door. He leaned out and shouted across Cloverdale Road to a uniformed white policeman who was lingering near gasoline pumps in front of a service station. "Hey!" the driver shouted. "I got a nigger on here who won't act right. I need your help."

As the officer ambled across the street to the bus, Jane Ann Thompson shifted nervously in her seat. The young black soldier stood no more than three feet from her.

Waiting and watching, Mattie Johnson and Alma Franklin felt suddenly hotter than they had moments earlier. Mattie recalls: "The heat's always hard on a body in August in Montgomery. But it was downright terrible on a bus. And when you're waitin' on something awful to happen, you feel it more than any other time. It feels like it's pressing down on you, gettin' tighter and tighter around you, cuttin' you off from everything else."

Jane Ann Thompson doesn't remember the heat. "It's always hot in the summer down here," she says. She does remember looking up into the young man's face and seeing his eyes glance over at her, "and it was kind of like a smile that formed on his face, a nice satisfied smile, like he'd had something good to eat."

When the officer stepped aboard the bus, the young man—twenty-year-old Private First Class Thomas Edward Brooks, who had born in west Montgomery in 1930—stood as still as a statue. Jane Ann Thompson remembers that his expression did not change until the policeman growled, "Git down here, nigger!"

The young soldier didn't move.

"I said, 'Get your black ass off the bus! Now!'"

Still, Brooks didn't budge.

Jane Ann Thompson remembers, "His smile kind of melted. His face became serene, like he was doing something he was proud to be doing. But I knew he was scared, too. But he didn't show it."

The policeman stepped toward Brooks. He quickly unsheathed his billy club, raised it, and swung it.

Mattie Johnson recalls, "When that wooden stick hit that boy's head, it cracked like a hickory-nut being snapped by a pair of pliers. My whole body jerked, like I'd been stuck by a pin. My elbows hugged my sides. I don't know whether I cried out or not, but I probably did. The policeman glared toward us in the back of the bus but didn't say nothing. He just looked. The little girl just cringed, she was so afraid."

Jane Ann Thompson says, "I pulled my feet up off the floor. When the black man went down on his knees, I jumped, out of pure fright. I hugged my knees, and I think I was shaking all over. The policeman said nothing to me, neither did the driver. All I can remember them saying was 'nigger, nigger, nigger.' My whole insides were quivering like a shaking bowl of Jell-O."

The officer grabbed Brooks and pulled him down the center aisle to the front door of the bus. Near the front, the driver helped pull him toward the steps. Brooks shook free, shoved the two white men aside, pulled himself upright, and bolted toward the door.

Off balance and leaning against a railing, the officer shouted, "Stop!" and drew his revolver.

As Brooks leaped from the front door, the officer fired. Brooks stumbled and fell forward onto the pavement.

Blood seeped through the back of Brooks's crisp khaki uniform. It spread, making a large splotch. He didn't move.

It was a living nightmare to Jane Ann Thompson. "I screamed. I was so scared. I didn't know what to do. I looked back at the women. I saw their faces filled with pure fright. I saw how awful they were feeling. I saw something I'd never seen before on the face of any human being. I jumped up and took off. I jumped off the bus and ran down Cloverdale Road. I didn't turn back. I ran all the way home, four blocks, and when I got there I tried to tell Mama what had happened, but all I could really do was cry. She tried to calm me, but I was shaking like a leaf."

Mattie Johnson remembers, "That poor little girl was so scared, she ran like a whupped dog. She took off down the street. Me and Alma didn't move. We stayed put, scared what the policeman might do to us. Finally, before they picked the boy's body up or anything, the driver got back on, looked toward us, grumbled something about 'niggers,' and started the bus up and took us on down the road."

Jane Ann Thompson states, "I never hated black people. I was afraid of them, until what happened on the bus that day. I went home and cried to my mama and told her what I'd seen. I had never seen a dead person before, but I knew that black man was dead. I was so scared, I wondered what the Negroes would do. Much later, I thought: *If I were they, I'd do something drastic.* I didn't think it then, although I saw the most terrible fear in the eyes of those women on that bus. Years later, however, the world forgot about the white children who grew up in that society. They forgot that we suffered, too. I had nightmares for years, and I still can't get it off my mind sometimes."

At home that night, Mattie Johnson telephoned her friend Edgar Daniel (E. D.) Nixon, a tall man with broad shoulders who attended the same church as Mattie and whom she knew as a leader among her people. He listened to her. When she finished, he said, "I'll look into it right away."

Sickened and angered, Nixon drove to the police department and demanded to know what had happened. When he was told that young Brooks was killed by a law enforcement officer who was protecting himself in the line of duty, Nixon issued a complaint. The official response was that the shooting was unavoidable. Hearing the words, Nixon felt a deep hurt. He told himself, *I'll keep a lookout on what they do. Some day they'll do something they will wish they hadn't. Some day.*

Mattie Johnson knew that E. D. Nixon would do what he could, but she wondered if anything could ever be done to make a difference. As she sees it, "There never was nothing done about the shooting, although it was a pure cold-blood hate killing. The police swept it under the rug, like they did a lot of other things back then. Said it was 'self-defense,' when anybody coulda seen the boy was shot in the back like he was a mad dog or something."

About an hour later Nixon called her back. From his friend Rufus Lewis, another outstanding leader in the black community, whose in-laws owned a funeral home, Nixon had learned that the young soldier's name was Thomas Edward Brooks. He was a Montgomery native. His family still lived on the west side. His wife, Estella, lived with the young man's parents. Mattie called the house. When she began to tell the mother what she'd witnessed that afternoon, Mrs. Brooks started weeping uncontrollably. Mr. Brooks took the phone and listened while Mattie told him what had happened. He thanked her and hung up.

After that day, neither Jane Ann Thompson nor Mattie Johnson ever rode a city bus again.

Brooks was not the only young black man to be killed on Montgomery city buses. At least two others were killed by policemen over the next three years. Nothing was ever done about
their murders. As far as I have been able to determine, only one
was reported in the daily newspaper. However, each minute of
every day, Jim Crow's hateful presence was felt in the black
community.

The germ of Jim Crow had actually been planted in the
Deep South at the end of Reconstruction in 1876. The South
had been devastated by the war. It was rebuilt under the heavy
guard of federal troops, who forced legitimately elected black
legislators upon the whites at gunpoint. When the federal
troops marched back home to the North, white Bourbon Democrats seized control of the political offices and began laying a
foundation that would solidify Jim Crow racism far into the
next century. Laws were enacted that locked black people into
second-class citizenship without access to the rights that were
guaranteed all people under the U.S. Constitution. What
African Americans had gained from the Emancipation Procla-
mation was taken away by a series of laws passed by angry, inse-
cure, devious white lawmakers in state houses and city halls
across the South.

I was born in December 1953, three years after this incident
that was kept quiet and two years before the incident that
would rock a nation and awaken the world to the horrible reality of forced segregation. I was raised by a mother who lived
by old virtues and without prejudices. She made me realize that
black people in the South had lived under laws of segregation
that persecuted them as a people simply because they were a
different color.

My father was primarily a skeptic. He never protested
against anything, as far as I know, and he did not encourage the

behavior. He told me that the South was not totally at fault for its racist attitudes. He believed the North was equally at fault for not treating black people fairly. But he also said that throughout our history in Montgomery we were sitting on a volcano. It erupted a number of times, but the reason it did not explode in a huge way was that the black people here had never had a hero to lead them.

My mother was the first to tell me about the young black man who was killed when he asked the bus driver to return his dime. For years I wondered if some of my mother's stories were true. This one I know is true, because I found the documents to prove it. When I first came across the document and read it, I remembered my mother's story. The first time I heard it we were sitting in lawn chairs outside in the front yard one evening. Hot and humid, it was one of those perfect Montgomery summer nights, and the stars were bright in the dark sky. Back then, we spent many nights outside, listening to my mother's stories.

Mama said that after the young soldier's mother buried her son she took her other children downtown to Union Station and put them on a train to Chicago, where they would live with relatives. She watched the train disappear down the tracks and turned away without shedding a tear. She knew that she was doing what she had to do, my mother told us. In a very quiet voice, Mama said, the woman told her, "I'll never see my children again."

The soldier's young wife went back home to her own mother. After the afternoon of her husband's death she never rode the buses again. But almost six years later she would surface to tell her story.

———

E. D. Nixon felt an emotional earthquake churning inside himself as he heard about the young black man's death that hot

August afternoon. Nixon was a man of his people. Every chance he got, he sat down among his neighbors and talked with them. His gravel voice was deep and disturbing as he talked about the travesties of Jim Crow. Women from Alabama State College for Negroes and local churches met regularly to listen to him. He was not an educated man, but when he spoke, his words were filled with emotion. He knew that when the time came, the black community had to be prepared to handle the situation. He became convinced that women would be the backbone and the ultimate strength of such a movement.

Among those who talked with Nixon regularly was Inez Jesse Baskin, who later became a part-time secretary to Dr. Martin Luther King, Jr. Baskin shared with me much of what happened during the last month of 1955 and throughout 1956.

Another woman who attended Nixon's talks was Johnnie Rebecca Carr. Carr was born in Montgomery on January 26, 1911, two years before her friend Rosa Parks. She recognized racial problems when she was still a little girl. As a student at Miss Alice L. White's Industrial School for Girls, Carr heard that black teachers made less money than white teachers and that almost no company would hire a black secretary. It was disheartening, but she kept plugging away.

Carr became aware of E. D. Nixon's leadership in the 1930s when he began work to organize the local chapter of the National Association for the Advancement of Colored People. She heard him talk about the need for each person to pitch in and help out. His words about black people pulling themselves up by their own bootstraps resonated with her, and she became a volunteer worker in the NAACP office. When the *Advertiser* did a story about Nixon and his helper, identifying Johnnie Rebecca Carr, Rosa Parks called the office and asked Carr if she was her old classmate from Miss White's school. (Back then they had been Johnnie Rebecca Daniels and Rosa McCauley.) Johnnie answered that she was the same girl.

In the early years of the 1940s Carr called Nixon whenever she needed help. "He was *the* person who we could call when we had a problem," she remembered. "I recall one instance when the city closed down all the stables around the city and they carried all the manure over to the park [Oak Park] across the street from where I lived. They were going to make fertilizer out of it. But it caused such a smell, and flies. I didn't think it was right, but I just tried to put up with it. We had called the health department, but nothing had been done. Then one day, I was cooking and the flies were all in the windows. And seems like I just broke down and cried. It just didn't seem right that we should have to live with that kind of situation. So I called Mr. Nixon, and he answered the phone in that big deep voice: 'Nixon.' And I said, 'Mr. Nixon,' and I told him what the problem was. And he thought it over for a moment and said, 'Sue the city.' And I started telling him how upset I was, and he broke in and said firmly, 'File a lawsuit against the city.' And at that time in the forties we didn't have any black lawyers, and so he told me which white lawyer to talk to. And it got taken care of the day after they got the letter from the lawyer. The city came out and cleaned up all that mess."

I know one thing. The civil rights movement did not happen as many Yankee journalists and out-of-state historians have led the world to believe: that Martin Luther King, Jr., was stricken by a sudden light, like Saul on the road to Damascus, and that he sprang up full-blown as the leader of his people, delivering them single-handedly from the bonds of racism into the broad open daylight of democracy. Too many academicians on vacation in the sunny South heard the fictitious tales of King's sudden sainthood and went home to fan the flames of myth.

What the tale of Thomas Edward Brooks's death on a summer afternoon shows us, among other things, is that terror was

building in the southland throughout the middle of the twentieth century. What happened on the bus early in the evening of
December 1, 1955, when Rosa Parks refused to give up her seat,
was a long time coming. It took the emotions and efforts of
many people like Mattie Johnson and Alma Franklin and Rosa
Parks; like Jo Ann Robinson and Johnnie Rebecca Carr and
Hazel Gregory; like Fred Gray and Edgar Daniel Nixon and
Martin Luther King, Jr. Individually and collectively, these people seethed with an overpowering mistrust of government in
general and of the local white government in particular. They
suffered the slings and arrows of unjust laws, and they were
overcome with the belief that they could change those laws.
When they sang the hymn "We Shall Overcome," they stood
together in a pride-filled crowd, ready to be unmoved, making
a noise like the thunder of angels in the old preacher's sermon.

2

His Own Man

EDGAR DANIEL NIXON was born on July 12, 1899, in a small shanty on Cane Street—within the shadows of the state capitol that had been the site of Jefferson Davis's inauguration as president of the Confederacy thirty-eight years earlier, and in a world lorded over by a mysterious but overwhelming ghost named Jim Crow.

Edgar quickly learned to take care of himself. He and six siblings slept on the floor; his baby sister slept in the bed with her mother and father. His mother, Sue Ann Chappell Nixon, who worked in white people's houses as a maid and a cook, died suddenly when he was a boy, leaving her husband, Wesley M. Nixon, with eight children. Wesley worked for a while at Sabel Steel. Later he began preaching in Baptist churches wherever his services were wanted, leaving his children behind to tend to themselves. Edgar remembered hearing a story about how his father became a dedicated preacher. His mother and father had rented a farm and planted cotton and corn there. At noon on a sunny July day, lightning struck the field, setting fire to every stalk of cotton on the place. Frightened by the sudden turn of nature, the couple ran out into the field and pulled every ear of corn they could find. With the wagon loaded, they headed home. As the wagon pulled up to the front of the house, Wesley stepped down. A crash of thunder rumbled. It seemed as though the earth shook. Wesley fell onto his back. It started pouring. As the rain fell, Wesley lay flat on his back and didn't move. When the rain finally let up, Wesley promised the Lord he'd start preaching and that he wouldn't stop until he died.

During Wesley's long absences, while he traveled around the countryside preaching, the children sought solace and sustenance in each other. Edgar paid particular attention to his younger sister, Josephine, who had been just a baby when their mother died. When the out-of-town trips grew longer, Wesley found a home for Edgar, Josephine, and several of the other children with his sister, Wynnie Bates, who lived in rural Autauga County, about fifteen miles northwest of Montgomery.

At Auntie Wynnie's house Edgar met his grandfather, Hamp Nixon, an old man who smoked a pipe when he sat on the porch and gazed out at the cotton fields he'd worked all of his long life. The old man told stories about the days when he was a slave—about being separated from his mother and father, and about how his mother showed up years later on the plantation he'd been taken to in the Black Belt of Alabama.

It was not long before Wesley found another wife, with whom he fathered nine more children. Edgar remembered those years without his mother or father as hurtful and lonely. His aunt satisfied his craving for nurturing as strongly as she could, but she was simply not his mother. A Seventh-Day Adventist, she took the children to church regularly and plied them with daily devotionals. They worked hard in the fields surrounding her unpainted old house when they were not attending the two-room schoolhouse ten miles away. Most of the time, they were not in school. Edgar remembered attending four months of school each year for four years. He learned firsthand the hard life of a sharecropper: people slaved away in the fields for long hours, day in and day out, and at the end of the year they owed the landowner more than their meager share of the harvest had earned. That debt usually grew larger and larger as the years rolled by. Young Edgar Nixon knew that he would remain a sharecropper if he didn't do something to pull himself up from that life.

He learned to read. He picked up his aunt's Bible and pored over the words. They did not come easily to him. "I read the Bible over and over again. Out in the field, I repeated verse after verse. Many words were not in me. I didn't understand everything, but I read it anyway. And I listened eagerly to the preacher's words. I would pick out phrases I seen on the paper and I'd make a picture of them in my mind and keep it there. When it was just me and row after row of cotton, the heavy old sun bearing down on my head and the sweat pouring off my forehead and stinging my eyes, the big old sack hanging around my shoulder growing heavier and heavier as I filled it with the cotton I picked, I'd think of the words of Genesis: 'In the beginning God created the heaven and the earth, and the earth was without form, and void; and darkness was upon the face of the deep, and the Spirit of God moved upon the waters, and God said, Let there be light: and there was light.' And while I worked, the whole creation thing swept over me and made me wonder. I knew that God had put me on Earth for a purpose, and that purpose was not to spend my life out there in that cotton field. There would be a day when I would find my way out of there. But I had my auntie and my sister. I was stuck off in a corner of the world where nobody else much cared."

Once his aunt sent him to the Swift Packing House, where "you could get a cow head for a dime. She put the dime in my pocket and put a safety pin on it. She said, 'Don't go and take that pin out 'til you get to the man. When he brings you the cow head, then you take the dime out and you give it to him.'

Nobody could have made me take that pin out. So, me and another boy went up there. We had a bag with two handles on it, and I had one side of the bag, the other boy had the other side. There was a man hollering to all the workers, 'Bring the cow head for this little nigger out here,' just like that. And I didn't know what he was talking about. But I went back and told her [Auntie Wynnie] that and asked her would she tell me [what he was talking about]. She said, 'He said that?' I said, 'Yeah.' And she never sent us back there no more to get a cow head."

When Nixon was fourteen, his aunt married a man named Nicholas Long, who did not care for the children. He was especially dissatisfied with young Edgar, whom he called "a slacker" and with whom he dealt not only harshly, but also violently. After the man beat him, Edgar gathered his few belongings and hit the road. He went back to Montgomery and stayed with a relative on Bell Street, sleeping on a couch in the kitchen and paying a dollar a day in rent. Since the wages he earned working at a nearby grocery store were also a dollar a day, he soon decided it was time to move on.

He caught a ride north back to Autauga County, then headed west. After several rides on wagons that were going his way on the two-path dirt road, he walked most of the thirty-some miles to Selma, a village on the Alabama River where cotton wagons unloaded onto steamboats, and where the Confederacy had operated one of its largest arsenals until it was burned to the ground by marauding Union troops at the end of the Civil War.

"I was a boy big for my age. I had muscles on top of muscles from pulling the cotton sack down long rows and filling it with bolls. I could lift my own weight and then some. While I was on the farm, I ate heaping corn bread and sorghum syrup, was my favorite. I was a hard worker, but I didn't plan to work for some man who was gonna beat me, even if he was married to my auntie. I could take care of myself, and that's what I took off to do. I knew I had to do what I had to do, to make a place for myself, my own. I still had those pictures in my head. I still had my words."

He wasted little time getting a job. With an old straw hat in hand, he approached a man who owned a small grocery store on the northern edge of Selma. He told him he'd sweep the floor, wash the windows, and carry groceries to people's houses. The man gave him a job for a dollar a day, plus a sandwich for lunch and some oatmeal for breakfast. Sometimes on Sundays he'd even get corn bread and syrup. There was a lean-to at the rear of the store where the boy could curl up and sleep. At least it was a roof over his head.

"I made do," E. D. Nixon recalled years later. "Weren't no steak and taters, but I developed a pretty fair appetite for sardines and crackers. And I could do a job on a fist-size hunk of hoop cheese."

One night, when it was raining, he felt something furry and damp slide up next to his leg. At first he felt a shiver of fright. Then he heard a deep moan and felt the lick of a dog's tongue on his cheek. It was a cur that had been hanging around the back door of the store looking for scraps. Nixon reached down and pulled the animal close, wrapping his arm around the dog's shoulders. After that night, the two were inseparable.

When men came to the store and sat in the rear and smoked their cigarettes or chewed tobacco, the boy worked nearby, quietly doing his chores while he listened intently to what the men were saying. If he got a chance, he would ask a question and listen while one of the men answered. If the men left a newspaper behind, Nixon would clean it up and take it to his lean-to, where he would read every word while the dog lay at his feet. He often read a newspaper two or three times, virtually memorizing the articles. He bought a secondhand dictionary and constantly looked up words he had never before heard or seen, building his vocabulary, every day adding two or three new words. In this way, the world became his classroom.

He lived in the lean-to behind the grocery store for almost a year, until one evening after work he exited the back door with a small sack of scraps. He rounded the corner, heading for the lean-to, when he found the long-haired animal lying inert in the shadows. Nixon dropped to his knees and cradled the dog's lifeless head. Behind him, the store owner said, "He was just a mangy no-account. He's better off dead."

The boy dug a hole and buried the dead animal. Then he gathered his belongings, including the dictionary and several old newspapers, and hit the road again. He headed north out of Selma. Several days later he arrived in Birmingham, Alabama's largest city. He took any job he could find. He gravitated to the vicinity of the train station in downtown Birmingham, where he picked up after workers and kept storage rooms clean. He met black men who told him stories about the road, and the thought of riding the rails began to appeal to him. He wanted to visit other places and see what life was like out there.

Already, Edgar Daniel Nixon had lost whatever boyish innocence he might have once possessed. He had a scar above his left eye from a fight with a hobo who had jumped him for a heavy coat that had been given to him by a white man he'd befriended in Selma. "I'm a fighter," Nixon said years later, while sitting in the shade of a scuppernong arbor during a lazy afternoon at the country place of his friends, Clifford and Virginia Durr. "I always have been. I don't think I ever hurt nobody. Not seriously, anyway. Out there where nobody has much of anything, some big men think they can take anything they want from you. It's a hard life. You've got to defend yourself and what's yours. I got beaten up sometimes when I was a boy trying to make my way. But nobody ever took nothing from me that was mine, that I didn't want 'em to take. When I found some poor soul suffering, I'd give 'em what I could give. I always was of a mind to share, when I had it to share. But they wadn't gonna take it just cause they wanted to."

When a white boy who was several years older than Nixon called him "a goddamn nigger," the black youth squared off and prepared to fight. A white foreman grabbed him by the shoulder, twisted him backward, and said if he didn't back down he'd be fired. Nixon dropped his fists but did not hang his head. "If I couldn't look a man straight in the eye, I might as well curl up in a ball and die. I already worked like a man. I knew I had to act like a man."

Some of the older workers around the train yard told Nixon about Mobile, where jobs were more plentiful in the early 1920s, and as soon as he managed to save a few dollars, he took off for the port city on the Gulf of Mexico. In Mobile, after drifting from job to job, never making more than two dollars a day and getting into fights with others who were down and out, he finally landed a position as baggage porter at the train depot near downtown in 1924.

After working hard around the yard for a year, he finally obtained a job as a Pullman car porter. All porters were black. They were paid little but regularly. And the job immediately elevated him to a prestigious position in the black community. He took runs from Mobile to Jacksonville, Florida, to Miami and up to Nashville. Soon he was stationed in his old hometown of Montgomery. "If they needed a man, I was ready. When they asked, I never turned down a run. I stayed with 'em morning, noon, and night." He was one of literally thousands of black men who worked Pullman berths around the United States, making the beds at night, fluffing pillows, folding the berths neatly into the metal walls of the trains during the day, carrying bags, lifting children from platforms of train stations up to the walkways between the cars, sweeping the cars, washing dishes, and polishing the brass hardware until it shone like a new penny. "We all worked for George Pullman. He was the big white boss. It was his name that was on every car. And sometimes we were all called 'George' by the white passengers."

According to varying accounts, porters were known among the whites as "George Pullman's boys"—a reference that harkened back to slavery days, and one that established another rung on the Jim Crow ladder of social mores in the South.

"Before I started traveling as a porter I thought the whole world was like Montgomery or Selma or Birmingham. I didn't know what was right or wrong with reference to the civil rights of people. Then I saw that things were different in St. Louis, Missouri. I was dumbfounded and shocked down to my toes when I got up there and found black people and white people sitting down at the same table eating in the railroad station. It had a heck of an impact on me. Here you have been conditioned traditionally to 'this is the way of life,' as they said, and all your life that's all you have known. And here I was, twenty-five years old, and I begin to think about the whole world out there that's different, and I see the blacks and the whites sitting down together and eating together, and all at once it's just like water that's been backed up behind a dam, and it breaks out and flows over. By the time I got back to Alabama at the end of my first four-day run, I started to think: 'What can I do to eliminate some of this?'"

On the trains Nixon and other porters were treated like faithful servants, even if an occasional passenger might spew a racist epithet or make unnecessary demands. When he stepped off the train and into the black community in Montgomery, he found that he was the subject of adoration. He wore his uniform proudly. He kept it cleaned and pressed. The brass buttons were polished until they glittered. His fellow black citizens began to ask him for advice. His preacher asked him to sit on the front pew. Women of the church began asking him to their houses for supper, and they wanted him to meet their daughters. When he accepted an invitation to dinner, he sat in the living room before the meal and talked with the man of the house. Edgar Nixon asked and listened, and older men asked him questions and listened to his well-thought-out answers. Nixon was a man who had traveled from one end of the nation to the other. When passengers left newspapers behind on the train, he took them to his cramped quarters and read the news under the twinkling of a tiny light. He discovered what was happening in Chicago, St. Louis, San Francisco, Buffalo, New York City, and Washington, D.C. Just as he had committed news from Selma to memory, he soaked up the news of the world. He didn't know perfect English grammar—he never would—but neither did the husbands and fathers he sat with and talked to. Most of them enjoyed the company of this unpretentious, solidly built young man.

During his first three years as a porter, Nixon logged nearly four hundred hours, or 11,000 miles a month, making sixty dollars a month plus tips. "Now and then a satisfied passenger, happy with his freshly polished shoes and tight bedding in his berth, would flip a dime my way, but that was indeed a rarity," he remembered. Porters paid for their meals, uniforms, and any necessary equipment, such as a shoeshine kit and bootblack polish.

Once a Catholic bishop gave him a folded bill after Nixon handled the man's luggage. Nixon unfolded the bill and discovered to his delight that it was a five-dollar bill. On another occasion he put Babe Ruth's bags on the train in Mobile. "He give me fifteen cents, and I thanked him. You know what he said? He said, 'Nigger, you don't know how to pull your hat off when a white man gives you a tip?' I said, 'Mister, if you expect me to climb for fifteen cents, you can keep it.' And everybody just hollered."

Sometimes Nixon would eat breakfast and nothing else during the day. If a passenger left a biscuit on his plate or a piece of ham on his tray, Nixon would sneak a bite. He took daily abuse from white passengers. He learned to stand silent and stoic, his eyes dull with hurt. Inside, he fought with his own feelings. "I knew I'd find a day when the world would change. I prayed a lot to myself, and I knew the Lord was with me. When I'd see other black people being treated badly, I felt a deep hurt inside—and I seed it often in my trips through the South. Of course, it wasn't just in the South that white people were cruel to blacks, but it was mostly in the South. It was here that we had the laws that were hanging over the heads of every black person. It was here that Jim Crow was commonplace. It was here that I saw it most blatantly. It was here that it had become an unquestioned way of life."

By 1926 Nixon felt secure enough with his life as a porter that, when he met a pretty, young Alabama State College student named Alease Curry, he not only courted her between train runs, but he also asked her to become his wife. The daughter of a Baptist minister from Greensboro, in the middle of Alabama's Black Belt, Alease Curry was deeply religious. She soon discovered that she loved the tall and handsome young man, and she accepted his proposal. Two years later she gave birth to their son, Edgar Daniel Nixon, Jr.

One evening in 1928, Edgar Daniel Nixon's life changed. He was in St. Louis, preparing for the next day's run southeast to Jacksonville and staying in a room at the YMCA. In an auditorium there, with about two hundred other porters, A. Philip Randolph, a well-known black socialist who had started the Brotherhood of Sleeping Car Porters three years earlier and who was now its president, explained his organization. A tall, slender, light-skinned black man whose eyes burned brightly when they looked a person in the eye, Randolph spoke clearly and delivered his message with verve.

Years later Nixon would tell Studs Terkel, "When I heard Randolph speak, it was like a light. Most eloquent man I ever heard. He done more to bring me in the fight for civil rights than anybody. Before that time, I figured that a Negro would be kicked around and accept whatever the white man did. I never knew the Negro had a right to enjoy freedom like everybody else. When Randolph stood there and talked that day, it made a different man out of me. He talked about all these things, about what people could do if they learned to do it together, things that black people didn't have to put up with if they learned to organize. From that day on, I was determined I was gonna fight for freedom until I was able to get some of it myself. I was just stumblin' around here and there. But I been very successful in stumblin' ever since that day."

When Randolph finished, Edgar Nixon dropped a dollar into the collection plate. He rose and started to leave. Randolph stepped down, reached out, and shook Nixon's hand. He asked, "Where you from, young man?"

Nixon replied, "Montgomery, Alabama."

Randolph said, "I need a good man down there. I'd like to talk to you."

On the spot, Nixon joined the Brotherhood.

This was the moment of his personal redemption. He felt a weight lifted from his shoulders. "As I walked back to my little room in the YMCA I realized that I was a new man. All of the experience I had been soaking up during my earlier years, all of the scenes I'd seen in my travels, all of the spit and backtalk I'd heard, all the names I'd been called—everything fell away from me. On that trip through the South, when I'd step off the train in stations in Nashville and Atlanta, when I saw White Only signs over water fountains or on restrooms, I knew that a day would come in the future when those signs would be torn from the walls and would fill the garbage cans of public facilities. Something inside me said: 'Edgar Nixon, you're gonna lead the way.'"

Nixon figured his association with the Brotherhood of Sleeping Car Porters might cause some trouble for him, and sure enough his boss was waiting at the station when he stepped off the train back home in Montgomery. "They tell me you attended this Brotherhood meeting." Nixon said that was right, he had. The boss said, "Well, I'm gonna tell you right now, we ain't gonna have our porters riding around here attending no Brotherhood meetings." Nixon nodded and said, "Maybe the guy who told you that also told you I'd joined the Brotherhood yesterday evening. Before I joined it, I thought about what lawyer I was gonna get to handle my case. Anybody mess with my job, I'm gonna drag 'em into court." The boss said nothing else. Although Nixon was bluffing, his voice was strong enough to make the white man believe his words. There were no repercussions.

Nixon began to look for ways to affect change in his own community. As a porter, Nixon was away from home for weeks at a time. When he was home, he met with other people, including women from the community, and preached what he had heard A. Philip Randolph say in his eloquent speech. Randolph became his hero. The union leader sent Nixon pamphlets and newspapers from Washington. He explained how the Brotherhood worked, how porters could make their lives on the trains better and more productive, and how they could all become better citizens by becoming more active in their communities. Randolph taught Nixon and others to become involved in the world around them. Through Randolph's long-distance teaching, Nixon learned how to organize people—how to pull them together and point them in the right direction.

Nixon decided to establish a local branch of the National Association for the Advancement of Colored People. Whenever his train pulled into Washington, D.C., Nixon would telephone Randolph, meet with him, and listen to his teaching. In New York he met with Randolph and leaders of the NAACP. He read about the organization that he would use to shore up black support and show the strength of his people. Back home, he preached the need for his people to pick themselves up by their own bootstraps. He went from door to door throughout the community and preached self-preservation. He believed that too many black people depended on welfare or government handouts. He told them to go out and get jobs, work hard and earn a living, and stand up for themselves. This, he said, was the only way that they could have total pride in themselves. If they worked and made a salary, they could take care of themselves and their families, and their lives would change, he told them.

But such involvement did not impress Nixon's wife, who was already uncomfortable with the marriage and distraught over the amount of time that Nixon was away from his family. Alease wanted him to be more involved in their home life, not necessarily in the community's, particularly since she suffered from health problems that had begun with the birth of Edgar, Jr. Finally, when she saw that her husband was stubbornly going in his own direction, disregarding her pleas, she told him good-bye, and she took their child with her.

In 1934 Edgar met a young woman named Arlet, who became totally devoted to him. A native of Pensacola, Florida, Arlet soon became Nixon's second wife, and she let him know immediately that she supported whatever he chose to pursue. In 1937, after Alease had died, Arlet welcomed Edgar, Jr., then nine years old, into their family. She had heard her husband's stories of growing up alone and lonely, and she was determined to make a good home for his son. Throughout his life, Nixon would brag about his dedicated wife. Arlet stayed at home and worked as a housekeeper and a mother. Her husband proudly stated that Mrs. Nixon, as he chose to call her, never had to go outside the family to earn a living. Unlike most uneducated black women at that time, she never worked as a maid cleaning up after white people—a fact that her husband talked about proudly. He often said that his earliest memory was that of his mother on her knees, scrubbing the floor of a white family's kitchen.

From the beginning, Nixon wanted to build a solid local foundation for both the Brotherhood of Sleeping Car Porters and the NAACP. Going beyond the necessary footwork required to establish a local branch, he delved into the background of the NAACP. On his long trips into the North, whenever he caught a moment, he would crouch in a corner and read. He learned how the organization was founded in 1909 through the leadership of W. E. B. DuBois, Mary W. Ovington, William M. Trotter, Bishop Alexander Walters, and Ida B. Wells. He read about the ideals of freedom, justice, and equality. He filled his brain with a yearning for more information that would give him ammunition to fight for such ideals. He believed deep down that those ideals could be realized, even in his hometown. He learned that justice and equality were seldom gained through the efforts of just one person working alone. It took a group of dedicated people, welded together by effective leadership and fighting for a cause they believed in, to achieve success.

In Montgomery, Nixon enlisted the aid of his minister at Holt Street Baptist Church, then searched out every other black minister in the town. He gathered them together and told them about the NAACP and its importance. The ministers, in turn, told their Sunday congregations about the organization and about Edgar Nixon. Within a short while, a few interested citizens began to trickle into his meetings. Among these was a young woman named Rosa Parks, who volunteered her services as a part-time secretary.

Nixon sat down with his groups and talked to them about the ways he found life being lived in Chicago, Detroit, New York, and St. Louis. "Now, mind you, I didn't want to move away from Montgomery, or Alabama, or the South. I didn't want to go Up-North, like so many others who'd taken off to find a new way of life, to escape the Jim Crow South. I didn't want to run. I wanted to make my home a better place. I wanted to make my folks understand what they had to do to stay on the right path."

His young son, Edgar, Jr., learned to recognize a hero when he saw one, but it took him a while. The message his father preached during his meetings was also preached at home. As a young teenager, the boy got a job that paid three dollars a week. His father made him pay a dollar in rent and put a dollar into savings, and allowed him to keep a dollar to spend. Young Edgar couldn't understand why his father made him pay rent. Other children teased him about the practice, but later he realized that his father was teaching him to be responsible. He was learning to be independent and self-sufficient.

During Nixon's train runs into the North, he talked endlessly with other Pullman car porters. To those who did not belong to the Brotherhood, Nixon would explain the necessity and the importance of the union. Speaking with the emotion that regularly fueled his preaching to the blacks down South, he told the other porters about A. Philip Randolph and what the man and the organization were doing for the workers. He explained how wages had increased under Randolph's leadership, how work had become less tedious and stressful, how train riders had become more courteous, and how personal benefits had increased. Nixon carried the shield for the Brotherhood and fought the battles as a soldier in the field. To gain freedom and recognition, he said, the membership rolls had to grow long and become fruitful. In other words, he said, it was easy for him to talk about ideals, but in order to be successful, the organization had to grow in numbers. New members had to go out and carry the message that he was sending to those who were ignorant of its possibilities. And when he was back home, he used the same argument with black people in the community to build the membership rolls of the NAACP.

In the 1930s Nixon heard about Myles Horton and the Highlander Folk School, which was tucked away in the hills of east Tennessee. He met Horton, a white man whom he immediately liked. Horton was just as enthusiastic about organizing poor people as Nixon. And when Horton told Nixon he wanted to organize itinerant cucumber pickers in rural Alabama, most of whom were white people living in the coastal plain, Nixon immediately realized that these, too, were poor people who had been used and abused by their big landowner employers. Nixon stepped forward and volunteered to do everything he could to organize these workers into a union. To him, it was another case of the rich and the powerful making huge profits at the expense of the poor, the downtrodden, the weak, and the oppressed. These people worked from before daylight until after dark. They made a pittance. They were always in debt to the company store, just as the sharecroppers Nixon had seen in rural Autauga County had been. To him, it was a shame.

Nixon realized he needed to learn everything he could from Horton to help organize his people back home in Montgomery. When he went home, he organized the Montgomery Welfare League the same year he married Arlet. It was the middle of the Great Depression. People were hungry; some were starving. In Montgomery and throughout the South, white people were quickly put on the relief rolls, but poor blacks were largely forgotten by the white establishment that doled out the federal relief that President Roosevelt was sending down. It was Nixon's idea to help the needy and disabled blacks. He took poor black women with children at their sides to the federal relief office in downtown Montgomery. He said, "You see this woman and these children? They deserve food just as much as any poor white family." Sometimes the bureaucrats reacted. Sometimes they didn't. But Edgar Nixon never let them forget. He always came back to them with more people and more stories.

In the same year, Nixon organized the Overall Committee to help black war veterans who had fought in Europe during the Great War to obtain their share of benefits and assistance owed to them by the government.

In 1935, ten years after A. Philip Randolph had begun to organize the Brotherhood of Sleeping Car Porters, the group was officially recognized by the American Federation of Labor as a union. In August 1937 the Pullman Company finally recognized the union and signed a labor contract that improved working conditions and raised the minimum wage of the black workers to $89.50 a month. After Randolph and the Brotherhood won these concessions, Nixon remembered, "Pullman wrote him and sent him a check. A blank check . . . At the bottom, it said, 'Not to exceed a million dollars.' [In the letter, Pullman] said, 'We've been fighting you about the Brotherhood, and if you want to, you can take a little rest. Put your own figures in this check, sign it, and forget about the porters.' [Randolph] made a copy of it and framed it, hung it up to his office, sent the written check back to Pullman with this phrase, 'Negro principles not for sale.' Now, I'm gonna tell you, I don't care what you say, or how you feel about it, whether it's white or black, it would have been mighty hard for a whole lot of folks, white or black, to send that check back when it said 'not to exceed a million dollars.'"

At Union Station in Montgomery, blacks could not use the water fountains. They had to go into the Colored Only bathrooms, bend down, and fold their hands to cup water from the faucet. After Nixon argued the point in the late 1930s, management installed electric water fountains for blacks.

At the large Sears, Roebuck and Company store there were no bathroom facilities for blacks. Once again, Nixon confronted the management and pointed out the problem. The management acquiesced and installed toilets for blacks.

During the 1930s Nixon met Joseph S. Gelders, a gentle, soft-spoken white man who lived in Birmingham and was the local representative of the National Committee for the Defense of Political Prisoners. Gelders had heard about Nixon and his work, and when Gelders helped in attempts to organize sharecroppers in Tallapoosa County, Nixon went into the fields to assist. He had been there, and he knew well the plight of the sharecropper. Nixon recognized Gelders as one of the few white men in the South who he could talk to about his people's problems.

On one of his many trips to Washington, D.C., Nixon was introduced to fellow Alabaman Aubrey Williams, a top official in Roosevelt's New Deal programs. Listening to Williams, Nixon recognized immediately that he was a man with a big heart and huge ideas. And, as a New Deal official, he had the power to help. Soon, Nixon was asking Williams's advice on how to fight many of his battles back in Alabama, and he received well-thought-out answers about how to chip away the obstacles that Jim Crow put in a black man's path. Besides, Williams looked him straight in the eye when they talked—something few white men ever did.

During World War II, young black soldiers who were stationed in and around Montgomery approached Nixon and explained that there were three United Service Organizations (USO) entertainment centers for white soldiers, but none for blacks. Nixon took action. After he talked to deaf ears on the local front, he telephoned the first lady of the United States, Eleanor Roosevelt, whom he had met while attending a Brotherhood meeting in Washington with Randolph. During that meeting she had told Nixon that she was interested in the fight he was waging down in Alabama, and she seemed genuinely concerned. After Nixon told her the situation, Mrs. Roosevelt interceded on behalf of the young soldiers, and a USO club was opened for them in the Montgomery area.

On a run to Washington, D.C., he asked another porter, "Who you got in that car back there?" The porter told him, "That's Mrs. Roosevelt." Nixon said, "Well, that's just who I wanted to see." The porter warned, "Man, don't make a fool out of yourself." Nixon paid no attention. "Just like that," he recalled years later, "I said, 'I won't.' So I went back and got the letter that she'd wrote me [about the USO clubs]." He knocked on the door to her car and told the first lady's secretary who he was. Mrs. Roosevelt spoke up, saying, "Let Mr. Nixon come in." He went inside and was invited to sit on the couch. She asked him question after question about what was happening in and around Montgomery. After almost an hour, he excused himself, saying he had duties he had to tend to.

When crosses were burned in the yards of black citizens, Nixon stood up, raised his fist in anger, and challenged the cowards to come out in broad daylight and try to pull such a stunt. "Of course, cowards like that never do come out and fight like men. That's why they hide behind masks. And I told that to my people, but it didn't do much to take away the fright that they'd known for a long, long time."

When he wasn't called elsewhere around the South to help organize railroad workers' unions in Tennessee, South Carolina, and Georgia, Nixon organized his own people with the Montgomery Voter's League, which he established in 1940. For ten years he had tried unsuccessfully to register to vote. Every time he'd entered the courthouse and attempted to register, he'd run into problems. The registrars, acting as judge, court, and jury, would ask Nixon questions about the Constitution. They would quote paragraphs and ask Nixon to explain them to their satisfaction. Of course, his answers never satisfied them. Finally, after he returned time and again, the registrars realized that he would never stop trying, and they allowed him to register. He had to pay the thirty-six-dollar poll tax. Until he was an old man, Nixon carried his voter's registration in his coat pocket, folded neatly but almost falling apart from the many times he'd unfolded it to read its words just one more time, or to show it to a black person who had not yet registered to vote.

Nixon led groups of blacks to the courthouse to register. More than once he was turned away at the door by city police officers or sheriff's deputies. He was warned again and again that he would be arrested if he didn't stop leading people to the registrar's office. But he didn't stop. "I kept telling the peoples that, sooner or later, they'd be allowed to vote. It was their right. They were citizens just like other people, regardless of the color of their skin. I told them to have faith. I told them, but sometimes it was hard for me to keep on doing, but then I'd tell myself, and Arlet would tell me at night, 'Just keep on, and it'll be right, it'll be done, sooner or later. It ain't ever too late.'"

On June 13, 1944, Nixon led seven hundred fifty blacks to the board of registrars and demanded that they all be allowed to register to vote. Many of them wore uniforms and had fought for their country overseas. Fewer than fifty were granted their request. The black lawyer Arthur A. Madison, Nixon's friend and a supporter of the defiant action, represented eight of the blacks who had been denied the right to register. Later five of the eight signed affidavits stating that they had not hired Madison and had not authorized him to represent them. Madison was subsequently disbarred on the grounds that he was representing a client without the client's consent, a trumped-up charge that would also be used when the atmosphere of demonstrations by supporters of the civil rights movement became heated. Madison didn't fight it. He moved to New York, where he became a successful attorney.

On leave from his Pullman porter's job in the early 1940s, Nixon traveled throughout Alabama, speaking and organizing black voters. Southern black voters increased from two hundred fifty thousand in 1940 to nearly six hundred thousand in 1946 to about seven hundred fifty thousand by 1948. Later, Nixon told *Advertiser* reporter Peggy Wilhide, "I wish that I could sell the people on this one idea of full citizenship and that we could be free if we make up our own minds that we really wanted to be free, but these crackers here have did a good job of keeping the Negro afraid and also keeping him unlearned."

Around this time, when three black men—Worthy James, John Underwood, and Samuel Taylor—were sentenced to death for allegedly raping a white woman in Prattville, Alabama, Nixon asked for and gained an audience with Governor Chauncey Sparks. Nixon argued that the only testimony against the men was the word of the victim, whose recollection was superficial at best. The men did not dispute the fact that they had had sex with the woman, but they insisted that it was consensual. The governor changed the men's sentences to life in prison.

Another time, after a thirteen-year-old black girl, Amanda Baker of Montgomery, was raped and murdered, Nixon went again to Governor Sparks, who, in an unprecedented move, offered a two-hundred-fifty-dollar reward for the arrest and conviction of the assailant. Nixon matched the figure with NAACP funds. Still, the guilty party was never found.

During the late 1940s Nixon worked to help other Pullman porters. When they were laid off or put on extended vacation because of a lack of railroad lines coming in and going out of Montgomery, he pleaded their cases. In 1949 he asked for another passenger line to be scheduled through the town to keep his men working. The white Pullman agent said the reason— "just to keep a few more niggers working"—wasn't good enough. Hurt and insulted, Nixon turned on his heels and marched away. He wrote to the president of the Brotherhood: "Brother Randolph, if you can help these men, they, their families, and myself will be grateful to you." It seemed a never-ending struggle. Even

Arlet wrote to Randolph, and he responded, "There are certain things I can't change and the Pullman Company can't change or the railroads for that matter." Later in the same letter, he stated, "I need not tell you that I have the highest admiration and affection for Brother Nixon and the great work he is doing, and I am greatly concerned about the lot of the porters everywhere and will do everything in my power to improve that lot."

In 1950, when Nixon heard about the killing of the young soldier Thomas Edward Brooks aboard a city bus, he was president of the Montgomery chapter of the NAACP. He was sickened and angered. "When I approached the police about the brutality, I got blank stares. It was like the boy never really existed. But I was persistent. Throughout this time, I was known as a troublemaker. When they saw me coming, they knew I had something for 'em. I didn't turn away and bow my head and look all defeated and victimized. I wasn't like that. Never was. Then some of the local police here started meeting me privately. When it was just me and them, they'd admit terrible things were happening. They knew that it hurt them just as much as it was hurting us. And most of 'em knew something was going to happen sooner or later."

In November 1954 Nixon and other black leaders gathered to cheer the victory of James Elisha "Big Jim" Folsom as a second-term governor of Alabama. They had heard his 1948 radio address to the people of the state, in which he said that all black citizens should be given their full rights. A few knew that Folsom, away from the view of the press, worked diligently to help black citizens to register to vote. On Saturdays, Sundays, and holidays, Folsom sent his chauffeur, Winston Craig, into the countryside to talk with local blacks in out-of-the-way county seats such as Monroeville, Hayneville, Chatom, and Alexander City. There Craig met with small groups of black people to tell them about their rights and to show them how to register to vote.

Nixon invited the black New York congressman Adam Clayton Powell to Montgomery to speak at a meeting of his Progressive Democratic Association, which was sponsoring Operation 5,000, a campaign to register five thousand black voters that had received national press attention. Folsom's chauffeur picked up Powell at the airport and delivered him to the front door of the Governor's Mansion, as he had been specifically instructed. Later Folsom, confronted with a barrage of questions from the press, said in his best good-old-boy fashion, "When I invite a congressman to have a drink of bourbon and branch with me, I don't expect him to come knocking on my back door with hat in hand. In fact, he didn't drink bourbon. The congressman preferred Scotch."

None of the reporters who questioned the governor about his hospitality to the black congressman (or to the young black attorney, Fred D. Gray, and the state president of the NAACP, E. D. Nixon, who were also present) realized that Powell had led a successful boycott of city buses by blacks in New York City in the spring of 1941. That night, after spending time with Governor Folsom, Powell spoke to the Operation 5,000 gathering on the campus of Alabama State College. His talk was focused not only on voting, but also on how the people could force social change by using economic pressure. Later Congressman Powell sat in the living room of Nixon's home on Clinton Street and told him about the effects of his New York City boycott: black drivers were hired and more routes were opened for minority riders.

Throughout his tenure as state president of the NAACP, Nixon heard many complaints, mostly from women, about the blatant racism they experienced from white bus drivers on Montgomery city buses. Many times, when he returned from the long train runs, he read over the sheet on which Mrs. Parks had written down the women's names and their problems. Few of the incidents, however, were as violent as the Brooks incident.

Nixon told the women that he was on the lookout for a perfect situation that could become a test case against the Montgomery ordinance that required separation of riders by race on city buses. That law required black riders to follow the instructions of the driver: if he told them to move, they were required by law to move, and to make room for white riders even when there was no room remaining in the back.

By the early 1950s Nixon had come to depend greatly on his part-time assistant, Rosa Parks. Judging by her appearance, the former Rosa Louise McCauley of Tuskegee, Alabama, seemed a most unlikely hero. A small woman with a frail frame and a whispery voice, she worked long hours Monday through Friday, laboring over a Singer sewing machine at her station in a back room at Montgomery Fair department store on Dexter Avenue in downtown Montgomery. On weekends she took in sewing at her home, an apartment at Cleveland Courts, off Cleveland Avenue, where she lived with her barber husband, Raymond Parks. Many times at night and on Saturdays, she devoted hours to her work in the NAACP office on Monroe Street. She typed letters on the old Underwood someone had donated to the organization. She called ministers to remind them about upcoming meetings, and she called members and nonmembers to gain their support for a project in the black community. She walked the streets, going door to door, soliciting volunteers and telling people about the work that she, Nixon, and others were doing. She met with the NAACP Youth Council at Trinity Lutheran Church near her apartment and offered guidance to the young people. Even when she was bone-tired from the job at the store, Mrs. Parks's strength seemed to increase when she started to rouse her people to embrace a new idea that might advance them one more notch toward freedom.

Sitting on the porch of his wood-framed house in the early 1980s, Nixon remembered, "Rosa Parks was not only a kind soul; she had a strength about her that was gigantic. She never turned away from a job that needed to be done. She was faithful as a good hound dog, and I mean that in the best way you can imagine. I never doubted her one minute. She was true as a compass. When I got home from long runs up North, she'd always have lists of people who'd called, who'd dropped by, who needed what and how quick I needed to do it."

Through both Nixon and Virginia Durr, a white woman who hired her to make dresses for her daughters, Parks learned about Myles Horton and the Highlander Folk School. At his integrated retreat in the thickly wooded hills of east Tennessee at Monteagle, Horton taught people about civil disobedience, the philosophy of the Golden Rule, and the importance of feeling equal in the human world. Horton had been in touch with Virginia Durr and told her that he had a scholarship open for two weeks in the summer. Mrs. Durr told Parks about the offer, and Parks sat down with Nixon to discuss it. Parks wanted to attend but didn't know when she would be able to. Nixon had been to Highlander, and he'd been impressed by Horton's gentle teachings. He thought it important that Mrs. Parks have the experience, and he insisted she take time off in the summer of 1955 and go to the school.

When Mrs. Parks returned, she and Nixon discussed her time at Highlander. Like Nixon, she was moved by her exposure to the teachings of nonviolent protest. She told Nixon that listening to Horton "made me want to reach out to all the little children of my world and to show them that they were equal to all other little children."

Early on the evening of December 1, 1955, a tired Rosa Parks finished a long day of sewing at Montgomery Fair department

store. It was one of those days before Christmas when everybody wanted their work finished so they could go on to more
shopping. Parks finished the last pile of sewing just before five
o'clock.

Bundled for the cold, wintry night air, Mrs. Parks trudged
a half-block to the bus stop on the corner of Court Street and
Dexter Avenue, where several dozen people waited.

Deciding to forgo the usually crowded 5:00 P.M. bus, she
crossed Dexter to do a little Christmas shopping for her own
family. At Lee's Cut-Rate Drug, she bought some aspirin and
took two on the spot. After milling around for a while and buy-
ing several small gifts for Christmas stockings, she again
crossed the wide boulevard of Dexter Avenue beneath colorful
Christmas decorations. Standing on the corner, she watched as
bus 2857 rolled to a stop in front of the passenger shed. In line,
she stepped aboard and paid her dime. She found an aisle seat
just behind the Colored sign and sat down. Sitting next to her
was a black man who said nothing to her. Across the aisle were
two women she knew. She nodded and spoke. They acknowledged her, then went on with their private conversation.

While she balanced her packages in her lap, the bus stopped
twice and picked up several white passengers. At the third stop,
in front of the Empire Theatre, known as the first totally air-
conditioned movie house in the South and the stage where
world-famous singer-songwriter Hank Williams gave his first
public performance, more white passengers filled the front of
the bus. One white man remained standing.

The bus driver, James F. Blake, stepped toward the Colored
sign. Seeing him, Parks realized he was the same driver who'd
been abusive toward her in 1943. He'd actually ordered her off
the bus after a disturbance among some of the other black riders. Since then, she'd made it a practice never to ride on a bus
that Blake was driving. On this evening, when she boarded the
bus, she paid no attention to the identity of the driver. Later,
she figured she had been just too tired to recognize him.

Blake gestured toward the row of seats where the four blacks sat. Even though there was only one white passenger standing, all four blacks would be required to move. That was the law. No blacks were allowed to sit on a row occupied by any white riders. "Now, y'all move," Blake said. "I've got to have those seats." He would simply move the Colored sign back one row. Blake knew the regulations. He had been driving city buses since 1942. After a stint in the U.S. Army in 1944 and '45, he had returned as a driver late in 1945.

Across the aisle from Mrs. Parks, the two black women rose. They lugged their packages with them down the center aisle toward the back of the bus, where they would stand for the remainder of their trip.

When the man next to Rosa started to move, she shifted in her seat, giving him room to stand and slide out.

Mrs. Parks slid into the space the man had vacated and gazed out the window at the marquee of the Empire. The marquee advertised a western movie, *A Man Alone*, starring Ray Milland.

Blake stopped short of the seat. He glared down at her and again ordered her to move.

Determined not to look down in defeat—a slave's vision— Mrs. Parks leveled her head and stared up into the man's angry face. His lips trembled slightly as he asked, "Are you going to stand up?"

She took a deep breath and let it out slowly. "No," she said with determination.

"Well, I'm going to have you arrested," Blake said.

She said, very clearly, "You may do that."

Later, talking to me at a friend's home in Montgomery, Parks remembers, "When I got on the bus that evening I wasn't thinking about causing a revolution or anything of the kind. I was thinking about my husband, how he'd spent his day at the barber shop at Maxwell Air Force Base, where he worked. I was hoping he'd had a good day. I was thinking about my back aching and about the pretty sights and sounds of Christmas. I was thinking about how we were going to have a good time this Christmas, and everybody was going to be happy.

"But when that white driver stepped back toward us, when he waved his hand and ordered us up and out of our seats, I felt a determination cover my body like a quilt on a winter night. I felt all the meanness of every white driver I'd seen who'd been ugly to me and other black people through the years I'd known on the buses in Montgomery. I felt a light suddenly shine through the darkness.

"I'd been happy early in the year when Claudette Colvin had been arrested for refusing to give up her seat on the bus. I'd been with Mr. Nixon when he'd declared it exactly what the black community needed. I'd seen the light in his eyes at the thought of being able to fight against the oppression of the laws that were keeping us down. I'd called my white lady friend Virginia Durr and we started calling folks to alert them to what was going to happen. We knew we were going to have to have help for a long struggle. Then I saw the hurt in Mr. Nixon's eyes when he found out the Claudette Colvin case wasn't the one we could use. I saw the silent hurt take over. But I wasn't thinking about all of that while I sat there and waited for the police to come. All I could think about, really and truly, was the Lord would help me through all of this. I told myself I wouldn't put up no fuss against them arresting me. I'd go along with whatever they said. But I also knew I wasn't gonna give up my seat just because a white driver told me to; I'd already done that too many times. As soon as they arrested me, I knew, I'd call Mr. Nixon and let him know what had happened. Then we'd see."

On March 2, 1955, a fifteen-year-old junior at Booker T. Washington High School named Claudette Colvin had refused to give up her seat on a city bus. She was riding home from school.

She and another black woman, Mrs. Ruth Hamilton, who was pregnant, sat next to each other on a seat just in front of the rear door, behind the Colored sign. A white couple boarded and sat in the last two open seats across the aisle from Colvin and Hamilton. When the driver, Robert W. Cleere, told the black women to move, both remained seated. Cleere called city police, and soon two officers arrived. Still, both women refused to move. Officers Thomas J. Ward and Paul Headley asked passengers in the rear to allow Hamilton to sit. A black man got up, giving the pregnant woman his seat. Then the officers told Colvin she would have to move. She refused. When the officers told her she was under arrest, she became hysterical, balling her fists and crying. The policemen lifted her and dragged her from the bus.

Nixon knew the young woman as a member of the NAACP Youth Council. He called the young black attorney Fred D. Gray, who took her case, and he asked Clifford Durr, the husband of Virginia Durr, to assist with the legal work. Durr, who assisted Gray in many cases, readily agreed. During Colvin's hearing in Montgomery County Juvenile Court, Ward testified that Colvin had hit, scratched, and kicked him. Gray, at the suggestion of Durr, questioned the constitutionality of the segregation ordinance, challenging it on the grounds that it violated Colvin's rights as guaranteed under the Fourteenth Amendment. Judge Wiley C. Hill, Jr., overruled his motion. Colvin was convicted not only of breaking the segregationist law, but also of assault on an officer. Gray appealed the decision. Soon it was discovered that Colvin, who was young and unmarried, was pregnant. Judge Hill placed her on indefinite, unsupervised probation. It was determined by Nixon and others that Colvin's case did not satisfy the requirements they needed to make an exemplary case with which to fight the law.

On October 21, 1955, another black teenager, Mary Louise Smith, had also been arrested for refusing to give up her seat on a city bus. When her father was called by juvenile authorities, he insisted she plead guilty and pay the five-dollar fine.

Later, however, in federal court, both Colvin and Smith would play significant roles in bus boycott history.

On the night of December 1, 1955, Arlet Nixon answered their home phone and was told by Mrs. Bertha Butler, who had also been riding bus number 2857, that their friend Rosa Parks had been arrested and taken to jail. Arlet called Nixon's office. The phone rang and rang until a neighbor from an adjoining office answered. Arlet told the man that something very important had happened and that Nixon should come home immediately. The man left a message on Nixon's telephone that read, "Call home, it's urgent."

As soon as Nixon walked into his office, he found the message and called home. Arlet said, "They arrested Mrs. Parks."

"For what?" Nixon asked.

"I don't know," Arlet said. "Go get her."

Nixon called the city jail, told the desk sergeant who he was, and asked what charges Mrs. Parks was being held on.

"It ain't none of your goddamn business," the sergeant said.

Nixon hung up. He knew that Fred Gray was out of town. He tried to call another young black attorney, Charles Langford, but there was no answer at either his office or his home.

Nixon then called Clifford Durr, the white lawyer who had tried several NAACP cases for Nixon. Durr's wife, Virginia, had helped Nixon and Mrs. Parks in the NAACP office.

Durr asked Nixon what Mrs. Parks was being charged with, and Nixon told him what the desk sergeant had said.

"Sounds just like 'em," Durr said. "Let me give it a try."

Durr called Nixon back several minutes later. "She's charged with violating the segregation law," Durr said.

"Well, can you go down there with me?" Nixon said.

"Mr. Nixon, I don't have anything to make bail with," Durr said. He earned only three hundred to four hundred dollars a month. It was barely enough to live on.

"That's all right," Nixon said. "I can make bail, if you'll go with me."

"Come by here, and I'll go with you," Durr said.

Nixon drove to the house at Two Felder Avenue where Durr rented an apartment. Durr came onto the porch, pulling on his suit coat. Before he got to Nixon's car, Virginia Durr burst out of the door and followed.

At the city jail on Lower Wetumpka Road, papers were prepared and given to Durr, who perused them carefully. "Looks like everything's in order," the lawyer said.

The sergeant asked Durr if he would sign the bond. Durr said he was not a property owner in Montgomery County, but Nixon was. Durr slid the papers to Nixon and said, "Mr. Nixon might want to sign the bond."

In the front corridor, Virginia Durr rushed to her friend Rosa Parks and surrounded her small frame in her expansive arms.

Outside, Raymond Parks drove up in a car with a neighbor. Rosa rode with him to their apartment on Cleveland Avenue. The Durrs rode there with Nixon.

Mrs. Parks, her husband, and her mother were gathered in the kitchen. The Durrs sat across from them at the kitchen table. Nixon paced and talked. "Mrs. Parks, your case is a case that we can use to break down segregation on the bus," Nixon said.

"Well, I hadn't thought about it," Mrs. Parks said.

Nixon gazed into her eyes. "I'm gonna ask you . . . I want to ask you: let us use your case for a test case. I'll tell you this: it won't be easy. It'll be long and hard. We might have to take it all the way to the Supreme Court, and that'll be a struggle."

Mrs. Parks turned to Clifford Durr, who told her he thought he could get the charges dropped, if that was what she wanted.

She looked up into Nixon's face.

Durr added, "Now, if you're going to fight this on a constitutional basis, you will have to get the NAACP to finance it because it's going to cost a fortune. It'll have to go all the way up to the Supreme Court of the United States, and it's going to cost a lot of money." He added that Fred Gray had connections with the NAACP Legal Defense Fund in New York.

Nixon said, "Mr. Durr's right; it'll be a long and hard struggle. It'll cost a lot of money. But we'll get the NAACP behind it, I promise you that. It won't cost you and Mr. Parks anything but time and misery. But I think it'll be worth all the time and all the misery."

During this time, Virginia Durr remembered, it was Raymond Parks "who was so reluctant. He kept saying over and over again, 'Rosa, the white folks will kill you. Rosa, the white folks will kill you.' It was like a background chorus, to hear the poor man, who was as white as he could be himself, for a black man, saying, 'Rosa, the white folks will kill you.' I don't remember her being reluctant."

Nixon, however, remembered that she was very reluctant at first. "I talked and talked. I answered questions for her. She looked at her husband, and her husband said, 'I think Mr. Nixon's right.' And her mother said, 'And I'll go along with him.' And she said, 'Well, in that case, we'll all go along with you.' And we agreed to use her case as a test case. And I went home that night and told Mrs. Nixon about it. She didn't think much of it."

Once Rosa Parks had agreed to the plan, Nixon knew he had people to see and things to do. He did not hesitate for an instant. This moment had been building within him throughout his adult life. For more than a year, since May 17, 1954, when the U.S. Supreme Court had ruled in *Brown v. Board of Education* (of Topeka, Kansas) that the concept of separate but equal schools was unconstitutional, Nixon had seen changes coming. In the mid-1960s, sitting under the arbor outside the rural Elmore County home of Clifford and Virginia Durr, Nixon recounted the earlier days. "After the Supreme Court ruled, the people started talking about integrating schools. Right about the same time, we began to get black policemen. We had never had nothing like that before. Of course, all those things made some changes. Lot of people thought that just because the Supreme Court ruled, they had it made; but I didn't agree with them. I knew that just 'cause the Court ruled, the people in Alabama weren't necessarily gonna go along with it. Up to the mid-1950s, my people were afraid. There was always fear. They figured if they spoke out, they'd be pushed around on their job, or they would just lose their job, so they kept silent. In my case, my paycheck came from Chicago, and they couldn't get me fired so easy. So, when I saw the opportunity, I knew I could reach out and grab for it."

Soon after he got home on the night of December 1, after he and Arlet discussed what had been decided, Nixon called Jo Ann Gibson Robinson, an Alabama State College English professor who was also president of the Women's Political Council. Nixon had a great deal of respect for Robinson and her ideas. Earlier in the year both she and Nixon had been excited about the prospect of Claudette Colvin challenging the Jim Crow law. Now they knew without a doubt that they had a situation that was worthy of making that challenge.

The twelfth child of a farming family in rural Georgia, Jo Ann Gibson was only six when her father died. It was not long before an older brother who'd moved to Macon persuaded her mother to move into town with him. Jo Ann entered school there and graduated from high school as valedictorian of her class. She became the only one of the twelve children to finish college when she graduated from Georgia State College at Fort Valley. She immediately began teaching in public schools in Macon. Gibson got married, lost a child, and suffered mightily from that loss. When her marriage broke up, Jo Ann Robinson, as she was now called, went on to graduate school at Atlanta University, where she received an MA in English. Later she went into the doctorate program at Columbia University in New York, but after a year she moved to Los Angeles, where she attended a semester at the University of Southern California.

After a year of teaching at Mary Allen College in Crockett, Texas, Robinson was offered a teaching position at all-black Alabama State College. She was not yet forty years old when she moved to Montgomery in 1949. There she met Dr. Mary Fair Burks, a fellow teacher at Alabama State College who was also president of the Women's Political Council (WPC). Robinson struck up a fast friendship with Dr. Burks, who taught her much about the nuances of life among mid–twentieth century intellectual blacks of Montgomery.

Robinson had known Jim Crow since childhood. Growing up black in small-town south Georgia was not much different from growing up black in Alabama. But she had spent little time as a professor in the Deep South until this year. Dr. Burks, who had founded the WPC in 1946 to help black women deal with the political world, welcomed any help she could find. And she recognized in Robinson a kindred spirit. Robinson listened as Burks described the work of the WPC, but she was not emotionally dedicated to its cause until an incident occurred on the first day of Christmas vacation.

Happy to have her first semester behind her, Robinson planned to take off during the break and leave the school and the town behind for several weeks. For a while, she would think about other things. As usual, she boarded a city bus near campus. She dropped her nickels into the slot and looked out across the length of the bus. A white woman was sitting near the front, a black man in the back. She walked a few rows toward the rear and took her seat.

Thinking about her vacation, she closed her eyes and prepared to relax.

Several minutes later, the bus driver stopped the bus, turned in his seat, and shouted toward her, "If you can sit in the fifth row from the front on other buses in Montgomery, suppose you get off and ride in one of them."

Robinson was stunned. She did not believe he was talking to her. She looked around the bus, thinking that surely he was talking to someone else.

At that point the driver rose, walked toward her, drew back his hand, and said, "Get up from there. Get up from there."

Afraid, she pulled herself up, ran to the front of the bus, and stepped down onto a lower level, just inside the front door. She wanted to hover close to the floor. By now, tears were streaming from her eyes. Her hands were shaking uselessly. She had forgotten that she was supposed to exit through the rear door.

Suddenly the front door opened and she stepped off, stumbling as her feet touched the asphalt.

In a daze, she made her way back to the campus and told friends about the experience. They comforted her, and later they drove her to the airport. She was off to Cleveland for her vacation with family members. But the vacation was not as pleasant as she had imagined it would be; all the while, she relived the nightmare on the bus.

By the time she returned to Montgomery, she had decided that she would be dedicated to working in every way possible to right the wrongs that were perpetrated on the city buses. She knew that many Montgomery women rode the buses daily. She had heard their stories. Before now, however, she had not personally felt the bitter anguish of their plight. They suffered the abuse of white drivers who treated them horridly. Now she knew firsthand the suffering that they had felt most of their lives. If there was any way it could be done, she knew that she would do whatever she could to change the system.

After Fred Gray studied law at Case Western Reserve University in Cleveland, Ohio, he returned to Montgomery and passed the bar exam. Soon after he returned, Robinson met him. He introduced her to his fiancée, Bernice Hill, a bright young woman who was equally passionate about change in the community where she was raised. Robinson told her new friends about her experience, and Gray said he was on the lookout for a case that he could possibly carry all the way to the U.S. Supreme Court to challenge the city ordinance requiring segregation on buses.

As they talked about the possibility of such a lawsuit, Robinson began thinking about the possibilities of using economic pressure to bring about changes in the system.

The WPC had been formed to instill in black women the idea that they were better than second-class citizens. The women were inspired to act without being afraid. They were encouraged to act together to raise their standard of living.

In 1950 Robinson became president of the WPC. She began organizing the women to be ready to act when the time came. The same year, she called Mayor William A. Gayle, told him who she was, and asked for a meeting with him and the two other commissioners. They met on several occasions, and the commission listened to Robinson's concerns, but few substantial changes were made. However, Robinson persisted.

In 1953 the WPC heard thirty complaints about problems on city buses. In 1954 Robinson wrote to Mayor Gayle with three demands concerning the buses: adopt the protocol used in Mobile, whereby seats were provided on a first-come, first-served basis, with whites filling seats from front to rear, and blacks from the rear forward; stop requiring blacks to pay at the front of the bus, then go to the rear door of the bus to enter; and see to it that buses stop at every corner in black residential areas, as they did in white areas. (In 1955 the requirement that Negroes pay at the front and enter in the rear was quietly dropped by the city and the bus company.)

In her letter Robinson stated, "More and more of our people are already arranging with neighbors and friends to ride to keep from being insulted and humiliated by bus drivers." That was the first time that Robinson made a subtle suggestion that a boycott might be in the works. After all, Montgomery City Lines depended on the black population for its profits: more than 90 percent of the riders were black.

As she and E. D. Nixon discussed Rosa Parks's case that Thursday night in December 1955, Robinson said she believed they should go further than simply challenging the constitutionality of the law.

"What do you mean?" Nixon asked.

She told him that she had been in the audience when Congressman Powell had spoken less than a month earlier. In his speech, Powell had described the boycott of the city buses in New York. "I think we ought to call a boycott," she said.

Of course, Nixon had heard Powell's speech. It was he who had introduced the congressman. And, later that night in his own living room, he had listened to Powell talk passionately about the changes the boycott had brought about.

"I can get my people behind it," Robinson said. "We'll start early tomorrow morning."

Nixon told her he agreed wholeheartedly. He would set up a meeting of the town's black ministers. They needed to preach the message from the pulpits. The community needed to start the boycott as soon as possible: Monday morning.

While getting ready for bed that night, Nixon remembered another person he should call. He had almost forgotten his trusted helper, Johnnie Carr, whom he knew should hear the news from him.

"Mrs. Carr," Nixon said.

"Yeah," she answered.

"Well, Mrs. Carr, they put the wrong person in jail."

"Who did they put in jail?" Mrs. Carr asked.

"They arrested Rosa Parks," he said.

"You don't mean to tell me they arrested Rosa Parks?" Mrs. Carr was dumbfounded.

"Yes," he said. "They arrested Rosa Parks on the bus today. They put the wrong person in jail." He told her there would be a boycott of the buses on Monday. There would be a lot of work at the NAACP office over the weekend. She and Parks would have to take care of things there. He would be heading out tomorrow on his train run.

The members of the Women's Political Council knew exactly what to do when the time came. They had been waiting. Robinson had been telling them that it wouldn't be long before the time was right. Early on Friday morning, they wrote a message to the black population of Montgomery: a boycott of the buses would begin on Monday, December 5. They cranked out mimeographed copies of the message, which they would distribute the rest of that day and Saturday. Preachers would talk about it from the pulpits on Sunday.

Nixon's first call early Friday morning was to Ralph David Abernathy, the young pastor of the First Baptist Church on Ripley Street. Nixon felt comfortable with Abernathy. The two men had a country upbringing in common, and they communicated easily. A heavyset, heavy-jowled man, Abernathy, like Nixon, had been raised on a farm in the heart of Alabama's Black Belt. He spoke in a deep, drawling baritone. When Nixon told him what had happened and the plans for a boycott, Abernathy said, "I'm with you, Nixon, all the way."

As he would say during a number of other calls he would make that morning, Nixon replied, "If this thing is going to work, we have to stand together. That's absolutely necessary. It's going to be a tough legal battle, long and drawn out, but it'll be worth it in the long run. And we're planning to call on the people to boycott the buses on Monday. That'll be hard on a lot of people who depend on the buses, but we all need to stick together on this thing."

Nixon commented years later, "There's one thing I know. I know how to organize. I ain't gonna argue with you about doing paperwork. I ain't never been a newspaperman. I ain't gonna argue with no schoolteacher about teaching school. I never taught school. I ain't gonna argue with no minister about preaching. I ain't never preached. But when it comes to civil rights and organizing, I know how to do it. I learned from the best in the land: Philip Randolph and Myles Horton. I been to their school and sat in their class and listened to their words. I been doing it since way back when I first put my mind to it."

However, Nixon realized that he had to be out of town too often to provide the full-time leadership necessary to sustain a full-scale boycott. Also, he was getting on in age. He was pushing sixty. The people needed someone who could grow with the boycott and give it a positive image; somebody who could speak strongly and with persuasion.

At a convocation at Alabama State College, Nixon had heard a speech by the new young minister at the Dexter Avenue Baptist Church, Martin Luther King, Jr. Listening, he thought, *Man, can he talk!* Standing nearby was his good friend Alabama State Professor James E. Pierce. They were standing in the back of an auditorium at the school. After King finished, Nixon said, "He is a wonderful talker, ain't he?" and Pierce agreed. Then Nixon said, "If he'll let me, I'm gonna hang that young man up yonder in the stars."

Nixon was not the only one who had heard King and been impressed with his oratory style. Two of the women who worked in the NAACP office with Nixon heard the young minister speak one Sunday afternoon at an NAACP meeting held at the Metropolitan United Methodist Church. In attendance were Rosa Parks and her friend Johnnie Rebecca Carr. Carr remembered, "Rosa Parks and I were sitting together in the church at the particular time, and when he got up and started talking, I told her, 'God, listen to that guy.' I said: 'He's something else!' We could see something in him, the way he even delivered the few words—that he was really somebody that had something people had needed."

So Nixon's next call that morning was to Reverend King, who at first hesitated. "When he heard me talk about how long it'd take and how hard the struggle would be, he wasn't sure. He was a young man just getting started in the ministry. His family was young. His wife had given birth to their first child, a little girl, less than a month ago. He said, 'Let me think about it a while and call me back.' After some more calls, I went to see him at the parsonage on South Jackson Street, and I told him straight out that I thought he was the man who should lead this thing. He paced the floor a time or two, then he turned to me and said in that strong and powerful voice of his, he said, 'Brother Nixon, if you think I'm the one, I'll do it.' I nodded and clasped his hand and held it, and I swear there was something stronger than ever in that handshake. I knew we'd all be one together."

Later, the preacher's wife, Coretta Scott King, would tell the *New York Times*, "If it had not been for E. D. Nixon, we would not have had the freedom movement as early as we did. If it had not been for him, Martin Luther King, Jr., would not have been involved that early."

Standing on the porch of the parsonage, a thought struck Reverend King. He told Nixon it might be a good idea to use Dexter Avenue Baptist Church for the meeting place that afternoon. Nixon laughed shortly. "I was hoping you'd say that, Brother King, 'cause I done offered it to everybody I called." Later King remembered telling Nixon that whatever they did, it was going to be without violence. Nixon, whose face was

scarred from old skirmishes and whose big fists were gnarled
from battles, said that whatever King said, that would be the
way. But, Nixon added, sometimes it was difficult for him to
remain nonviolent when he looked Jim Crow in the face.

As soon as Fred Gray arrived back in town, he was told about
the arrest of Rosa Parks. He was eager to get to work on the
case. For him, it would be a tough but great beginning to
changing bus company practices and breaking down segregation throughout his community.

Born in Montgomery on December 14, 1930, Fred Gray was
raised by a hardworking mother who cooked for white families
after his father died when Fred was only two years old. He was
brought up in the Holt Street Church of Christ, which his
father, a carpenter, had helped build. His life with four siblings
revolved around church activities: a born orator, who in his
early life had already acquired a useful vocabulary, he began
preaching when he was still a boy. His mother wanted all of her
children to obtain an education, become good Christians, and
make something of themselves. She taught her children that
they could be anything they wanted to become. At age fourteen, Fred was sent to Tennessee's Nashville Christian Institu-
tion, an African American Church of Christ high school. After
graduation, he returned home to Montgomery with the idea of
becoming a Church of Christ minister.

At Alabama State College for Negroes (which would later
become Alabama State University), Gray was encouraged by
E. D. Nixon's close friend, Dr. James E. Pierce, a political science professor, to apply for law school. Gray's first choice was
the University of Alabama Law School. But black students were
not allowed to attend the only public law school in the state.
Instead, Gray received financial aid from the state because no
black institutions of higher learning offered a law degree. The

state not only paid his tuition to Case Western Reserve in Cleveland, but it also sent him regular checks for extracurricular activities. After graduating from Case Western, he took the three-day Ohio bar examination. And, after arriving back in Montgomery, he prepared to take the Alabama bar exam.

To stand for the Alabama bar, he was required to file character affidavits from five lawyers who had been practicing in the state for at least five years. But he did not know five lawyers. With strong determination, a quality his mother had instilled in him many years earlier, he went to see E. D. Nixon, whom he knew as Mr. Civil Rights and who had been solving problems for black people for years.

When Gray was a youngster, E. D. Nixon had asked him to organize the Young Alabama Democrats (YAD) to help get young people involved in the political process. It was through this effort that Gray became associated with Inez Jesse Baskin, a woman who worked as the assistant editor of the Colored News section of the *Montgomery Advertiser* and as an unofficial stringer for black magazines such as *Jet* and *Ebony*. Baskin wrote about Gray's efforts in the local paper, spreading the word throughout the black community, and she also brought national attention to his work in *Jet* and other magazines that were targeted at black audiences. Nixon supervised the young man's work and helped him to organize a plan to interest young people in both registering to vote and insisting that their parents register. On election day, YAD had assisted in the transportation of people to polling places.

As soon as he heard of Gray's dilemma, Nixon went to work to obtain affidavits. He made up his list and started checking off names. Arthur Shores, of Birmingham, was the best-known black lawyer in the state. Charles V. Henley, the grand master of the Masons, didn't practice law, but he held a law license. Both signed affidavits for Gray. Gray's fiancée, Bernice Hill, worked for the wife of Nesbitt Elmore, a white attorney. Elmore introduced Gray to his uncle, Clifford Durr, who signed an affidavit after he'd become acquainted with the young man and realized not only that Gray was very smart, but that he also had outstanding personal credentials that would stand him in good stead in the practice of law. Other white attorneys who signed affidavits for Gray were Woodley C. Campbell, Henry Heller, and Kenneth McGee, all of whom practiced in Montgomery.

Soon thereafter, Gray and Durr became especially close. After Gray opened his office in 1954, he persuaded Durr to serve as his legal adviser.

When he heard the details of the Rosa Parks case, Gray felt as strongly as Nixon that this was indeed the case they had been looking for. He went directly to Durr and asked him to join in the effort. Again, Durr readily agreed.

Sitting on the wooden pew in the Dexter Avenue Baptist Church that Friday afternoon, Inez Jesse Baskin waited for the meeting to begin. She was accustomed to waiting: she knew that not every meeting started exactly on time.

Now she looked around the interior of the old church. She knew its history, just as she knew its people. A holding pen for African slaves had sat on this very spot a hundred years earlier. Nearby there had been an auction block on which the slaves were paraded in front of prospective buyers, who would inspect the wares: check the teeth, pinch the skin, slap backsides, and examine heads to make sure the property wasn't infected with lice. And Inez Jesse Baskin knew, too, that after the Civil War, it was the freed slaves themselves who'd torn the pen and block down and ripped the material to shreds. It was the black people of money and position, the teachers and doctors and lawyers and business leaders who lived mostly on nearby Centennial Hill, who put up the money and built Dexter Avenue Baptist Church with bricks and hand-hewed timbers in 1878.

Sitting there, Inez Jesse Baskin listened to the black ministers arguing about who would do what when. She noticed that the young minister who'd recently taken over the church's pulpit was sitting in a pew behind the older, more experienced preachers, listening to their talk. Holding her reporter's notebook in her lap, her pencil poised, she wondered where E. D. Nixon was. He'd called the meeting, and now he was late.

When Nixon walked through the doorway, having been held up at home with some last-minute packing and a phone call he couldn't avoid, he stopped for a moment and listened to the conversation taking place in the church.

Inez Jesse Baskin watched, wondering, a little apprehensive about what was about to take place. She had known Edgar Daniel Nixon for years. She'd grown up in his neighborhood and in the Holt Street Baptist Church, where he was a leader to whom the congregation turned when they wanted everyday truth beyond the pulpit. He was their strength when they needed him. Through all of her dealings with him she could not remember ever hearing him raise his voice. But she could see by the fire in his eyes and a tremble in his heavy cheek that his temper was rising beyond annoyance as he listened to the men bicker.

All of the preachers seemed to be talking at once. One minister said that the blacks needed to keep everything to themselves. "We don't need to let the white people know what we're doing," he said. Another said they needed to conduct business in the churches, not out in the open or in the streets. Another said he was worried about what the situation was going to cost the black community. "If the white people know what we're doing," he added, "a lot of Negroes are going to be fired."

Inez Jesse Baskin made notes.

Nixon sat and listened. Finally, after Baskin saw his cheek twitch for the third or fourth time, Nixon rose to his feet and stepped in front of them. He shook his head. "Gentlemen," he said in a quiet voice.

All other talk ceased. The preachers' heads turned to him.

"You can't keep a boycott secret," he said. "You all ought to know that. What good is having a boycott if you gonna keep it to yourselves? The whole idea behind a boycott is making the other side know you mean business."

"But if we shout it from the rooftops, Mr. Nixon, a lot of Negroes are gonna lose their jobs," one said.

"You know, the white folk ain't gonna sit still for this," another said.

Nixon squeezed his thick brows into a frown. "This morning I was down yonder with some of the women who been maids and housekeepers all their lives. These womens been treated worse than animals by white bus drivers all their lives. You know what they doing before they go outside and get on the bus to go to work?"

Nobody said a word.

"They helping Jo Ann Robinson and her folk print up and put out flyers so every Negro in Montgomery will know we gonna boycott them buses on Monday morning. They doing what it takes to do to make sure that task is done.

"While y'all sittin' here fussin' over who's gonna take credit for what. You say you want ever'thing secret. You want to keep it out-a newspaper, off-a TV. Well, I'm here to tell you, you can't have no boycott in secret. Fact is, I'm gonna take stuff downtown to a newspaper reporter right now in a few minutes. I want it all over the newspaper Sunday morning. I hope and pray it is."

Several preachers started to protest.

Nixon raised his hand again. "I'm here to tell you, we gonna shout it out to the nation. If need be, we'll go worldwide. Y'all know we got to make the world know where we is and what we all about. You know that, don't you Reverend Abernathy?"

Abernathy nodded. "I know it, Brother Nixon."

Another said, "We know it."

"Now let me tell you something else," Nixon said. "Those washwomen work they fingers to the bone. That's what they do! All the Negro mens in this community been living off the sweat of those washwomen for years. The mens done nothing to help. Well, now you can help! They need you to stand tall and be counted! Now, you gonna be with us? You gonna stand on your feet? Or are you gonna sit here and whimper? Mens have to be mens, or they wear aprons all their lives.

"I say we need to turn history around and stop hiding behind these women who do all the work for us. I say we stand out there in the open and hold our heads high and quit all this bickering.

"I know one thing: we can't crawl in a hole. The word is already on the street. The white folks that own the bus company, they know what we doing. If they don't know it now, they gonna know it. How you gonna not let 'em know? Right now, we better make up our minds: We gonna be men enough to stand on our feet and discuss our grievances out in the open? Or we gonna admit to the world that we just a bunch of cowards?"

In a rear pew, Reverend King stood. Without hesitation, he stated loud and clear, "I'm no coward. I'll stand up, and I'll be counted."

The men nodded with him and mumbled, "Amen." Then they stood and went to Nixon and shook his hand. "We're with you, Brother Nixon," they said.

A Reporter's Scoop

ON THE MORNING of December 2, 1955, the *Montgomery Advertiser* ran a short, one-column article about Rosa Parks's arrest the night before. The story was buried on page nine of section A of the paper. It gave no signal of the far-reaching events that would take place in the year ahead.

Negro Jailed Here For 'Overlooking' Bus Segregation

A Montgomery Negro woman was arrested by city police last night for ignoring a bus driver who directed her to sit in the rear of the bus. The woman, Rosa Parks, 634 Cleveland Ave., was later released under $100 bond. Bus operator J. F. Blake, 27 N. Lewis St., in notifying police, said a Negro woman sitting in the section reserved for whites refused to move to the Negro section. When Officers F. B. Day and

D. W. Mixon arrived where the bus was halted
on Montgomery street, they confirmed his
report. Blake signed the warrant for her arrest
under a section of the City Code that gives
police powers to bus drivers in the enforcement of segregation aboard buses.

Joe Azbell did not write this story. At the time, although he was city editor and chief reporter at the *Advertiser* and arguably knew more about the everyday goings-on in the city than any other individual, he was not aware of the significance of the arrest. However, he would soon learn from an old friend.

Joe Allen Azbell, a lanky, stoop-shouldered young man from Vernon, Texas, was an old-fashioned journalist who considered himself a tough, hands-on, capable, street-smart reporter. He had learned the newspaper trade in the late 1930s and early '40s from an elderly editor of his hometown weekly. Like E. D. Nixon, Azbell had known hard times as a child and had left his family home when he was still very young. After receiving numerous beatings, he ran away from home in his early teens and lived in a tiny room at the rear of the newspaper office. As a result of the violent abuse he'd suffered as a child, he said later, he developed a distinctive tongue-tied lisp that he could never shake.

Under the strict tutelage of his mentors, Azbell learned to write succinct, declarative sentences. Early in his career he accomplished the nearly impossible task of writing directly into type: lifting letters from a font box and placing them into a handheld stick. As he meticulously set the type, he would form his composition, using simple sentences with strong active verbs, before placing the finished story into the form, and then putting it to bed, rolling the ink and printing the final product by hand; as such, he was not only a reporter, but he also doubled as a printer's devil at the Vernon weekly.

As a result of this early training in composing directly to the cold type, he never learned to type. He used the hunt-and-peck system, his extended forefingers slamming down onto the keyboard. Still, he could rip out finished copy faster than most trained typists could copy a transcript, doing it while an unfiltered cigarette dangled from his lips. With smoke puffing out of the edges of his mouth and ashes falling onto his chest, Azbell looked like the clichéd tough-guy reporter on the cover of a 1950s pulp-fiction paperback.

Azbell joined the army in Texas. During his tenure as a soldier, while he was stationed at Craig Field, near Selma, Alabama, he met Betty Jackson. Jackson came from a family that had lived in Dallas County, in the heart of Alabama's Black Belt, for several generations. She was a lovely young woman who had studied ballet from a local teacher.

At the time, Joe was tall and gawky. His sweetheart thought he was "nothing much but skin and bones." But he was a hard-working young man, and his intellect impressed her. Betty also appreciated Joe's industrious nature. Having spent most of his early years unsure of the next dollar or meal, he took a job off the army field, working part-time for the *Selma Times-Journal.* He also salvaged thrown-away cardboard from alleyways behind downtown businesses, which he sold to a west Alabama factory by the hundred-pound load. With the extra money he bought a wedding ring. He and Betty married, and as soon as he left the armed service, they moved to Montgomery.

At the *Montgomery Advertiser*, Azbell quickly became a well-known reporter. He was fascinated with his new world. He familiarized himself not only with the political hierarchy, but also with the underbelly of the lazy town. He regularly walked the downtown streets between the *Advertiser* offices and Union Station, passing the cotton warehouses and the alcoves where hobos curled up in balls to stay out of the wind that sometimes whipped off the Alabama River. He knew the gamblers who hung out at Willie's Pool Parlor and in the late-night joints along Lee Street. He knew the girls of the night who worked the Steamboat Lounge and carried their customers around the corner to the Exchange Hotel, where Jefferson Davis had stayed the night before he was inaugurated president of the Confederate States of America and where poet Sidney Lanier had written "The Song of the Chattahoochee" while working as a night clerk in the days after the Civil War. Azbell knew Johnny Connor, a legendary gambler and nightclub owner who'd hosted another world-class gambler, Titanic Thompson, when he swept through town and took thousands of dollars from the rich businessmen at the Montgomery Country Club. In the late 1940s Azbell sat in a booth in the Crystal Cafe, the all-night restaurant on the corner of Lee and Montgomery streets, and listened to a thin-faced young man with a melodious voice tell him about life on the road, playing honky-tonks and being on the stage of the Grand Ole Opry in Nashville, where he was known as an erratic star because of his drunken, rowdy ways. And when country music star Hank Williams died at age twenty-nine on New Year's Day, 1953, Joe Azbell, by then city editor at the daily morning newspaper, devoted an entire front section to the singer-songwriter's demise. "Old man Hudson [the publisher of the *Advertiser*] called me into his office and chewed me out. He was embarrassed, he said, that I would go over his head to spend so much time and space on the death of a sorry, no-good, carousing sonofabitch like Hank Williams. He fired me on the spot and ordered me to write the story of my firing. I walked out, left the paper, didn't write the story, and went home to Betty to tell her I was without a job. The next day, Mr. Hudson called me back to the paper. He discovered that more than twenty thousand extra copies of the Hank Williams edition of the paper had been sold on the streets, and people were clamoring for more. He didn't apologize, but he said, 'Print all you think will sell, but make sure they do sell.' We printed ten thousand more and they all sold." Williams's funeral, which was held in the auditorium at City Hall, was the largest in the town's history.

In his off hours, Azbell loved to sit at his favorite booth in the Sheridan Cafe on South Perry Street, across from City Hall, where he would brag to politicians, policemen, and other reporters about the way he'd learned his trade. He chided the young college-trained journalists, like Tom Johnson from Florence, in north Alabama, and recent graduate Steve Lesher from New York, saying they were soft and didn't know the game the way he knew it. And when a politician or a policeman wanted to leak an important story, get headlines on page one, or make a story disappear, they knew where to find Azbell.

Through the early 1950s, Azbell had become aware of the changing political scene in the capital city. He wrote a number of articles about the emergence of east Montgomery's middle-class voting power in city elections. In 1947 a young teacher and football coach at Capitol Heights Junior High, Earl D. James, had challenged and defeated General William P. Screws, a member of the stalwart old-south Montgomery political machine that had ruled city politics for nearly all of the twentieth century, in a bid for city commissioner. The defeat of Screws, a wealthy resident of Cloverdale who'd been a city commissioner since 1931, shocked most of Montgomery's political insiders. After all, Screws had been state commander of the Rainbow Division in World War I, and he was a member in good standing of the "Gunter machine," a highly organized local political group named for William A. Gunter, Jr., who'd served as mayor from 1910 to 1915 and from 1919 until his death in 1940. Azbell enjoyed telling stories about how William Gunter came to power after a long battle with another rich and powerful family, the Hills, descended from the Reverend Luther Leonidas Hill, who arrived in Montgomery shortly before Jefferson Davis and the Confederate congress. As for Screws's defeat, Azbell said he'd seen it coming.

Throughout the early days of the 1900s, poor whites and blacks suffered from discrimination in the city. As early as 1900, a city ordinance requiring separation of races on city trolleys provoked a Negro boycott. It lasted through the summer, when the city council amended the law to offer concessions to the boycotters and even to provide black drivers for trolleys carrying black passengers. At the time, few blacks were registered to vote. However, the number increased rapidly through the 1940s.

Under Mayor Gunter's long reign—during the four years he was out of the mayoral office, he served in the state senate—Montgomery's city government was changed to that of a commission. Its officials now consisted of the mayor; a commissioner of public affairs, who presided over the city's fire and police departments; and a commissioner of public works, who oversaw the operation of parks, libraries, street maintenance, and garbage collection. The city had no merit system; everyone who was employed by the city of Montgomery was hired by Gunter. The only jobs that went to blacks were those of garbage collectors and janitors.

When William A. "Tacky" Gayle was elected commissioner in 1935, he was Mayor Gunter's fair-haired boy. A former adjutant general of Alabama's home troops, a veteran of World War I, and a lifelong resident of Cloverdale in south Montgomery, Gayle was the heir apparent when Gunter died in 1940. While serving as an air corps colonel in Britain during World War II, he was elected to his third term on the Montgomery commission in 1943. After he returned home, he was reelected once again in 1947, and he became mayor in 1951.

In 1953, when Earl James resigned his commission seat to go into private business, a special election was called to fill his term. Young state representative Joe M. Dawkins received the backing of Gayle and the Gunter machine. He was opposed by Dave Birmingham, a diminutive, dapper politician given to

overstatement and demagogic innuendo. An outspoken supporter of Governor "Big Jim" Folsom's opposition to the "Big
Mules," Birmingham's term for powerful big business and util-
ities, Birmingham campaigned against the "ringmasters," his
term for the Gunter machine, which he also called "that
cesspool of gangsters at city hall." Thanks to the votes of the
poor and lower-middle-class whites of Capitol Heights, in east
Montgomery, and Highland Gardens and Boylston, in north
Montgomery, as well as to the steadily growing black vote, Birmingham won.

Two years later, Azbell wrote that city politicians now won
with "the silent vote," no longer depending on the personal
acquaintance of the powerful families, the Gunters and the
Hills of south Montgomery, but depending on an impersonal
advertising-style campaign. "No one seemed to care how the
Hills were moving," he wrote. "No one seemed concerned
about the political blocs. Twenty years ago a political observer
would not dare comment on an election without first determining how the blocs were going. For the first time in city
political history, ring politics played no important part in the
local election, because the old ring politics had been overshad-
owed by a growing city where there is no control or method of
determining how the voters will cast their ballot." With each
change in Montgomery's political climate, E. D. Nixon and his
fellow blacks began to exercise more power.

It was during Birmingham's short term, which lasted only
two years, that the city finally hired its first black police officers. However, in the spring of 1955, when Birmingham came
up for reelection, he was opposed by Clyde C. Sellers, a south
Montgomery businessman. Azbell was present at a meeting of
E. D. Nixon's Progressive Democratic Association at the Ben
Moore Hotel, where all candidates for municipal offices were
invited to share their points of view on issues concerning blacks.
At that meeting, Sellers first voiced opposition to a proposal to

change seating arrangements on buses, saying that it was illegal. Later, he campaigned openly and loudly against the mounting black unrest, pledging that he would oppose appointing any blacks to city boards. If the commission complied with a request from blacks that they be allowed to register for civil service jobs, he stated, "It would be only a short time before Negroes would be working alongside of whites, and whites alongside Negroes." In campaign speeches Sellers said, "There are places in this nation where civil service jobs for Negroes are available, but not in Montgomery. I will expend every effort to keep it that way." The electorate chose Sellers over Birmingham, who took a moderate stand on the racial question.

———

Neither Joe Azbell nor E. D. Nixon could remember who had initiated their friendship. By 1955, however, they had known each other for several years, and each respected the other. On Friday, December 2, 1955, they met in an area between the white and black waiting rooms at Union Station. Built in 1898, the old depot had been the scene of thousands of young soldiers returning home from the Great War in 1918 and '19, and of thousands more leaving to go to World War II in the early 1940s. Union Station was a neutral spot where both the white reporter and the black civil rights activist felt comfortable. Besides, meeting Azbell was the last thing Nixon had to do before climbing aboard the train for a two-day run, heading for Atlanta and New York. He would return Sunday night.

Azbell listened intently as Nixon outlined the plans for a boycott to begin the following Monday—the same day that Rosa Parks would go to trial in municipal court. Nixon gave the newsman copies of the leaflets that Jo Ann Robinson and her team of women volunteers had created, pieces that would be handed out on the streets Friday afternoon and all day Saturday, and tacked to every bus stop shed in town. Nixon told Azbell that, if everything worked according to plan, Monday would be the most important day in the history of Montgomery. It would be the most memorable day since Jefferson Davis sent the telegram ordering his Confederate troops to fire on Fort Sumter. Both men had read the brass plaque that resided on the side of the National Shirt Shop in the Winter Building, on the southeast corner of Dexter Avenue and Court Street, where the telegraph office had been located in 1861. No historian had ever disputed the significance of that event in the annals of Montgomery, Alabama.

On the eve of the boycott, Azbell's Sunday morning page-one story in the *Advertiser* stated that the blacks were planning an all-out boycott of the city buses. Azbell reported a "top-secret" meeting called for Monday night at a local Baptist church. Couched in the immediacy of lurking danger, Azbell quoted the leaflet that had flooded "Negro sections" of town on Saturday: "Another Negro woman has been arrested and thrown into jail because she refused to get up out of her seat on the bus and give it to a white person.

"It is the second time since the Claudette Colvin case that a Negro has been arrested for the same thing.

"This must be stopped. Negroes are citizens and have rights.

"Until we do something to stop these arrests, they will continue.

"The next time it may be you, or you, or you.

"This woman's case will come up Monday.

"We are, therefore, asking every Negro to stay off the buses on Monday to protest . . . Please stay off the buses Monday."

When E. D. Nixon arrived back in Montgomery that Sunday, he read Azbell's front-page article. He began calling his preachers, asking if they'd read the newspaper. Most had. Several had not. "Get it and read it," Nixon told them.

Throughout Montgomery that morning, black preachers raised their voices, telling their congregations to stay off the buses Monday morning.

Anxious, Nixon drove around town that afternoon, visiting various churches. Every time he saw more than two black people on a street corner, he stopped and talked, preaching his own sermon about the pending boycott. During his drive, he stopped at Two Felder Avenue and paid a call on the Durrs. He sat in their living room and told them what had taken place during his absence. Virginia Durr was particularly thrilled that a boycott of the city buses would actually take place on Monday morning. "Is there anything we can do?" she offered. Cliff had already talked with Fred Gray, who would be defending Rosa Parks in city court on Monday morning. He had already begun researching what they would file on appeal.

When Nixon finally went to bed that evening, he told Arlet that, surely, the people listened to their preachers. Arlet didn't tell him, but she was skeptical.

Azbell awakened before daybreak on Monday. As he slid out of bed in the dark, Betty mumbled something and turned over. By now she'd become accustomed to his reporter's hours, and to him getting calls in the middle of the night and taking off at any time, morning, noon, or night. It was still dark when he drove into town. The early morning streets were ghostly quiet. Few stirred.

As he drove west on the wide boulevard of Dexter Avenue, a smoky cloud of vapor, like a sleeping giant's breath, rose from the open grates along the curb. Only one car was parked near the shed where the buses stopped. Azbell slowed his car to a creep, then came to a stop, and noticed a white man sat in the driver's seat of the parked car.

Azbell sat in his car and watched the empty bus stop. Usually on a weekday morning, several dozen people would be waiting for the first bus. This morning a cluster of black men stood at the far corner next to the First National Bank. Others stood across Commerce Street next to the old brick Exchange Hotel and near the glass-fronted National Shirt Shop on the south side. These men stood still, like statues. They were talking in hushed tones.

To the east, under streetlights haloed in cold moisture, he saw a city bus heading down the hill away from the white-domed capitol. With his window rolled down, smoking his third cigarette of the morning, Azbell jotted thoughts in his reporter's notebook, a journal so narrow that it fit comfortably into his breast pocket. He was seldom without his notebook. Just as he was about to reach a conclusion, one woman walked around the southwest corner of Court and Montgomery streets. She walked slowly toward the benches at the bus stop shed. She stood near the benches and looked up as the bus came to a stop within twenty feet of her. She gazed into the windows of the bus. Azbell saw the front door of the bus open. Lights inside the vehicle showed that the only person aboard was the driver, who called out something. Azbell could not hear the words. The woman did not move. She said nothing. The groups of black men gazed in the direction of the bus.

One man moved toward the bus. Azbell watched his dark profile, tall and thin and erect, his head held aloft.

The driver shouted, "You gonna get on?"

The man said nothing. He stood still in the crisp December morning, his breath visible, like smoke.

"You gonna get on?" the driver asked again.

With a defiant twist of his head, the man declared, "I ain't gettin' on until Jim Crow gets off."

Azbell heard the driver's laugh echo through the empty bus.

The would-be rider marched away toward the other blacks who were standing nearby and who were listening to his declaration. None of them said another word.

The diesel engine within the bus belched. Smoke coughed from its underside. A screech sounded through the cold morning as the folding door closed with a thud. Then the bus continued along its route, heading around Court Square Fountain and up Montgomery Street, toward the spot where Parks had been arrested four days earlier.

Behind the bus, on Dexter Avenue, Azbell heard the driver of the car say something to the black men nearest him. Three of the men sauntered over to the car. More words were exchanged. The men walked around the car. One got into the shotgun seat and two slid into the back. The white man drove off with his passengers.

"I stayed there about twenty to thirty minutes," Azbell later testified in Montgomery Circuit Court. "Negroes were all around the corners, and cars were coming along and picking them up as if there was a migration of Negro people. They were hanging around on every corner, came up one by one, two by two; some came from that direction, and some were going in another direction. The buses were empty, except for a few white passengers."

As the sun came up behind him, Azbell proceeded to Cleveland Avenue, out to Fairview, through the ritzy, turn-of-the-century subdivision of Cloverdale to the Negro section of Bogge Homa, then to Capitol Heights, Washington Park, and down to the shanties of White Dog and Peacock Park. In all of the places he knew were predominantly Negro neighborhoods, he witnessed black people standing and walking, but none were riding the buses. "Most of the Negroes early that morning were walking and singing to themselves, 'We are not riding the buses,' and making a lot of hell," the reporter later told the court. He passed several pickup trucks with black people in the backs, singing the same song.

E. D. Nixon was pleased that morning when he saw only one black rider on all of the buses that came through his neighborhood. He and his wife drove to Rosa Parks's house, picked her up, and together they went to Fred Gray's office downtown. It was agreed that, in recorder's court, Parks would plead not guilty.

Less than an hour later they proceeded to the courtroom on Madison Avenue, behind City Hall and the police department. As they entered, Nixon did not notice the number of black people who lined the halls. Parks's case was called, and she pleaded not guilty. The bus driver testified that she had refused to move when ordered. Municipal Judge John Scott found her guilty, and Gray stated that the defendant would appeal the fine of ten dollars plus court costs. When Nixon turned, he looked out at the many blacks who lined the walls. In all the years he had been going to city court to help people in trouble, the only blacks he had seen there were defendants whose cases would be tried, or relatives or close friends of those defendants. This time, when he walked out with Parks, there were black people all the way down the hall to the clerk's office. After the papers were signed and Fred Gray was satisfied that everything was in order, about twenty blacks crowded around the door. "What happened, Brother Nixon?" one of the men asked. Nixon said, "They found her guilty and they fined her ten dollars, and we're gonna appeal the decision, and I'm gonna make a second bond for her, and I'm gonna bring her out." Another said, "Well, if you don't come on out, we'll come in there and get you."

Years later, on a Sunday afternoon at the country home that Clifford Durr had built with his own hands, Nixon remembered, "I couldn't believe it. There were all these people down there just to back us up. Well, I went on in the clerk's office, signed her bond, and came outside with Mrs. Parks next to me. We looked out there and saw more than five hundred black men up and down the street and all around the courtyard. I'd never seen nothing like that before. Then I put Mrs. Parks in the car and told Mrs. Nixon to take her home. I just wanted to stand there and look at the sight. I still couldn't believe my eyes.

There was a couple of police with sawed-off shotguns in two or three of the windows upstairs. I said to the men, 'How many of you men know me? Hold your hand up.' It looked to me, everybody held their hand up. I said, 'All right, don't spit on the sidewalk. Don't throw no cigarette butts, or paper, or anything. You see those men with those sawed-off shotguns? They'd go on and use them. Don't give them a chance. Now, if you really want to do something, go back to your neighborhood and ask at least five people to be at the Holt Street Baptist Church tonight.' Some of them said they were gonna ask more than five. Some said they were gonna ask all they can."

Nixon thanked the people for their support. Several slapped him on the back before he walked south on Perry Street toward his office. On the way Nixon was met by E. N. French, pastor of the Hilliard Chapel AME Church, and Reverend Abernathy, who'd been looking for him. Following him to his office, they wanted to know what had happened with Parks. Nixon told them. He said they needed to do some planning before the meeting that afternoon. Sitting in the NAACP office, they began to talk about a new organization. Nixon later recalled that Abernathy came up with the name—the Montgomery Improvement Association, which seemed perfect to Nixon and French. "He was sitting right in front of me," said Nixon. "He reached over and put his hand on my knee and said, 'Brother Nixon?' I said, 'Yeah.' He said, 'You're gonna serve as president, ain'tcha?' I said, 'No, not unless you-all don't accept my man.' He said, 'Who is your man?' I said, 'Well, first I'm gonna tell you the reason. This is going to be a long, drawn-out affair. It's gonna need somebody who's gonna be on the scene every day. My man for this spot would be Martin Luther King.' He said, 'I'll go along with you.' French said, 'I'll go along with you.'"

To make the boycott successful, E. D. Nixon, Martin Luther King, Jr., and the others who gathered at the Mount Zion AME

Church on Jeff Davis Avenue at 3:00 P.M. that Monday knew that a great deal more planning would be necessary. What had been started had to be finalized. Still, they did not have time to study every detail before they put their plan into action.

At the suggestion of Reverend Abernathy, the group decided to call itself the Montgomery Improvement Association (MIA). Rufus Lewis stood and nominated Reverend King as president. King said he'd agree to take the position. Various committees were named to oversee operations during what Nixon had already said would be a long, drawn-out, difficult journey. Appointed to the executive committee was Rufus Lewis. He was also named chairman of the enormously important transportation committee, which was made up largely of bright and energetic women including Jo Ann Robinson and the members of her Women's Political Council. Also helping were the members of the Ten Times One Is Ten Club, a group of dedicated older women whose organization had celebrated its sixty-seventh anniversary about a month before Parks had been arrested.

An active member of the Dexter Avenue Baptist congregation, Rufus Lewis had been a football coach at Alabama State College, earning the lifelong nickname of Coach Lewis, and he had married the daughter of the owner of the city's largest black funeral home. He was not only a businessman with considerable experience, but he was also a highly respected leader in the community. Like Nixon, he was passionate about voter registration, and he hounded his fellow citizens, insisting that everybody of age register. He reiterated his philosophy, "A voteless people is a hopeless people," every chance he got. Also like Nixon, he personally transported everyone he could find who had not registered to the courthouse and accompanied them to the registrar's office.

Other officers of the MIA who were elected that afternoon were Reverend L. Roy Bennett, first vice-president; Moses W. Jones, M.D., second vice-president; Erna Dungee, financial secretary; Reverend Uriah J. Fields, recording secretary; Reverend

E. N. French, corresponding secretary; E. D. Nixon, treasurer; C. W. Lee, assistant treasurer; and Reverend A. W. Wilson, parliamentarian.

The resolution that Abernathy and French had written in Nixon's office was presented. It stated the purpose behind the organization, calling for a full and complete boycott of city buses that would continue as long as necessary.

Such an immense undertaking did not simply happen. A complex infrastructure had to be devised, put into operation, and maintained at a high level of efficiency. Lewis, Robinson, and others began the intricate organization of a massive city-wide system of daily pickups and deliveries of thousands of would-be bus riders. More than forty dispatch stations were set up at various service stations, church parking lots, and appointed intersections of well-known streets. A list of these stations was mimeographed and distributed.

On Monday night, 5,000 hymn-singing blacks, Joe Azbell, and several television crews packed into the Holt Street Baptist Church to hear the Reverend King and others speak about the boycott. The multitude sang the rousing hymn, "Onward, Christian Soldiers," after which the Reverend W. F. Alford prayed for safety, honor, and loyalty. To Azbell, "the voices thundered through the church."

Nixon stood at the pulpit and told the crowd, "My friends, you who are afraid, you might as well get your hat and coat and go on home right now. This is gonna be a long, drawn-out affair. Before it's over, somebody's gonna die. Maybe even me, for all I know. The only thing I ask is: don't let me die in vain. For years and years I have fought because I didn't want the children to come along behind us to have to suffer the indignation that we have suffered all these years. That's what I've fought for for a long time. But tonight I have changed my mind. I've decided I want some of that freedom myself."

Not one person left the church.

In his first speech as the leader of the civil rights movement, Martin Luther King, Jr., rose to the moment. In the powerful, resonant voice that would soon become known to people
across the entire world, he told the crowd that the "tools of justice" must be used to attain the "day of freedom, justice, and
equality." His voice rallied them. "We must stick together and
work together if we are to win—and we will win by standing
up for our rights as Americans."

Then Reverend Abernathy read at length the resolution,
which stated that "over a number of years, and on many occasions, citizens have been insulted, embarrassed, and have been
made to suffer great fear of bodily harm by drivers of buses. . . .
The drivers of said buses have never requested a white passenger riding on any of its buses to relinquish his seat and stand
so that a Negro may take his seat. However, said drivers have
on many occasions, too numerous to mention, requested Negro
passengers on said buses to relinquish their seats and stand so
that white passengers may take their seats." The resolution
asked that all citizens refrain from riding buses operated by the
Montgomery City Lines, Inc., and that they help in transporting citizens to and from work by providing free rides. It ended
by stating that "we have not, are not, and have no intentions of
using any unlawful means or any intimidation to persuade persons not to ride the Montgomery City Lines buses. However,
we call upon your conscience, both moral and spiritual, to give
your wholehearted support to this undertaking."

At the end, they sang, "My country, 'tis of thee, sweet land
of liberty, of thee I sing."

Nixon was overwhelmed by the outpouring emotions of the
crowd. At a symposium celebrating the occasion thirty years
later, he remembered, "We took up a offering that night, passing the plates. We collected seven-hundred-and-some-odd dollars that night. I told the police commissioner sitting right
there in the meeting, 'You're gonna have to send me home in a

car with all this money. I ain't gonna drive by myself.' He told one of the colored policemen to carry me home."

In the *Montgomery Advertiser* the next morning, Joe Azbell wrote, "As I drove along Cleveland Avenue en route to the Holt Street Baptist Church Monday night, I could see Negroes by the dozens forming a file, almost soldierly, on the sidewalk. They were going to the Rosa Parks protest meeting at the church."

He rode by silent people, who were bundled in suits and overcoats. To Azbell, they seemed to be performing a ritual. When he parked a block from the church, he noted the time was 6:45 P.M. There were so many cars parked six or seven blocks from the church, the scene reminded the reporter of the massive lot next to Cramton Bowl during an Alabama State–Tuskegee football game. But the demeanor of the crowd was not one of jubilation. The people were stone silent.

After one minister stated, "We will not retreat one inch in our fight to secure and hold our American citizenship," the crowd, which filled the church and spilled onto the street, roared with applause. Again, when he stated, "The history book will write of us as a race of people who in Montgomery County, State of Alabama, Country of the United States, stood up for and fought for their rights as American citizens, as citizens of democracy," the multitude whooped and clapped.

Throughout the meeting, more and more cars arrived, and the crowd grew until it covered the streets and sidewalks for more than a block in all directions.

The meeting reminded Azbell of an old-fashioned revival. As he left, he watched as the black throng filed orderly out of the church. Outside, they marched down the sidewalks, got into their cars, and drove away without incident. The reporter wrote, "It proved beyond any doubt there was discipline among

Negroes that many whites had doubted. It was almost a military discipline combined with emotion."

Three days later another mass meeting was held, this time at St. John AME Church, and four nights after that, another was held at Bethel Baptist Church. Every three or four days for months, the ministers called their people together to hear the resounding voices of leadership, trying to keep the spirits up, repeating their rhetoric that, regardless of what the white politicians were saying, the boycott was succeeding. Day in and day out, people were hurting. E. D. Nixon witnessed them as they walked miles and miles every day. One of the women later told writer Howell Raines, "My feets are hurtin' but my soul is rested." For Nixon, that was what it was all about. To him, their souls were vibrating with new energy. He knew it was easy to slip and fall, but he saw them pick themselves up and keep going. Sitting in the shade of the Durr arbor years later, Nixon said, "As I told 'em all along, it's a long, hard, tough road, so you gotta keep on trudgin' and keep on movin' toward the promised land. Of course, Martin King was tellin' 'em the same thing, only he was saying it better'n I ever could. He had poetry in his voice, and he could snatch scripture outa the air and make it hum like one of them old hymns we all like to sing. It was that kinda joy we had to keep alive, and that's hard sometimes, 'specially when the goin's rough. And it's rough a lot of the time. But that's what organizing is all about. It's not just getting folk together in the beginning, it's holding 'em together through thick and thin. They got to stay together all the way."

On some of his runs into the North, Nixon would meet with his old mentor, Philip Randolph, who put out the word around the nation about the boycott and who set up meetings to raise money for it. One banquet in New York raised more than thirty-five thousand dollars. And in Detroit, the United Automobile Workers raised another thirty-five thousand dollars. A black doctor's wife in Detroit asked, "How many cars are you driving?" Nixon answered, "I got one, and I can't hardly keep that one." The woman told him she had a brand new Buick Special station wagon she would like him to use until the end of the boycott.

Few of Nixon's fundraisers received publicity. At the same time that Nixon was meeting quietly with various groups, Reverend King was traveling around the nation, speaking at headline events. He gave a big speech in Chicago that was covered by the local papers and the Associated Press. Back home in Montgomery, the boycotters read the headlines about their leader and saw the television reports on network news. Each time they read King's name as he traveled through Chicago, New York, Washington, or Baltimore, they were cheered on by the publicity.

Every time he got home, Nixon would drive around town. If he saw anyone who looked as though they needed a ride, he would pick them up. One day he was driving the Buick Special station wagon through Cloverdale. It was pouring down rain. He saw a white man walking. He pulled up and asked if he could give him a ride. "Where are you going?" the man asked. Nixon replied, "I'm going where you want to go. Where do you want to go?" The man said he was going to town. "Well, I'm going to town," Nixon told him. In the car, Nixon introduced himself. The man told him his name and then said, "You know, it takes a whole lot of courage for a man to keep a promise on a morning like this." Nixon asked, "What promise?" And he answered, "I promised myself I wouldn't ride the bus again 'til all of your demands have been met. And I don't own a car." Nixon said, "Mister, I'm not in town always, but I'm going to put a notice in each of our pickup stations. I don't care when it is, if you call, they'll see that you get transportation where you want to go. All you have to do is call." Nixon gave him his card.

Several weeks later Nixon stopped by the Bethel Baptist pickup station and a man there said, "The other day when it was pouring down rain like nobody's business, the telephone rang and a white man called and told me his name. He said he was the man you drove and told him we'd pick him up whenever. He said he had a bunch of groceries and needed assistance." Nixon said, "What did you do?" He said, "We sent a man out there to get him and carried him home." Nixon praised the man, saying that was exactly what he wanted.

Nixon remembered, "That man I picked up that day was one of the only whites that rode with us. Now and then, one would take a ride. Sometimes they just wouldn't.

"It was all a day-to-day thing. Sometimes spirits were high. Sometimes they were dreary. We kept on having our meetings. Reverend King, Reverend Abernathy, all the rest of 'em, they talked and talked, doing their best to keep spirits as high as they could.

"Now and then, out of nowhere, a white driver would pick up a Negro walking down the street. But that didn't happen on a regular basis. Now and then, a white woman would go pick up her maid over in west Montgomery. That usually happened when they needed help and they were afraid they wouldn't have the help unless they went to get 'em."

Following Azbell's first articles in the *Advertiser* that announced the beginning of the boycott and that described himself as being among the blacks in the first mass meeting, Azbell received numerous threats. At home, Betty heard an angry voice cursing into the phone and telling her that her husband was in danger. At the county courthouse, a man spat at Azbell's feet and called him "nigger lover." The next morning he found copies of his articles cut into ribbons and scattered across his front lawn. He comforted Betty and told her not to worry, that these threats were meaningless and nonsense, but inside he wondered silently if they were not seriously dangerous. He knew that Inez Jesse Baskin had also received threatening telephone calls. As the black writer who did stories about the boycott in national black magazines, she became the target of hate-filled white callers who would not identify themselves. Azbell told her not to worry. At home, he told Betty about Baskin's calls and said that such callers were cowards. He had lived with danger before. In the early 1950s he'd gone to New York as an undercover journalist with the *New York Herald-Tribune*, for which he'd been a southern stringer since his days in Selma with the *Times-Journal*. For several months Azbell had infiltrated the longshoreman's labor union in New Jersey. He ferreted out facts of payoffs, under-the-table deals, and general corruption among union bosses. He reported back to the editors for whom he worked, and a series of articles ran under his byline. Later, television's *Big Story* ran a dramatic retelling of Azbell's work. He was proud of that work, just as he was proud of his journalism involving the boycott. He was not about to stop just because a few anonymous cowards were threatening him and calling him names.

Years later, when he looked back on the boycott, Azbell downplayed his courage and his importance. "My work told the first story, alerted the community about what would take place on Monday, and I did some day-to-day reporting. But the most important coverage of the boycott was the television camera. The television camera took the story to the world and showed the world what was happening in Montgomery."

4

Hanging from the Stars

AT FIRST, Martin Luther King, Jr., was reluctant to be thrust into the position of president of the Montgomery Improvement Association—a position that entailed leading a massive boycott that would rock the Cradle of the Confederacy. He was a young husband, a new father, and a busy minister at his first church.

As a precocious youngster raised in the comforting arms of Atlanta's middle-class Ebenezer Baptist Church, where his father ruled the pulpit during the days of the Great Depression, young M.L. (as he was called as a boy) was known as the brilliant child with a beautiful voice who, on occasion, would rear back and sing a hymn. He grew up listening to his maternal grandmother tell stories from the Bible, and to his Daddy sharing recollections of the rough old days of growing up on a sharecropper's farm in rural central Georgia. King recalled later that his newfound friend and benefactor in Montgomery, E. D. Nixon, reminded him of his father's rough-hewn country ways, although both of the older men had reached maturity in an urban South they wished to change.

Young King had seen poverty in the soup lines of Atlanta and had witnessed racism from a distance, but he had never felt its sting on his back, as his father and E. D. Nixon had. But Martin Luther King, Jr., knew what it meant to be black-skinned. He had heard the word "nigger" spoken by twisted white tongues, and he had felt a deep-down hurt at the Colored Only signs in downtown Atlanta department stores and public buildings. The youngster's home turf was the few blocks between the church and Auburn Avenue, where he grew up not only in his own home but in the home of his mother's parents, whom he loved dearly. And his own mother, Alberta, whom M.L. and his two siblings called Mother Dear, doted on her children, particularly M.L., the eldest son.

At the dinner table, M.L. heard his father expound on the virtues of the NAACP. Martin Luther King, Sr., served on the executive board and social action committee of the organization's local chapter. Also like E. D. Nixon, the Reverend King, Sr., fought the system and gained his right to vote. While the elder was known for his boisterous sermons, his suppertime speeches could be just as meaningful, especially to the boy who seemed to live to hear his father's words of praise.

M.L. was riding in the car with his father one day when a patrolman stopped them and strolled to the window. Looking down at the driver, the policeman said, "Boy, show me your license." Without hesitation, Daddy gestured toward M.L. "That's a boy there. I'm a man. I'm Reverend King." When they continued on their way, Daddy King said, "Son, never talk like a slave. Stand tall. They might talk down to you, but you don't have to stoop to their level."

The boy told his father that he understood. What he didn't understand was the day when he was twelve and his grandmother, Alberta Williams, died of a heart attack. When he was a baby he had nuzzled in her lap. When he was late with his homework and his father got angry because of a teacher's scolding note, her understanding warmth had comforted him. His father assured M.L. that his grandmother's passing was not the end of the world. "Think about what she would want from you, then do it," Daddy King told his son.

From that moment on, M.L. excelled as a student. He had always been bright. He knew more words than boys twice his age. But suddenly his intellectual ability and achievements soared. He entered Booker T. Washington High School a year later and graduated when he was fifteen. That summer, before entering Morehouse College in Atlanta, he got a job working on a Connecticut tobacco farm as a day laborer. It was his first time away from home alone. On weekends in Hartford, he found that he and other black students could actually sit at a counter in a diner and eat next to whites. However, on the train south, he entered the dining car where a waiter took him to a seat in the rear, away from the white people, and dropped a curtain to hide his presence from the others.

At Morehouse he fell under the spell of several outstanding professors. Walter Chivers taught sociology and stated, "Money is not only the root of all evil; it is also the root of the particular evil: racism." Gladstone Lewis Chandler spoke with a crisp British West Indian accent when he taught English and was one of the most articulate, knowledgeable, and brilliant professors at the school. It was Chandler who urged the young man to enter the Webb Oratorical Contest during his sophomore year. With Chandler's coaching, M.L. won second place.

When he was seventeen, Martin Luther King, Jr., decided to become a minister. He went to his father and asked for his blessing. Daddy King said that he wanted first to see what the boy could do and told him that he could preach in the small chapel at Ebenezer. It would be his trial. The day came. Young King took the pulpit. He began speaking. Word spread to those in the larger sanctuary of the church that M.L. was speaking. Soon there was standing-room only in the chapel. The father halted the sermon and moved his son to the larger sanctuary. M.L.'s trial was a rousing success. Parishioners talked about it all week. Although the father did not tell him in so many words, he was very proud of his brilliant son.

In 1947 M.L. was ordained. He became his father's assistant pastor at Ebenezer, and he continued his studies at Morehouse, where he was recognized as an outstanding student leader. A year later he graduated with a degree in sociology.

Wanting to free himself of his father's watchful eyes, King decided to leave the South. He attended seminary at Crozier in Pennsylvania, where he read the Communist philosophers and decided they were inherently atheistic, and that they drained their constituents of spiritual salvation. To King, they offered no positive outlook, an attitude he wanted to sharpen within himself. In a sermon titled "the challenge of Communism to Christianity," he warned the church to stop "pious irrelevancies and sanctimonious trivialities." In it, he preached for "a world unity in which all barriers of caste and color are abolished." It was the beginning of what would one day evolve into his unforgettable "I have a dream" speech.

Several times as a student he had brushes with racism. Once, with several other students from Crozier, he stopped at a roadside diner in New Jersey. They sat and waited, but the waitress never approached them. After complaining to the management, they were told to leave. The students explained that New Jersey law forbade racial discrimination in public places. The manager ordered them to leave and even drew a gun. King and his friends reported the incident to police. The local NAACP pressed charges, but three white witnesses, all students at the University of Pennsylvania, refused to testify. The case was dropped.

When a white Crozier student from North Carolina who was known to use racial epithets broke into King's room, shouted insults, blamed King for wrecking his dorm room, and even pulled a gun, King stared him down. In a calm voice, King explained that he had nothing to do with the wrecking of the boy's room. King kept talking until the enraged young man put away his revolver and retreated to his room. The incident became part of school lore, and King developed a reputation as a peacemaker.

At a speech by famed pacifist A. J. Muste, executive secretary of the Fellowship of Reconciliation, King began to question his thoughts about war. Muste preached that war was evil in and of itself. However, King knew that the Civil War had ended slavery and that World War II had stopped Nazi Germany and the continuation of the Holocaust. If this was true, he asked himself, how could deep-seated Christian love defeat evil? Didn't it take war to end many horrible evils? He read Nietzsche's glorification of war, which ripped apart democratic government and damned Christianity. The super race would rise up, Nietzsche predicted, and it would gain power over all. Exploring many philosophical angles and ideas, King wandered, metaphorically speaking, in the wilderness until he sat in a lecture by the president of Howard University, which was known for its black scholarship. Having just returned from two months in India, Dr. Mordecai W. Johnson spoke in quiet, dramatic terms about the life of Mahatma Gandhi. Using the power of love, Gandhi had affected great social change in his world.

Young King was so moved by the talk that he began reading everything he could find by and about the great Gandhi. Louis Fischer's biography showed how an angry man with a fiery temper became a soulful leader whose quiet words would be adhered to by the masses of India and the world. King learned that Gandhi's transformation did not happen overnight, but through years of self-taught guidance. Gandhi had read Henry David Thoreau's theory of civil disobedience. Where Gandhi had turned, so King went: he, too, read Thoreau. He, too, delved into Hindu teachings. Intellectually, he followed the path of Gandhi and saw how the Indian leader discovered that love can bring about justice.

After more than a year of reading about and examining the depth of Gandhi's world, King came to the conclusion, he would write years later, that "he was probably the first person in history to lift the love ethic of Jesus above mere interaction between individuals to a powerful effective social force on a large scale."

In the spring of 1951 King went home to Atlanta. As in summers past, he preached in the sanctuary of Ebenezer Baptist Church when his father was away. At summer's end, he told his father of his plans to enter Boston University's graduate program. Daddy King agreed and sent him on his way in a brand-spanking-new green Chevrolet.

Once again, young King immersed himself in his studies. As always, he was an eager student. Only twenty-two, he climbed the intellectual mountain of spiritual scholarship, taking it apart from the varying perspectives of Judaism, Buddhism, Hinduism, Islam, Sikhism, Taoism, Confucianism, and other worldly religions.

His bent for academics notwithstanding, King was a sport in his new car. Handsome, always nattily dressed, he and another Morehouse graduate, Philip Lenud, sampled the soul-food restaurants and jazz nightclubs. Soon he and Lenud became roommates. They enjoyed talking late into the nights, discussing their reading and their most recently molded philosophies. They discovered to be true something that both had heard since graduating: once a Morehouse man, always a Morehouse man. Wherever he might find himself, King knew he could count on a Morehouse graduate for moral or physical support. It was a truth that would be proved over and over again through the years.

Although King had been on many dates with attractive young women, he was not bowled over by any of them. A married female friend told him about a young woman named Coretta Scott, but added that he probably wouldn't be interested because she wasn't a frequent churchgoer.

Nevertheless, he took Scott's name and number, and early in 1952 he called. After a brief chat that didn't go as smoothly as he'd hoped, he persuaded her to go out with him for a little ride.

He found her very attractive. He liked her hair, with bangs cut across the forehead and a flip curl below her ears. Their conversation moved rapidly from awkward questions and answers. He learned that, after growing up in rural Perry County, Alabama, near Marion, Scott had attended Antioch College and won a scholarship to study music at the New England Conservatory. Scott listened to the lilt of King's baritone voice telling her about his studies and his beliefs. They talked and talked.

On their way back to her dorm, he told her that she had everything he was looking for in a wife: character, intelligence, personality, and beauty.

They dated for a year. Every time King made a new intellectual or spiritual discovery, he discussed it with Coretta. They went to the symphony, and after a long evening of music, she told him she had always wanted to be a singer. She sang for him. He loved the sound of her voice.

In the spring of 1953, he proposed, insisting that they travel south to meet his family. In Atlanta, Daddy King greeted her cordially, but he told his son he expected him to marry a girl from a good family from Ebenezer. Martin told his father that Coretta was the girl for him. On June 18, Daddy King married the young couple in the front yard of her parents' home in rural Alabama.

At home in a tiny apartment in Boston, he cleaned house while she completed her hours toward graduating. But he did not relinquish his own pursuit of a PhD in theology, bringing piles of books home from the library. Having completed course work, he failed his final in German, asked for another examination, and passed it.

What would he do now? His thesis was not yet written. He would not have his doctorate until he finished it and passed his oral examination. That would take time.

Several of his professors argued that he should take a teaching position. His faculty adviser, L. Harold DeWolf, thought King should remain a scholar and contribute on the university level. Several academic institutions, including Morehouse, offered him positions on their faculties.

Also, several churches expressed interest in him as a pastor. Among these was Dexter Avenue Baptist Church in Montgomery, Alabama, a place about which both the young man and his young wife had doubts. They knew the South. Both had come face-to-face with Jim Crow. Coretta remembered her early years, of going into Marion on Saturdays and seeing the main street crowded with hayseed farmers, the Colored Only water fountains in the courthouse, the demeaning looks on the white faces when they glared at the young black girls playing on the sidewalk. She had not liked it as a child, and she knew she wouldn't like it as an adult. As for Martin, he'd never lived in a Southern town the size of Montgomery. He didn't know the ins and outs and idiosyncrasies of a black minister's life in the segregated society of a relatively small town. He knew it would be different from Ebenezer, where his father had doubled the congregation in his first years as a minister there and had made it one of the largest and most respected black churches in Atlanta and the South. Still, there was a challenge and an opportunity at Dexter. The board of deacons invited him to come down and preach a sample sermon. They wanted to hear him in person. He decided he would give it a try.

He flew south to Atlanta in January 1954. Daddy King warned that he should preach the sermon, listen to the church's offer, then refuse it politely. After his father loaned him his automobile, the young man drove southwest through Alabama. He passed through the hard-scrabble, sandy loam of rural Macon County and through the small town of Tuskegee, where Booker T. Washington had built a thriving institute for blacks. It was here that black scientist George Washington Carver had discovered hundreds of ways to use peanuts and sweet potatoes that grew easily in this earth. It was a part of every educated black person's history.

The terrain changed to open bottomlands, where cotton plantations had thrived in the rich Black Belt since a half-century before the Civil War. It was a land that slavery had made flourish. Driving into Montgomery on U.S. 80, he passed the large rock with the words Cradle of the Confederacy etched on the flat surface.

He turned in front of the gleaming white capitol high on Goat Hill onto the wide boulevard of Dexter Avenue. A block west of the capitol steps he pulled into a parking space on Decatur Street next to a relatively small red-brick church.

Inside a sanctuary that was not even half the size of Ebenezer's he was met by a team of parishioners. They were led by a dapper coffee-and-cream-complexioned man whose soft-spoken voice and easy manner quickly charmed the young preacher. An insurance executive, Robert D. Nesbitt was also church clerk and head of the pulpit committee. Seldom outspoken, Nesbitt was even-tempered and analytical in his approach to finding a new minister. King was very impressed with this businessman, who exemplified the high-quality individuals who would fill the pews on Sunday morning to hear him preach. As he was welcoming King, however, Nesbitt was fighting a battle of church politics. The chairman of the board of deacons favored hiring another, older minister who had preached at Dexter two weeks earlier. Martin was only twenty-five years old. In the opinion of the chairman, Dexter needed a more mature, seasoned pastor, someone who could relate to the problems of the older congregation. After all, Dexter was not a start-up church, but a pulpit with great tradition, where Montgomery's finest black families had been worshiping since its founding.

Nevertheless, as the glorious stained-glass windows poured forth multicolored light from the sun on Sunday morning, Martin Luther King, Jr., rose from his seat and strode toward the pulpit. With a handsome face dominated by big brown eyes, a prominent nose, and strong African lips, he gazed down upon the small crowd that had come to judge his performance. He hesitated a moment. Then he read the Scripture from Revelation: "Love yourself, if that means healthy self-respect. That is the length of life. Love your neighbor as yourself; you are commanded to do that. That is the breadth of life. But never forget that there is an even greater commandment, 'Love the Lord thy God with all thy heart, and with all thy soul, and with all thy mind.' This is the height of life."

His words put the text of his message into everyday terms. Although only twenty-five years old, he appeared relaxed and polished. His words and his demeanor captured the listeners, and they proudly slid their hands into his as he bade them farewell at the door.

Nesbitt and the members of his committee stayed behind. They took King to lunch, where one of the parishoners fed him fried chicken, butter beans, squash, turnip greens, and hearty corn bread. He ate like a starving man, Nesbitt remembered later, "And that, as much as his words, made the lady of the house very happy."

During the following week, in an office in the church's basement, the chairman of the board of deacons pounded the table and reminded the deacons that they had already made a decision. He was determined to have the older man as their pastor. But the deacons, including Nesbitt, told him that it was their prerogative to change their minds. In no uncertain terms, they pointed out that no final vote had been taken. The chairman insisted that they ratify the earlier decision immediately, but the board members stated they were not prepared to make such a move after having heard the dramatic sermon "the three dimensions of a complete life" as it poured from young Martin King's mouth.

They argued throughout the afternoon about what to do and finally struck a compromise: The older candidate would be invited to preach a second sermon, after which the board would make its final decision.

The next Sunday the chairman's candidate returned for a repeat performance in the pulpit. The chairman of the board had obviously related to him the situation; when the deacons walked from their cars to the church the next Sunday morning, they read the candidate's sermon title on the bulletin board outside: "the four dimensions of a complete life."

When the older minister finished his sermon, a warmed-over version of what young King had given them, the deacons and congregation knew without a doubt that King was their man. They wanted the original, not an old phony. They confronted the chairman, who stubbornly held to his own opinion. He said they had not given the older man a chance.

The drama continued for several weeks, but the board of deacons was satisfied that they wanted King and no one else. Finally, the chairman gave in, and King was offered the job as pastor, as well as the princely sum of forty-two hundred dollars a year, the highest salary of any black minister in the town.

Once again, Martin and Coretta had to face the reality of moving back to the South. They knew it was an important decision, and they did not make it without much talk, consultation, and prayer. They wanted a family. Did they truly want to raise their children in the kind of environment that they knew existed there? Coretta recalled other childhood experiences. He listened. Hers were much worse than his. He closed his eyes and took her hands in his. He spoke. If they went south for a few years, he said, they could escape while they were still young. They would not stay in Montgomery forever. They would not grow old there. And perhaps, if the time presented itself, he could do something that might help and even change that evil environment that persisted in the South, and in Alabama particularly.

For a month they mulled over their prospects. Finally, they made up their minds. And, on April 14, 1954, King accepted the job with the provision that the church provide time and money to allow him to finish work on his doctorate. The church accepted his proviso.

King flew to Atlanta to tell his father in person. Daddy King ranted. Why would his son choose to begin his career in a place like Montgomery? Why in a tiny, out-of-the-way church like Dexter? Martin listened, then told his father quietly that he and his wife had made up their minds, and that was that. They would remain in Boston, where he would work at the university library on his dissertation, until September; then they would move to Montgomery.

The parsonage was a pleasant white-framed house with a wide front porch on South Jackson Street, halfway between the white-domed capitol and the red-brick buildings of Alabama State College. A block to the south, on the corner of Jackson and High, was the five-story Ben Moore Hotel, where influential blacks who lived on Centennial Hill sometimes met for coffee and conversation.

Since his first days away from Atlanta, King's life had been shaped by self-discipline. Married life did not change those habits. He rose early. He wrote for several hours on his thesis. Coretta fixed his breakfast. He and his wife talked every morning. He shared his thoughts, which focused these days on the latest U.S. Supreme Court ruling, *Brown v. Board of Education* (of Topeka, Kansas), which made the practice of maintaining "separate but equal" schools illegal. He told Coretta that there must be something that he as a minister could do to help facilitate enforcement of the new law. He wanted to be active in bringing about social change. She warned against his becoming too active, reminding him that he was a preacher and not a lawyer, a man of the cloth and not a politician. He nodded, but she could tell his mind was working, sifting through his knowledge of social and political problems that persisted among their people.

King's was the mind of a scholar. He treated his first year in Montgomery as if he were in a classroom, and he studied hard. Every morning he met, sat down with, and talked to the members of his congregation. Soon he began to know them as individuals. Each had his or her own problems. Young married couples were having a hard time communicating. Some had money problems. He drew them together. He delved into their worlds. Older members suffered from various diseases. Some were just old. He reserved at least two afternoons a week for hospital visits.

During the first year, Martin and Coretta became friends with Ralph and Juanita Abernathy. Ralph, twenty-nine, was little more than three years older than Martin. The two young women shared problems as wives of ministers. Ralph, a rough-hewn farmer's son, was pastor of the First Baptist Church, Colored, an offshoot of the First Baptist Church on South Court Street, where black slaves had attended services in the balcony before the Civil War. They were never allowed on the main floor of the sanctuary unless they were sweeping or mopping. After the war, the black parishioners were given a plot of land at the edge of town at the corner of Ripley and Columbus streets. The first portion of the First Baptist Church, Colored was constructed with bricks the members picked up from the streets of downtown. In the mid-1800s, many of Montgomery's streets were paved with bricks. When a member found a loose brick, he or she would pick it up and carry it to the spot where their church would be built.

During his first year in Montgomery, King attended a local meeting of the NAACP and met its president, Edgar Nixon, who talked an emotional but unschooled brand of social activism. King admired Nixon's labor union–style approach to organizing the community, and he shared Nixon's concerns about black people who would not or could not reach out and help themselves, but he did not know quite how to react to the older man's down-to-earth, even crude way of expressing his heartfelt beliefs. King sensed a hard, violent nature at Nixon's core, and he did not appreciate such a reaction to social problems. When the NAACP chose its leaders that year, Martin Luther King, Jr., was elected to its executive committee. Early in November, Nixon, who was impressed with King's powerful oration, sharp wit, and natural leadership ability, asked King to become president of the local chapter. King refused, saying he had more duties as a minister, a husband, and a soon-to-be father. Also, he was busy as an active member of the Council on Human Relations, in which he served with other black and white ministers as well as businessmen.

Throughout the year, while racial unrest pulsated across the South; while White Citizens councils met periodically; while the Ku Klux Klan donned their white robes and hoods and marched and burned crosses; while blacks felt more abuse being heaped upon them, word about the beautiful and stirring sermons of Martin Luther King, Jr., spread across the nation. On trips to Boston to visit the university where he would submit his dissertation for final review, he preached in churches in Washington and across New England and the Midwest. After he talked, the people talked about him. They told others who had not been fortunate enough to hear him that this young man from Dexter Avenue Baptist Church in Montgomery preached magnificent sermons.

Hearing the heart-wrenching stories from women at NAACP meetings who told about their awful experiences riding the city buses, King organized an effort with Jo Ann Robinson to confront the town fathers about the terrible problem. The city commissioners listened. The officials at the bus company listened. Neither made a move to alleviate the problems.

When women were arrested for refusing to give up their seats to whites, Nixon faced the problem and questioned ways to solve it. In each case, Reverend King followed up with meetings with officials, asking that the Jim Crow laws and strict rules concerning buses be changed. He led a committee of concerned black citizens, including the Women's Political Council, whose pleas were heard but basically ignored. Public Affairs Commissioner Clyde C. Sellers told them that such changes would never happen while he was in office. It was not only frustrating, King felt; it was also demeaning. After years of meetings between the Women's Political Council and the city commission, the only concession the bus company deemed to make was to forgo the practice of making black riders pay in the front of the bus and enter from the rear. The rule was removed so quietly that many riders continued the practice long after it had been dropped.

On Friday morning, December 2, 1955, Nixon called King. After explaining what had happened with Rosa Parks, Nixon told him, "We have took this type of thing too long already. We got to boycott the buses. We got to make it clear to the white folks we ain't taking this type of treatment any longer." Nixon told him he'd already touched base with several ministers, including Abernathy. He said it would be a long, hard, uphill struggle, "But it'll be worth it in the end."

After listening, King explained that he had been working very hard at his job. "Let me think about it a while." He asked Nixon to call him back later.

Nixon said he would.

But Nixon didn't call him back. Several hours later, Nixon knocked at the front door of the parsonage on Jackson Street. King invited him inside.

Nixon took a seat opposite King. He leaned forward and anchored his elbows on his knees. He stared directly into the young man's face. "Reverend King, I got to tell you this straight out. Ain't no other way. I been studying on it, and I think there's no other way to go but to have you as the leader of this whole thing."

King stood. He looked back toward the rear of the house, where Coretta was tending to the baby. He walked into the dining room, turned, and walked back toward Nixon, who had not moved. King gazed into Nixon's big face. As he spoke, he nodded. "Brother Nixon, if you think I'm the one, I'll do it."

Nixon nodded. He reached out and took King's hand into his own gigantic paw. Their hands squeezed together.

They walked together onto the porch. Nixon smiled and nodded.

That afternoon, Nixon showed up at the Dexter Avenue Baptist Church and heard the preachers arguing about how they were going to conduct themselves with the boycott. He took them to task for their squabbling and their doubts, then left them to handle the meeting on their own.

After a long prayer from Dr. H. H. Hubbard, an elderly, highly respected minister, Abernathy turned the meeting over to Dr. L. Roy Bennett, president of the Interdenominational Ministerial Alliance, which sponsored the annual Easter sunrise service.

Bennett rambled on about what they had done in the past, how they had always been turned away by the white leadership, but he never once mentioned Rosa Parks or her arrest or anything about a possible boycott. The ministers listened. Some shifted in their seats, checked their watches, and glanced toward the exits. Bennett went on and on.

Inez Jesse Baskin stopped taking notes. She wondered if Nixon had left too early. As long as he had been present, the ministers seemed under control. As soon as he left, they drifted back into chaos.

Several people in the back of the church rose and slipped out. Finally, when only twenty or so were left, Abernathy went to the pulpit. He said, "Brother Bennett, we've got to settle this thing."

Abernathy began to outline the situation. The ministers who were left nodded and said "Amen" when he told them everyone was needed to support the Monday boycott. "You've got to preach it loud and clear on Sunday morning. Make 'em realize we need every last one of them. Not just a handful. Every Negro in this community has got to agree." Again, they nodded. Again, they uttered, "Amen." They also agreed to hold a mass meeting Monday night to decide whether or not to extend the boycott into the week or even longer. That meeting would be held at Holt Street Baptist Church.

The *Advertiser*'s story of the pending boycott came out on Sunday morning. That same day, church services throughout the black communities of Montgomery emphasized the importance of participation in the boycott. By Sunday night, all the leaders could do was pray that their people would go along with it. On Monday morning, seeing the empty buses pass their respective houses, both King and Abernathy were elated. Late that morning they drove around town just to see if their first impressions were holding out. They were. Only now and then did they see a single rider in a city bus.

The first meeting of the Montgomery Improvement Association was held that Monday afternoon. King was elected president and a slate of officers was named. E. D. Nixon was tired from a long day of going to city court with Rosa Parks, participating in the meeting that afternoon, and being a part of what he hoped would become a historical occasion. He went home to Clinton Street, dropped his big body into his favorite old chair in the living room, and took a cup of coffee from Arlet, who sat opposite him and listened while he told her of the day's activities. As he talked, he realized that he had gained strength and vitality. The tiredness that he'd felt when he walked through the doorway was lifted from him. As he talked, he became more and more reinvigorated. He looked forward to the evening. He wanted to once again gaze into the eyes of the people just as he had seen them that morning outside the city courtroom.

At about 6:00 P.M. King arrived at the parsonage and told Coretta about his being elected president. The new mother clasped her husband's hands in her own, looked him in the eyes, and assured him that, whatever he chose to do, "You have my backing."

King cloistered himself in his study for almost thirty minutes to relax and think. He closed his eyes and prayed. He wanted to be perfect tonight. His congregation would consist of more than the well-to-do, well-educated group that he spoke to every Sunday morning at Dexter. These would be people from east, west, north, and south Montgomery. These would be people from all over the city. They would be maids and cooks, housekeepers and housewives, janitors and junk dealers, and mechanics and bricklayers, as well as schoolteachers and professors. He did not have all week to prepare a sermon. He had only a few minutes.

As he drove toward Holt Street Baptist Church, King's eyes beheld block after block of parked cars. Several police cars drove slowly around the block where more than a hundred people milled around the front of the church. He parked nearly a block from the entrance and made his way to the back door. Inside, he found Abernathy, Nixon, and several others preparing to take the pulpit. He was told that the sanctuary of the church had been packed for more than an hour. People were still arriving when the moment arrived to begin his sermon.

Not only was *Advertiser* editor-reporter Joe Azbell seated in the front pew, but several television cameras were also situated in the far aisles to the left and right. This was Martin Luther King, Jr.'s, first public encounter with the television media. After several of the older ministers offered prayers, Abernathy, who acted as the master of ceremonies, asked Gladys Black, the minister of music for Holt Street Baptist Church, to lead them in "Onward, Christian Soldiers," the first hymn sung during what would soon become known as the civil rights movement. Abernathy then introduced Reverend King as the new president of the MIA. As King strode to the podium, applause and shouting rang across the room. He stared out at the crowd. He looked to the right and then to the left. He gazed into the lenses of the cameras.

He raised his hands with open palms, signaling for quiet. Momentarily, they fell silent.

"We are here this evening for serious business," King stated.

Outside the church, where several thousand black people had gathered, loudspeakers brought them every word that was uttered inside. King's baritone voice lifted, bringing waves of nods and a chorus of "Amen" from those standing in the shadowed darkness outside.

"We are here also because of our deep-seated belief that democracy transformed from thin paper to thick action is the greatest form of government on Earth."

His words reached far more than just these thousands gathered in a church and on the street in a poor neighborhood of west Montgomery. As he would discover in the next few days, the power of television would carry his message across the nation and into the world. Oppressed people everywhere would hear his words. Later, he told the press in Chicago that the boycott was part of a worldwide movement.

"We are here in a specific sense because of the bus situation in Montgomery. We are here because we are determined to get the situation corrected."

Listening to the young minister succinctly recounting the trials and tribulations of black bus riders—and the specific abuse heaped on Rosa Parks the previous Thursday—it was difficult for E. D. Nixon to believe that only four days had passed since she was arrested. Now she sat in a chair behind Reverend King, and her eyes watched him. "When I heard him speak that first time," Nixon said later, "I knew. I knew that we had made not only the right choice, but the only choice. His words almighty stirred the folks, made their hearts burn with a fire that could not be put out in just a day or two or a week or longer. He set a fire that wouldn't ever go out, as far as I was concerned."

King told them, "We have no alternative but to protest. For many years we have shown amazing patience. We have sometimes given our white brothers the feeling that we liked the way we were being treated." Now, he said, black people didn't want "anything less than freedom and justice."

The crowd roared. "Amen, brother!" "Amen!" "Amen!"

He told them they had to stick together, that unity "is the great need of the hour." If they were unified, they would show power, and they would be able to attain many of the freedoms they had been requesting.

Then the refrain came to him. His voice sang, "If we are wrong, the Supreme Court of this nation is wrong. If we are wrong, the Constitution of the United States is wrong. If we

are wrong, God Almighty is wrong. If we are wrong, Jesus of
Nazareth was merely a Utopian dreamer who never came down
to Earth. If we are wrong, justice is a lie."

King told his listeners to always be mindful of Christ's
words. If they failed to follow the teachings of Christ to be
nonviolent, he warned, "Our protest will end up as a meaningless drama on the stage of history, and its memory will be
shrouded with the ugly garments of shame. In spite of the mis-
treatment that we have confronted, we must not become bitter." Regardless of what happened, he said, they should not hate
their white brothers. "As Booker T. Washington said, 'Let no
man pull you so low as to make you hate him.'"

As he ended, the voices erupted. They jumped to their feet.
They shouted praise. For more than fifteen minutes, the black
people gathered in the church and outside on the street poured
forth their adoration for their new leader.

In the congregation at that evening's mass meeting was
Johnnie Rebecca Carr, who later said, "God sent Moses to the
children of Israel to get them out of Egypt. He sent Martin
Luther King in this particular instance to lead our people. And
he did a magnificent job of leading our people."

When King finally sat, he clasped his hands together. He
closed his eyes and bowed his head. Only hours ago he had been
a mere minister. Now he was the leader of a people.

While King, Abernathy, Robinson, and others scheduled more
meetings with the city's politicians and the officers of the bus
company, Nixon was in and out of town on his rail runs. At least
twice a week, mass meetings were called in various black
churches around Montgomery. Ministers would speak. People
of all walks of life took the pulpit and told why they were boycotting the buses. After some talked, tears streamed. It was not
easy to listen to some of the agonizing stories.

On Thursday, December 8, a delegation of the Montgomery Improvement Association met in City Hall with Mayor Gayle, Commissioners Sellers and Parks, and representatives of Montgomery City Lines, Inc., including its attorney, Jack Crenshaw.

Mayor Gayle asked, "Who is your spokesman?"

All of the MIA members looked at King, who raised his hand. Once again in the glare of television camera lights, he squared his shoulders and stepped forward to face the officials.

"What is it you're asking for?" Gayle asked.

King spoke out loud and clear. As Jo Ann Robinson and Fred Gray had said at previous meetings, first among their demands was first-come, first-served seating. "We want reforms of existing rules and regulations," he explained. Also, he stated, "It seems to me that it would make good business sense for the company to seek employees from the ranks of its largest patronage." Finally, he promised there would be no violence from the black demonstrators.

During a quiet discussion among the officials, Commissioner Parks recounted that other Southern cities—Atlanta, Mobile, and Nashville—had first-come, first-served seating. Going against the hard-line denials previously expressed by Commissioner Sellers, Parks added, "I don't see why we can't arrange to accept the seating proposal. We can work it within our segregation laws." Crenshaw replied, "Frank, I don't see how we can do it within the law. If it were legal, I would be the first to go along with it. But it just isn't legal." Parks interjected, "Well, it's legal in Mobile. If they can make it legal in Mobile, why can't we do it up here?" Crenshaw shook his head. He added, "The only way that it can be done is to change the segregation laws. If we granted the Negroes these demands, they would go about boasting of a victory that they had won over the white people, and you know we can't stand for that." Sellers nodded in agreement.

King rose and stated that the blacks would not boast a victory if these demands were met. If the changes were made, he said, blacks would ride the buses.

Crenshaw said he did not believe it.

Asked if the bus company would meet them halfway, Crenshaw stated, "We will certainly be willing to guarantee courtesy. But we can't change the seating arrangement because such a change would violate the law. And as far as bus drivers are concerned, we have no intention, now or in the foreseeable future, of hiring negras."

As Abernathy pointed out, this time the delegation's demands would be made public. There were at least a half dozen reporters and three television cameras in the room. Besides, it was obvious that Parks had been moved to attempt a compromise. In that respect, the group felt it had made at least a small dent in the armor of segregation. "Surely the world will see that our demands are not out of line," Abernathy said. "Perhaps they will see what we're facing."

In the back rooms of City Hall, Mayor Gayle and Commissioner Sellers were just as sure of themselves as they had been earlier. "This bunch of niggers aren't going to rule this city," Sellers stated. "We're gonna watch 'em like hawks. They'll break the law, and we'll swoop down and put 'em behind bars. Won't we, Frank?" he asked Parks, who was silent on the matter. Sellers told the others, "There's a lot of mad white people all over town who are not going to stand for this mess. I tell you, we better not give 'em an inch." Crenshaw agreed.

The first *Montgomery Advertiser* reporter to interview King was Tom Johnson, a young native of Florence, Alabama, in the northwest corner of the state. Johnson had worked for the local newspaper, the Florence *Times-Daily*, before moving to North

Carolina, where he worked with radio stations in the Raleigh-Durham area. Later he became a reporter for the *Commercial Appeal* in Memphis, then moved to the capital of Alabama. Years later, after he became editor and publisher of the *Montgomery Independent*, Johnson said that the King interview was his first big story. It was the first time the people of Montgomery read about the new leader of the black boycott.

Under the headline "The Rev. King Is Boycott Boss," Johnson quoted the twenty-seven-year-old minister, who looked and acted older. "Most people would guess him to be about thirty-five," Johnson wrote.

King told the reporter, "Frankly, I aim for immediate integration. Segregation is evil, and I cannot, as a minister, condone evil."

In his January 19, 1956, article, Johnson wrote, "King speaks openly and with an authoritative air on the Negro view of the bus boycott. He is convinced the boycott will not end so long as the present arrangement exists. Moreover, whatever effect the boycott has had on the bus company and on race relations in Montgomery, King says the Negro has profited—he has gained a 'dignity' that he never knew before. He has discovered the voice of the protestant."

King told him, "A minister should attempt to improve social conditions of men at every point where they are not proper—educational, cultural, and economic. He must not only change a man's soul, but a man's environment, too."

The young preacher said that he believed the boycott "is part of a worldwide movement. Look at just about any place in the world, and the exploited people are rising against their exploiters. This seems to be the outstanding characteristic of our generation. Why it had to happen at this time in history, I don't know. But it's happening."

Explaining his interest in various philosophers through history, King quoted Will Durant's definition of dialectics in his

Story of Philosophy: "Struggle is the law of growth; character is built in the storm and stress of the world; and a man reaches his full height only through compulsions, responsibilities, and suffering."

Asked if he would settle for compromise, King stated, "We began with a compromise when we didn't ask for complete integration. Now we're asked to compromise on the compromise."

Explaining the difference between the White Citizens Council (WCC), which championed one race, and the NAACP, which championed another, King answered that the aims of the latter were, "to get full rights for Negroes, to abolish injustice, to obtain the vote, to obtain protective legislation, improve the cultural life of Negroes, and stop lynching," all by efforts in the court system. On the other hand, he said, the WCC, "Seems to be an organization to preserve the status quo and to buck the law of the land." While King stated his stance against violence, he was not sure about the WCC. So Johnson pointed out that official WCC statements "reject violence of any kind." In short, King said, while the NAACP was "constructive," the WCC aimed to "block progress in race relations."

When the boycott began, E. D. Nixon had been hoping for one successful day: December 5, 1955. If that could be accomplished, he thought the boycott would be considered a success. After the mass meeting at the Holt Street Baptist Church that evening, his hopes had expanded. If Reverend King's call for nonviolence worked—and if the passion of his people stayed at a fever pitch—maybe, just maybe the people would stay off the buses and Jim Crow could be defeated. "Although we raised a lot of money in those first days and weeks, I knew we had to keep on organizing, tightening the nuts and bolts of our operation every day," Nixon recalled as he sat under the arbor at the Durr's country place. "And the preachers had their hands full, keeping the folks who were being threatened every day with violence or jail or the loss of their jobs from being worn down and giving up. It was a hard row, believe me. We all had it rough in those days, but it was the women more'n anybody else who kept the spirits high and wouldn't give in. They was the ones who were the backbone, the heart and soul, who had the most to lose but kept their heads high. Without them, it might have folded in those first days."

Rough Days and Dangerous Nights

DURING THE FIRST WEEKS of the struggle, each side accused the other of using violence. Joe Azbell reported in the *Advertiser* that, according to Police Commissioner Clyde Sellers, many blacks were "threatened with physical violence" and "goon squads" were on patrol to keep them from riding buses. Sellers said that many people, white and black, throughout Montgomery were afraid. "I and members of the police department have gotten these reports and I assure anyone who has any idea of using goon-squad tactics that they will be arrested and brought to trial."

A Montgomery City Lines driver, George Henderson, said that his bus, traveling on Early and Hill streets in a black neighborhood, had been fired at six times. Police said a large-caliber pistol was used. A shot smashed the bus window about two feet from Henderson. Another struck the side of the bus. At the time, no passengers were on board.

H. A. Burks, another bus driver, told police that his vehicle had been hit twice by gunfire while traveling on Holcombe and Jeff Davis streets. One shot broke out a window. Police found no evidence of the second shot. On the bus with him were his wife and two children.

Police Chief G. J. Ruppenthal told the *Advertiser* that fifteen armed Montgomery reserve police officers had been assigned to follow city buses to provide protection.

The White Citizens Council offered a hundred-dollar reward for the arrest and conviction of a person firing into a city bus.

A month after the boycott started, on January 5, 1956, Montgomery City Bus Lines transportation superintendent James H. Bagley sat in his office at 701 North McDonough Street in downtown Montgomery. In a telephone conversation with his home office in Chicago, he reported that company business was down so much that expenses far exceeded income during the past month. Although few people had been riding the buses, drivers had to be paid and gasoline had to be purchased. According to his estimation, it cost between forty and forty-four cents every mile to operate a bus. Since the boycott had started, he estimated that the company had lost about twenty-two cents for every mile of operation. Multiplied to its fullest, with twelve buses operating sixteen hours a day, the company was losing at least four hundred dollars every day. Bagley knew that his estimation was on the low side. In truth, the company was losing much more.

Because the company had a contract with the city to provide public transportation, buses had to continue to run their regular routes. On January 4 the vice president of Montgomery City Lines, K. E. Totten, and the company's attorney, Jack Crenshaw, had gone before the city commission and asked to be allowed to double the adult fare from ten cents to twenty. Crenshaw also asked the commissioners to abolish free transfers and to double the current five-cent school fare for children. Totten told the commission that if the company was not allowed such an increase, it would be forced to reduce the number of buses presently serving the city.

Saying that the commission would take the request under advisement, Mayor Gayle took the opportunity to criticize the boycott and its leaders and to ask the white people of the town to ride the buses more frequently.

Totten called the mayor and personally pleaded for action, telling him privately that whites had also stopped riding the buses because they were afraid of the violence that had been reported. At its next regular session the following week, the city commission issued an order to increase adults' fares by five cents, and children's fares from five cents to eight cents.

Still, Totten and Bagley realized, if white citizens of Montgomery did not ride the buses, the company would continue to lose far more money than it was making.

In mid-January, after meeting with several black ministers (but not King), the city commission announced that a compromise had been reached to end the boycott. Gayle and the other two commissioners said the ministers they'd spoken with wished to remain anonymous. The commission agreed to provide ten reserved seats for whites in the front of each bus and ten in the back for blacks. Special buses would be used during rush hours to transport black riders only along predominantly black routes.

King told the press that the city commission had "hoodwinked" the three unnamed black ministers into a private meeting, then issued a misleading statement indicating that a compromise had been reached. King said that such a compromise had not been presented to him or to the members of the MIA. He added that it was not satisfactory, and he stated that the boycott would continue.

Following the exchange, Mayor Gayle issued a public statement that there would be no more discussions with boycott leaders until they were ready to end their protest. "We have pussyfooted around on this boycott long enough," he said, and he announced that all three commissioners had joined the Montgomery White Citizens Council.

In a stance that would play a major role in the ongoing controversy, the mayor explained that the city commission had attempted "with sincerity and honesty to end the bus boycott in a businesslike fashion." He insisted that Reverend King, in a telephone conversation, had told him that the compromise would be accepted and that the boycott would end. King said they had had no such conversation.

Gayle also insisted that the boycott was being run by a group of black radicals "who have split asunder the fine relationships which have existed between the Negro and white people for generations," indicating that these were outside agitators who had come into the town to destroy "the social fabric of our community."

Until the boycott, he said, "the Montgomery Negro rode the bus cheaper than Negroes in the vast majority of cities in the nation. Now, the boycott has been fabricated by the Negroes into a campaign for forcing the white people of our community to accept their demands or else they will not ride the buses. We attempted to resolve their reasonable complaints but they proved by their refusal to resolve the reasonable ones that they were not interested in whether the bus service was good or not. What they are after is the destruction of our social fabric."

Gayle outlined what he said was the prevailing position of whites: "They do not care whether the Negroes ever ride the buses." He did not reveal information about the closed-door meeting in which bus company officials had asked the city commission to allow them to initiate the first-come, first-served seating plan that had operated successfully in Mobile for years. But bus company attorney Jack Crenshaw had told them that "this would not be legally possible." In this secret meeting, company officials said it was a vital concern to them that this matter be quickly resolved. The simple fact remained: the company was losing too much money very quickly.

King, Nixon, and Gray recognized Gayle's statement as the same Old South rhetoric they had heard for years. They hoped that the rest of the black community would see through the falsehoods. They also hoped that they could show them to the community and the nation if they could ever get Gayle and the other commissioners into a court of law, where they would be required to testify under oath.

The next day, at a regular city commission meeting, Mayor Gayle said that white Montgomerians should immediately stop the practice of using their private automobiles as a free taxi service to transport their maids and cooks to and from work. By now, it was no secret that many well-to-do white housewives were regularly picking up their servants in the black neighborhoods, giving them rides into the white subdivisions, and taking them home at night.

Just as he had accused black radicals of destroying the social fabric of the community, Gayle now warned white Montgomery citizens that they were doing the same if they continued the practice of giving free rides. "The Negroes are laughing at white people behind their backs. They think it's very funny and amusing that whites who are opposed to the Negro boycott will act as chauffeurs to Negroes who are boycotting the buses."

Every chance he got, the mayor called Azbell with a new twist on that theme. "When a white person gives a Negro a single penny for transportation or helps a Negro with his transportation, even if it's a block ride, he is helping the Negro radicals who lead the boycott. The Negroes have made their own bed, and the whites should let them sleep in it," Gayle told the reporter.

Police Commissioner Sellers told Azbell, "We have received complaints from white homeowners that Negroes are loitering in groups on the sidewalks outside their homes and that the habit has become rather chronic. A person has the right to wait for a ride, but the practice of six or eight Negroes huddling together for an hour or more, trampling lawns and making loud noises in white residential districts, must cease."

Commissioner Parks said he had heard from dozens of white businessmen who told him they were going to fire or lay off Negro employees "who are being used as NAACP instruments in this boycott."

Azbell wrote that he had talked with white residents, in stores and on downtown streets, who praised the mayor and the commissioners for their "leadership in cutting the legs off the Negro boycott." One man told Azbell, "I hope the Negroes walk until they get bunions and blisters."

City Hall switchboard operator Katherine Brown told Azbell, "In my nineteen years, I can remember only once or twice when there were more telephone calls." The mayor's secretary, Kate Barnett, told Azbell, "The telephone hasn't stopped ringing, and there have been so many people in here this morning to thank the mayor that we haven't been able to do a thing." In his office, Mayor Gayle showed the reporter a thick stack of telegrams from people throughout the state congratulating him on his stance.

In February Azbell reported ongoing violence in his column, "City Limits": "A white girl was knocked down, her dress torn, and her books scattered by a group of Negro children recently. A group of white youths was bombed with bricks tossed by Negroes as their car stopped at a light signal. One of the rocks cut a gash in the head of one youth. A group of white youths tossed rotten potatoes at a car filled with Negroes. A hot rod, loaded to the bumper with teenagers, zoomed through downtown Montgomery one night last week as a chorus boomed from the car: 'We're looking for a big fat nigger.'

"These occurrences are vivid illustrations of the current juvenile problems in Montgomery. As yet the racial pranks and vandalism acts have been much like Halloween assaults on a Chic Sale. But they are serious enough to cause Police Commissioner Clyde C. Sellers, juvenile court judge Wiley Hill, Jr., and local youth and social workers to ruffle their brows with justified concern."

Azbell continued, "Both white and Negro youths have been guilty of repeated acts of petty vandalism that have drawn more taut the line of racial conflict. Explosion of water balloons and tossing of dirt bombs are major incidents of the past week."

***

About a week after Mayor Gayle made his statement, Reverend King was driving through west Montgomery. With him was Professor Robert E. Williams from Alabama State College. King noticed that two uniformed motorcycle patrolmen were following his car.

Just before reaching the intersection of Dericote and East Grove streets, one of the patrolmen sped up, turned on his siren and flashing lights, and pulled to the side of King's car, motioning him to pull over.

After King halted his car at the curb, patrolman Grady L. Arnette walked to the driver's side, asked for King's driver's license, and told him he was under arrest for speeding.

Exiting the vehicle, King told Williams, "Take the car and go home."

Williams got out of his side of the car. King told him to contact several people. Williams wrote the names on a pad, slid behind the wheel, and drove away.

The patrolman called for a squad car. King was cuffed and slid into the back seat. The car took off, heading toward north Montgomery. Later, King's wife wrote, "Martin told me later that he had been a little frightened that first time in jail. He had not even known where the jail was before, and he thought they might be taking him out to lynch him. He cheered up when he saw all his supporters waiting outside."

In city recorder's court several days later, Arnette testified that he'd clocked King's automobile traveling thirty miles an hour in a twenty-five-mile-an-hour zone.

King's attorney, Charles Langford, asked Arnette if this was the first time he'd arrested a black man for going only five miles over the speed limit.

City attorney D. Eugene Loe objected.

Recorder's court Judge Luther H. Waller sustained his objection, then warned Langford not to ask about previous happenings between the police and King.

Langford said he wished to "show that a previous occurrence—"

Judge Waller cut him off: "You are a licensed attorney and should be familiar with court procedure. There is no necessity to show bias or hate or anything else. Please limit yourself to the facts at the time. Is that clear?"

Arnette's partner, R. H. Houlton, also testified that King was speeding.

King told the court that he had been aware that two motorcycle policemen were following him and he kept his car within the speed limit.

After arresting him, King said, the two officers frisked him from head to toe. "That is customary procedure," the judge stated.

After Langford rested his case, Judge Waller found King guilty and fined him ten dollars, plus four dollars in court costs. King filed notice of appeal and posted a fifty-dollar bond.

Early on an evening in late January, two days after King's appearance in court, a group of frustrated white men huddled in a back room of a service station on Norman Bridge Road to talk about what they were going to do "about this mess with the niggers," according to one of the participants. Most of the men were members of the Ku Klux Klan, and they knew they weren't going to stand for what they saw as lawlessness among blacks and the black leaders. "We didn't care what the city was going to do with them; we knew they were doing what they wanted to do: they were not riding the buses and they were standing up in City Hall and talking like they owned the place. We knew damn well we had to do something. This whole thing was getting out of hand."

These words are Leonard Toliver (L. T.) Green's. Unlike most KKK members, Green was a college graduate. The first in his family to graduate, he attended Livingston Teacher's College on the GI Bill after World War II and earned a degree in history, specializing in what he called "the War Between the States." The more he read about the Confederacy, the more he believed that it represented the grandest moment in Southern history. To Green, the leaders in the South should have succeeded. And he insisted that the South would have, if it hadn't been for an element of the Southern population who were dead set against the separate government prospering. To Green, the South was a paradise before the war. In his inimitable way, the student of Southern history believed that the South needed to be apart from the federal government. It needed to control slavery and keep power to itself. It needed to make its own rules to live by. After the War Between the States, when the Confederacy no longer existed, that power was taken away. And during Reconstruction and throughout the twentieth century, the federal government had become more and more powerful, which irritated L. T. Green. The way he saw it, the federal government squeezed the South economically, politically, and socially. "Then, when the Negroes started gaining more and more power through the iron-fist rule of the U.S. Supreme Court controlled by Chief Justice Earl Warren, the South—

because of its way of life not understood and not appreciated by the rest of the country—once again became the target for leftists and Communists. We knew that the Jews and the Communists and labor unions were behind the bus boycott and E. D. Nixon and Martin Luther Coon and all the rest. We knew that the money they were operating with was funneled directly from the big Jew billionaires in New York and the labor unions in Detroit and Chicago."

Leonard Toliver Green was from the rural Black Belt, not far from the farm where Ralph David Abernathy was born. Green grew up picking cotton, like Edgar Daniel Nixon, and, like Nixon, he didn't enjoy that life. His parents sent him and his three siblings to school, but he left before graduating, got a job in the largest nearby town (Demopolis), and joined the army shortly after the Japanese attack on Pearl Harbor. After undergoing basic training in South Carolina he served on a troop train between South Carolina and California. From there, he was shipped out to the South Pacific, spending most of his time working on Jeeps, tanks, and other vehicles. "And we shot every gook we could find in the islands," he remembered.

Back home, he took advantage of the GI Bill. After graduation, he found a position teaching in a junior high school in Montgomery. On weekends, he returned to his favorite pastime, working on automobiles. Soon, he discovered he could make a better living as a mechanic than he could as a teacher.

Green had been raised in a segregated world. As long as blacks stayed to themselves, they were all right by him. In Demopolis, he remembered, blacks stayed at their end of town, and he and other white people went where they wanted to go. Neither messed with the other. Blacks had their own schools; whites had theirs. They didn't mix and mingle. To Green, that was the way things were supposed to be. He knew that at one time the blacks had all been slaves. They worked in the fields and in the houses. They didn't do a white man's work. They didn't live a white man's life. And when they decided they were just as good as whites, Green and his friends decided to take matters into their own hands.

In early 2000 Green, now a great-grandfather, looked back nearly fifty years to a time he remembers almost fondly. He expressed no regret, other than what he saw as a failure on the part of white Montgomerians to stop integration. As he drove through downtown Montgomery, he pointed out places where he and the others had met. Most of the establishments had been torn down or were closed and empty. One had been a restaurant on Jefferson Street called the Kountry Kitchen; another was the service station near the convergence of Decatur and Union streets.

With Green behind the station that night were men who were born and raised in the Jim Crow South. They liked it. They thrived in it. Although they would never admit it, they were frightened by the idea of the blacks gaining freedom. It challenged their world. If the black citizens climbed out of the social, political, and economic cellar, where would Green and his cohorts be? They shook their fists at the prospect of change in a world they had ruled simply because they were white.

During the second week in January, 1956, they had attended a White Citizens Council meeting, where more than twenty thousand white people had listened to the group's self-proclaimed leader, state senator Sam Engelhardt, say, "The niggers are getting out of control. They think they can do anything they want. They think they are just as good as me and you. Well, we know damn well they aren't! We know they are lily-livered, lowlife descendants of blue-gum slaves from the African coast. Well, I'm here to tell you we ought to send 'em back where they came from.

"They think just because one little ol' pinheaded nigger said 'no' to a bus driver they can do anything they want to do. They think just because one nigger leader name Martin Luther King stands up in front of 'em and waves his black hand they can march down the street without being run over. Well, I'm here to tell you we got to drive straight and steady. We got to make sure they don't take over the streets—or the schoolhouses—or the city buses."

The twenty thousand whites stomped their feet, clapped their hands, and screamed as loud as they could.

Engelhardt, the scion of an old family from Macon County, was plantation-born and bred. He was brought up in the big house, and he believed strongly in the superiority of the white man. Like his cofounder of the White Citizens Council, Senator Walter Givhan of Dallas County, he believed in doing whatever was necessary to keep "the ignorant Negroes ignorant." The two had founded the organization in Alabama in the spring of 1954 after the Supreme Court ruled in favor of school integration in *Brown v. Board of Education*. To the plantation house born, Givhan, too, was predisposed to the teachings of his Confederate ancestors. "We were raised on smoked ham and buttered biscuits, made by a mammy who muttered 'yes, suh' or 'no, suh' and knew her place in this world. We believed in the romantic adventures of the heroes of Sir Walter Scott," Givhan once told a reporter. "When we were children we read books about Negroes being lazy, dumb, subservient people, and that's the way we want to keep 'em. We should have never educated 'em to begin with."

In his column "Around Alabama," political journalist for the *Mobile Register* Ted Pearson wrote that Montgomery, the old capital of the Confederacy, was once again an arena of conflict between blacks and whites. To preserve the sanctity of Southern tradition, Engelhardt and Givhan had organized the White Citizens Council. Now, according to Pearson, the WCC was "dedicated to the pursuit of all peaceful and legal means available to preserve racial segregation, which is the base roots of all fields of social endeavor, whether it is in the North or in the South."

Pearson described the WCC headquarters as a modest frame office building on Perry Street near the Governor's Mansion, where "the Council's chief organizers are quietly mapping plans for extending the councils into every hamlet and to every branchhead in Alabama. . . . Engelhardt, like thousands of other Southerners, deeply resents the attempts of the federal government to destroy those traditions."

Engelhardt predicted that the membership of fifty thousand would grow to two hundred thousand in Alabama alone by the end of the year. If this happened, Pearson wrote, "The Citizens Councils will constitute a formidable factor in state politics." In Alabama, where only about four hundred thousand citizens were qualified to vote, any candidate for public office would have to have the WCC's endorsement to win.

A person who joined the WCC pledged to "help defeat the NAACP, integration, mongrelism, socialism, Communist ideologies, and one-world government, and to help preserve the U.S. Constitution and the bill of rights, states' rights, segregation, and our God-fearing American nation."

In his ringing endorsement of the White Citizens Council, the columnist made Engelhardt sound like a scoutmaster. However, when the men who gathered in the back room of the service station recalled the WCC meeting they'd attended, they seethed with anger. For them, the speeches were a call to action. In essence, they wanted to take the law into their own hands, like vigilantes in the Wild West.

In a booth in a downtown Montgomery café, Terry Leon Hall recounts how the men in the back room of the service station considered themselves a posse going after outlaws. "Like Mayor Gayle said, the niggers were trying to destroy our way of life— and we liked the way we had always been living."

Hall had driven a wrecker for the service station where the men were drinking beer and talking about what they had heard at the meeting at the Garrett Coliseum, Montgomery's largest auditorium. His muscled arms covered with tattoos he'd gotten while serving in the U.S. Navy, Hall liked to show off his strength by crushing a beer can with one hand after he'd chug-a-lugged the contents in less than ten seconds.

"It was a time to act," Hall recalls. Still a rugged-looking man with dark hair barely touched by a few threads of gray, he has no regret for anything he and the others did in the black neighborhoods. "I don't look back on it with one bit of shame. I'm just sorry we couldn't-a stopped them. What we wanted to do was make 'em quit all their carrying on and go home and let us go home and act like they'd always acted. Up to that time, I'd never done a thing to a Negro. But I was hot and tired. I wasn't gonna stand for them to keep on doing this thing they called a boycott. What the hell, it was un-American!"

***

Tommy Joe Long was the youngest in the group. He was sixteen. Raised in an area of north Montgomery called Boylston, Long had grown up racist among racists. His father and his two uncles had been Klansmen as far back as he could remember. A tall, skinny boy with blond hair that he combed in a ducktail style, he liked to brag on the mid-morning smoking court at Sidney Lanier High School. He told his buddies about how he had been with the older guys when they drove through the black sections of Montgomery, "nigger-knocking" and throwing anything they could get their hands on, from balloons filled with water to Coke bottles filled with gasoline, at Negroes who were walking on sidewalks or hanging out on a corner.

Long sits in a Montgomery café near a place where he and others regularly met over coffee and biscuits thirty years ago, back when the older guys told him he was too young to belong to the Klan. Now, more than thirty years later, married with grown children of his own, Long wraps his knotted fingers together. Occasionally, while he talks, he balls his fists and hits them, not so gently, on the tabletop. "We should have been throwing bombs, that's what it should have been. If it had been, they wouldn't be controlling everything in this country today, from national TV to the politics. Look how the niggers have taken over our lives. Well, it started back there in 1955 with that damn bus boycott.

"And then we found out that a white preacher was right there in the middle of it, helping the Communists win their fight against the white people of the world. What we wanted to do was find that white sonofabitch and string him up in a tree in Oak Park, just to show the rest of the lily-livered whites what'd happen if they turned on their people."

When a man known to them all as an officer in the local Ku Klux Klan showed up in the room behind the service station on Norman Bridge Road, Green, Hall, Long, and their pals gathered close to listen to what he had to say. A scrawny roustabout with a close-cropped flattop and a rawboned face, the man grinned as he told them, "We got boys roaming all over town with what I'm gonna give y'all." He motioned toward a pasteboard box sitting at his feet. "Now, you got to be careful with this shit I'm about to give y'all. If you ain't, we'll have white blood blown all over niggertown." They all laughed nervously.

After he picked up several homemade bombs with sticks of dynamite tied to a makeshift box, he showed the men how to detonate the weapons.

L. T. Green and the rest of his bunch had never seen anything like the homemade bombs. They had heard about explosives. They knew what they had seen in movies. Several had thrown grenades when they were in the armed service. One had been in World War II. Several had been in Korea.

The skinny Klansman passed out the bombs to teams of three. There were six teams in all. Before they dispersed, an older man who owned the station took the floor. "Now, only you boys know who you are, so the first thing you got to do—starting right now—is forget who you are. Do you understand?"

Nobody answered. All nodded.

Later, Montgomery Police Department detective Jack Shows, who had been on the force since the days following World War II, when he'd served in the U.S. Navy, sat in his house showing his oversized scrapbook with page after page of clippings about his 1950s investigations. He remembered that the gang that had met in the back room of the service station were a ragtag bunch of amateur crooks. To Shows, who chuckled when he talked about them, they didn't know what they were doing. He knew they were a hateful group, but he thought they were basically harmless. "It's a wonder they didn't blow themselves to kingdom come," the veteran detective said. "All they knew was, they hated Negroes. Only they didn't say 'Negroes.' They didn't swear any kind of oath not to talk. But they were told not to. Once I talked to them, it wasn't hard to get them to tell all about what they were hoping to do that night.

"As far as I know, after talking with all of them, they had a pretty uneventful night. They threw some bottles, scared some Negro girls, did some loud hollering and some fast driving. Best I could tell, they were about half drunk and raising hell, and that was all."

Everything was quiet in the six-room, white-frame parsonage on South Jackson Street. Reverend King's wife, Coretta, sat in the living room at the front of the house, talking with Mary Lucy Williams, a twenty-five-year-old friend and one of the most devoted members of her husband's congregation. They were speaking softly so as not to wake the baby, who slept in a back bedroom. It was a little after nine o'clock, Coretta noted, and she told Mary Lucy that Martin would be home soon. As he did on most Tuesday and Thursday nights, he was speaking at a mass meeting to cheer the crowd of boycotters, assuring them that their staying off the buses was furthering the cause of all black people. Tonight the meeting was at Reverend Abernathy's First Baptist Church, only a little more than five blocks away.

As they continued their gossipy talk, they heard footsteps in the front yard. The steps were too rapid and too loud to be Martin's; at night, he always entered the house quietly, aware of his tiny daughter's sleeping habits. Then the two women heard a sound from the front porch, only feet away from them. Coretta said the sound was a "thud, like a brick hitting the porch." Both women jumped to their feet, thinking it might be "something dangerous."

Coretta quickly led the way toward the rear of the house, where her seven-and-a-half-week-old daughter, Yolanda, lay sleeping. The women moved fast, straight back to the guest bedroom. They were in the middle of the bedroom when they heard a loud blast. The women stopped abruptly as they heard glass exploding from the front.

Mary Lucy grabbed Coretta and started screaming. Coretta hesitated momentarily, then rushed toward the back bedroom where Yolanda lay in her bassinet. Coretta grabbed the baby and held her tightly, rocking and comforting her. But the baby did not seem frightened at all.

From the front, the doorbell rang. Coretta shouted, "Who is it?"

Mary Lucy stood nearby, shivering with fright.

A voice outside the door asked, "Is anybody hurt?"

Coretta opened the front door for her neighbors, then called the First Baptist Church and told a member that their house had been bombed.

When the bomb hit the porch about two feet past the concrete steps, it exploded, ripping a hole about a half-inch deep, four inches long, and two inches wide in the tile-like covering on the porch floor. The explosion shattered four windows in the front of the house, scattering glass through the living room, where Coretta and Mary Lucy had been sitting. The floor of the room used as a den and music room was also covered with splinters of glass.

Joe Azbell was in the *Advertiser*'s newsroom when he heard an alert announced over the city police radio. The police radio was always on in the newsroom. The journalist seldom paid attention to the words that were announced, in a monotone, over the apparatus. But when something unusual was said, his ears perked up. That night he heard the word "explosion" over the monitor, followed by the words "309 South Jackson Street." Azbell knew the location. He had been there several times before. He grabbed his jacket, hollered for someone to order a photographer, and took off down the stairs.

When Azbell arrived on the scene only a few minutes later, he saw police cars pull to the curb near High Street, a half-block to the south. He parked, and other black-and-whites parked behind him. Together, the reporter and the police officers walked rapidly down the block on South Jackson toward the parsonage.

Azbell was on the porch with detective Jack Shows, making notes, when Reverend King drove up. Another plainclothes detective met King on the sidewalk and spoke quietly to him. Then King rushed toward the house. As always, the minister was immaculately dressed in an overcoat, suit, and tie.

After King acknowledged Azbell, he went inside to find his wife. He went directly to Coretta, who was still holding the baby. He caressed them and listened as Coretta told what had happened. Then he explored the damage while Jack Shows and an assistant state toxicologist, Vann Pruitt, examined the scene. Later, Pruitt told the press that he believed the bomb was either a hand grenade or a stick of dynamite.

Interviewing the next-door neighbor, Ernest Walters, Azbell learned that Walters had seen a light-colored car stop in front of the King house, then move away "in a terrific hurry" shortly before the bomb exploded. He saw only one man in the car.

Mayor Gayle and Commissioner Sellers arrived on the scene, spoke briefly to police, then went inside the house, where they met Reverend and Mrs. King, Police Chief Ruppenthal, and Fire Chief R. L. Lampley. All of the officials assured King that the city would do everything in its power to find the culprit and bring him to justice. Sellers told the Kings that he hated violent acts such as this. "I will certainly do everything in my power to bring the guilty parties to court and put them in prison." Looking into King's face, he added, "I do not agree with you in your beliefs, but I will do everything within my power to defend you against such acts as this."

Outside, Azbell suddenly found himself surrounded by several hundred angry blacks. "I felt electricity in the air. It seemed as though the people appeared out of nowhere, like they came out of the darkness. They didn't say anything threatening, but I saw in their faces that these weren't just good old Negroes coming to pay a house call. They were seething. For the first time since the boycott started, even when I was in churches with several thousand black people, I felt totally and absolutely scared. I knew if somebody didn't do something, this would turn into a mob, and somebody, perhaps me, would get hurt. Then, at that very moment, King stepped out onto the porch. It was as though the porch lights were suddenly spotlights. He shone in their brightness. He raised his arms. His palms opened to them. Whatever murmur that had been going through the crowd hushed."

Flanked by four uniformed policemen, the mayor, Commissioner Sellers, the police chief, and the fire chief, King stood on the porch. He spoke. His voice lifted over the crowd. "Brothers and sisters, we believe in law and order. Don't get panicky. Don't do anything panicky at all. Don't get your weapons. He who lives by the sword will perish by the sword. Remember that is what God said. We are not advocating violence. We want to love our enemies. Be good to them. Love them and let them know you love them. I did not start this boycott. I was asked by you to serve as your spokesman. I want it to be known the length and breadth of this land that if I am stopped, this movement will not stop. If I am stopped, our work will not stop. For what we are doing is just. And God is with us."

"Amen!" the crowd cried.

"God bless you, Brother King!"

The Reverend King nodded and stepped back.

Mayor Gayle moved forward. As he began to speak, the crowd became quiet. "I am for law and order. The entire white community is for law and order. None of us condones or believes in these sorts of acts in any way. I am going to work with my last breath, if necessary, to find and convict the guilty parties."

Azbell remembered, "That night King made a believer out of me. He stood there and quieted that angry mob. I know that if he had not spoken as he had, violence would have erupted. And I'm not so sure violence would not have rushed through Montgomery like a wildfire. Those people were so angry, you could feel it. Tension was in the air. It was about to explode. After King spoke, I knew this whole thing was about Jesus."

Still, the crowd did not disperse. After the officials left, the people sang "America," which was followed by several hymns. At 10:45 P.M., Reverend Abernathy, who had heard about the explosion and had come to make sure Coretta and the baby were OK, stepped onto the porch. He said he had a message from Reverend King. "We feel it is best not to sing, and for you all to go home. The police are investigating and everything is under control." Soon, the crowd began to break up and move on.

On the following morning, the city commission offered a five hundred–dollar reward for the capture and conviction of the person or persons who had bombed the King home.

IN THE SUMMER OF 2004, while cleaning out a storage area in the basement of the old Montgomery County Courthouse, Chief Deputy Sheriff Derek Cunningham discovered a box of old photos of people who'd been arrested nearly fifty years earlier. Searching through the box, Cunningham soon realized that the bulk of these black-and-white pictures were actually mug shots taken in February 1956, when nearly one hundred leaders of the black community were arrested and charged with conducting an illegal boycott of the buses. Also in the box were several legal-sized pads, on which the names and arrest numbers of those who had been arrested were handwritten.

Here are some of those mug shots:

Fred D. Gray was indicted and arrested on February 1, 1956. He was charged with a misdemeanor (under the Alabama Code, as an attorney "appearing without authority") for representing a client who claimed she had not hired him as her lawyer.

Reverend Ralph D. Abernathy.

E. D. Nixon.

L. R. Bennett.

H. H. Hubbard.

Reverend S. S. Seay.

Reverend W. F. Alford.

Jo Ann Robinson.

Rosa Parks.

J. E. Pierce.

Reverend E. N. French.

P. E. Conley

Reverend Martin Luther King, Jr.

On Monday morning, December 5, 1955, Rosa Parks leaves Montgomery City Court, where she was fined ten dollars and court costs for violating the city's segregation ordinance for city buses. With her are E. D. Nixon (left) and her attorney, Fred D. Gray. (Associated Press)

OPPOSITE PAGE: (top) A lone driver guides his empty city bus through the down-town streets of Montgomery, Alabama, on April 26, 1956, five months after the boy-cott began. The sign on the side of the bus, Ease That Squeeze, refers to traffic problems in the city, not to congestion on the buses. (Associated Press)

(bottom) The Reverend Martin Luther King, Jr. (at pulpit), was convicted on charges of participating in an illegal boycott in Montgomery Circuit Court in March 1956. He was fined five hundred dollars and court costs. That night he spoke to a mass meet-ing at the Holt Street Baptist Church. (Associated Press)

The Reverend Martin Luther King, Jr. (right), and the Reverend Ralph David Abernathy wait to be booked by Lieutenant D. H. Lackey on February 22, 1956. King and Abernathy were part of a mass arrest of nearly one hundred black Montgomerians who were charged with conspiracy to conduct an illegal boycott. (Associated Press)

An unidentified black woman watches white-robed Ku Klux Klansmen walking on the downtown streets of Montgomery on November 24, 1956. That night the Klan held a rally outside Montgomery to protest the U.S. Supreme Court ruling that the Montgomery segregation ordinance was unconstitutional. (Associated Press)

On December 21, 1956, Montgomery City Lines resumed full service on all of its routes. Among the first passengers to ride in the section formerly reserved for whites were the Reverend Ralph David Abernathy (first row, left), Inez Jesse Baskin (first row, right), the Reverend Martin Luther King, Jr. (second row, left), and the Reverend Glenn Smiley, of New York (second row, right). (Associated Press)

OPPOSITE PAGE: (top) Rosa Parks (right) smiles at a comment from Virginia Durr at a reception held on the campus of Auburn University at Montgomery to celebrate the publication of Durr's autobiography, *Outside the Magic Circle,* in 1985. (Alabama Department of Archives and History)

(bottom) Chosen as one of the Outstanding Women of Montgomery by the *Montgomery Advertiser* in 1994, Virginia Durr is seated second from the right. Standing (from left to right) are Essie Buskey, Johnnie Rebecca Carr, Eunice Davis, Dr. Jane Day, and Irma Moore. Seated (from left to right) are Zecosy Williams, Circuit Judge Sally Greenhaw, Virginia Durr, and Guin Nance. (Alabama Department of Archives and History)

Johnnie Rebecca Carr, photographed in front of her home on Hall Street in the fall of 2004, after she'd spoken to the One Montgomery Breakfast Club. (Wayne Greenhaw)

OPPOSITE PAGE: (top) E. D. Nixon was honored for his fifty years as a leader for civil rights on December 4, 1982. Vernon E. Jordan, Jr., president of the National Urban League, told the group in Montgomery, "It was the E. D. Nixons who got out the troops, who strategized, and who were the backbone of our victories. And it was E. D. Nixon who picked Martin. E. D. Nixon was a leader, a man of foresight and strength." (Alabama Department of Archives and History)

(bottom) Frank M. Johnson, Jr., had been appointed to U.S. District Court in Montgomery only days before Rosa Parks refused to give up her seat on the city bus. Fred D. Gray's lawsuit that challenged the city's laws segregating public transportation was Johnson's first major case as a federal judge. (Penny Weaver)

Bus number 2857, on which Rosa Parks was riding on December 1, 1955, was built by General Motors Corporation in 1948. Twenty-nine feet long, nine feet high, and eight feet wide, it accommodated thirty-six passengers. It's transmission had been rebuilt to accommodate driver James F. Blake, so that he could drive the bus smoothly up and down the city's only hilly route. It is pictured here in 2000, before it was purchased and fully restored by the Henry Ford Museum. (Donnie Williams)

A few nights later, on February 2, while he was out of town on his regular train run to Chicago, a bomb was thrown onto the front porch of E. D. Nixon's house. It bounced off the porch and landed on the ground before exploding. Only one corner of the porch was destroyed. Still, Nixon, who had had KKK crosses burned in his front yard on numerous occasions during the 1930s and '40s and who had received dozens of threatening phone calls through the years, was afraid for his wife. "I was gone so much. I knew she'd be alone, and that bothered me," he said.

Concerned for her safety, when he returned the next day, Nixon suggested to Arlet that she pack up and go home to her parents for a while, until the violence calmed. Arlet told him, "I ain't going nowhere." And later, when the going got tougher, Arlet told him, "They're trying to make you quit, but don't do it. I'd rather be the widow of a man who had the courage to fight than the wife of a coward."

6

The White Preacher

WHEN TOMMY JOE LONG was talking about the white preacher, he was referring to the Reverend Robert S. Graetz. One of the least understood of all the strong supporters of the boycott, Graetz, a short, slender minister of an all-black church, first heard about Rosa Parks's arrest from her the morning after she was taken to jail.

Graetz was a native of Charleston, West Virginia, where, as one letter writer to the *Advertiser* pointed out, the radical abolitionist John Brown was hanged, and where, the same pundit suggested, the residents should do the same with Graetz. Of German heritage, he had attended all-white public schools—the only blacks he knew personally were the janitors.

But in his junior year at Capital University in Columbus, Ohio, while doing research for a paper on discrimination against Jews in higher education, he discovered that black people had been almost completely excluded from many U.S. institutions of higher education. "That revelation altered my life and my ministry forever," he recalls. He switched his major to social science, started a race relations club, and joined the

NAACP. "I was full of zeal to eradicate racial injustice and discrimination wherever it existed."

In fact, he was so enthusiastic, he wanted to become black himself. He had a plan: he would transfer to a black school and live his life as if he were black. He realized that he would never be accepted as a black only many years later, when a black friend told him, "You always have the option of walking out. We don't."

At Capital he met Jeannie Ellis, a pretty Pennsylvania country girl who shared his strong feelings for society's underdogs. Like Robert, she was gentle and kind. Being a farm girl, she had worked hard. Like her future husband, she felt a strong kinship with Jesus, and she wanted to treat people as he would have treated them.

They were married on June 10, 1951. She continued her education at Capital while he attended Evangelical Lutheran Theological Seminary across the street. He was drawn to St. Philips Lutheran Church, on Columbus's black east side. When the church's white pastor, Edward Keim, recruited student volunteers, both Robert and Jeannie joined the church, working Saturdays stacking bricks and Sundays teaching classes. It was there that Graetz met Nelson Trout, a young, black seminary graduate who preached at Trinity Lutheran Church in Montgomery in the early 1950s.

After Graetz graduated from Evangelical, he entered an internship program to serve as lay pastor of a small church in a predominantly black section of Los Angeles, California. While intern ministers were usually well supervised, he was left alone to complete his duties at Community Lutheran Church. Jeannie was pregnant again after having suffered a miscarriage, and her physician suggested that she not drive all the way across the country. She initially stayed with her family, but she later flew to the west coast to be with her husband. Their first child, Margaret Ellen, was born in November 1952 in Los Angeles. The Graetzes' next child, Robert Sylvester Graetz, III, arrived in March 1954.

By the time the Graetzes left to go back to Columbus, they had witnessed racial unrest among their flock. Members of Graetz's congregation had moved into a previously all-white neighborhood; they received threats and their homes were vandalized. Graetz, in his gentle and kindly way, ministered to these families.

After finishing seminary, the call came to go south to Trinity, to an all-black congregation in the middle of Montgomery, Alabama. Neither Robert nor Jeannie hesitated. In fact, they looked forward to the challenges that such a position posed. Neither had ever experienced life in the Jim Crow South of the mid-1950s.

Years later, Robert's and Jeannie Graetz's smiling faces and lilting voices portray the positive attitude that gave their marriage and their joint effort as pastor and pastor's wife their rosy glows. In 1955, with two small children in tow, they headed into the new territory knowing very little about the delights and the dangers ahead.

In addition to Trinity, Reverend Graetz was also given the responsibility of leading two rural Alabama churches: St. Paul's Lutheran, in Clanton, about forty miles north of Montgomery, and St. Mark's, near Wetumpka, about twenty miles northeast of Montgomery. Both churches revealed the rural idiosyncrasies of black farming communities. Sometimes the parishioners came to church; sometimes they didn't. When they had crops to gather, the residents of these small towns sometimes considered Sunday just another day to get the work done before the rainy season or winter set in.

It didn't take long for the Graetzes to become immersed in south Montgomery's black community, in which they lived. As they had in Los Angeles, they joined organizations that involved other churches and their members. They joined the

Montgomery Council on Human Relations and soon became friends with its state director, Bob Hughes, and his wife, Dottie. At one of the first meetings, held in the fellowship hall in the basement of Dexter Avenue Baptist Church, Graetz met the church's minister, Martin Luther King, Jr., who was little more than a year younger than Graetz. They talked eagerly about their churches and their congregations.

Graetz was astounded when he heard that the husband of a white woman who was a member of the Montgomery Council on Human Relations had bought an advertisement in the *Advertiser* to state that his wife's public position on human rights did not agree with his own. The man had added that he "had nothing to do with the organizations she supported."

Another member of the council, Jane Katz, who was Jewish, soon became friends with the Graetzes. She and her husband, Warren, worked hard throughout the town to better racial relations. Mrs. Katz introduced the Graetzes to Cliff and Virginia Durr, whose company they found endearing.

Graetz joined the all-white Montgomery Ministerial Association, although he was looked on as one of the most liberal— if not *the* most liberal preacher—in Montgomery.

As a pastor, Graetz heard many stories of the abuse heaped on the black riders of the city buses. He heard about the riders who'd been killed by police officers, including the young man who had been shot in August 1950. He knew about the riders who had been arrested for refusing to give up their seats when told to do so by drivers. However, he didn't know those women personally.

When, in early December, he heard that another woman had been arrested for refusing to give up her seat, he was not surprised. Sitting in the church office, he called his friend Rosa Parks to find out more about what had happened. He had worked with Parks, who lived just around the corner in the Cleveland Court apartments, and he respected her abilities as an adult adviser to the Montgomery NAACP Youth Council, which met regularly in the Trinity church.

After the two exchanged pleasantries over the phone, Graetz said, "I just heard that someone was arrested on one of the buses Thursday."

Parks answered, "That's right, Pastor Graetz."

"And that we're supposed to boycott the buses on Monday to protest."

"That's right, Pastor Graetz," Parks said.

Graetz asked, "Do you know anything about it?"

"Yes, Pastor Graetz."

"Do you know who was arrested?"

"Yes, Pastor Graetz."

"Well, who was it?"

Graetz remembers, "There was a moment of silence. Then, in a quiet, timid voice, she replied, 'It was me, Pastor Graetz.'"

Years later, Graetz recalls, "It would have been unlike her to respond in any other way. Mrs. Rosa Parks was dignified and reserved, one of the most highly respected people in the Negro community. For years she had quietly grieved over the harsh treatment her people had received at the hands of whites, and she worked hard as secretary of the Alabama chapter of the NAACP to bring about changes in the segregation system."

With the boycott imminent, Robert and Jeannie talked about what they would do. He had promised church officials back in Ohio that he would concentrate on being the best pastor he could possibly be. He would not start any trouble in the community. Like other pastors, he and Jeannie prayed. He sought God's guidance about what he would say to the congregation on Sunday morning.

The young couple talked well into the night for several nights. Because they were pastor and pastor's wife, they decided, they were involved. It wasn't as though they were causing the problem. The problem was present without their doing anything. As far as they were concerned, the problem belonged to the town's government and its unlawful and immoral ordinances. If they didn't join in the fight, they might as well go back north and forget these people whom they had come to minister. If they didn't participate, they'd be giving their approval to bad government and Jim Crow laws.

———

In mid-January, *Advertiser* reporter Tom Johnson interviewed Graetz. His article began, "A young white minister clad in the vestments of the Lutheran Church stood in his pulpit on a Sunday last month and calmly urged his congregation to give its fullest support to the Negro boycott of Montgomery buses.

"He told of his plans to make his own car available to a 'share the ride' pool, organized to transport Negroes unable to afford taxis, and indicated he was about to assume an active part in the conduct of the boycott.

"He said: 'Let's try to make this boycott as effective as possible, because it won't be any boycott if half of us ride the buses and half don't ride. So if we're going to do it, let's make a good job of it.' Then he began his prepared sermon, 'The Blessings of God's Covenant,' taken from the 31st chapter of *Jeremiah*."

As Graetz outlined his plans to participate in the boycott and urged his people to do likewise, his words met with enthusiastic approval from the 210 members of the Trinity Lutheran Church. Soon after his December 4 sermon, Graetz was working sixteen hours a day carrying out church duties and helping to organize and operate the boycott. He hauled passengers in his new Chevrolet from 6:00 to 9:00 A.M. As a member of the transportation committee of the MIA, he helped to organize a pool of 250 to 350 private cars and to establish pickup and dispatch points for transporting blacks to and from work.

In a letter to other white ministers he copied on his church office mimeograph machine, he outlined many of the problems of the past and detailed the history of abuse of black riders of city buses. He concluded, "Please consider this matter prayerfully and carefully, with Christian love. Our Lord said, 'Inasmuch as ye have done unto one of the least of these my brethren, ye have done it unto me.'" On his church stationery he printed the biblical quotation, "And the Angel of the Lord spake unto Philip saying: 'Arise, go toward the South,' *Acts 8:26.*"

The boycott leaders, including Graetz, attended mass meetings on Tuesday and Thursday evenings, where they presented progress reports. Meeting at a different church each night, they passed the collection plate to raise money for operational expenses for the car pools.

In his interview with Johnson, Graetz called himself and other ministers "first lieutenants" to "the general," referring to Reverend King.

In Johnson's article, the young journalist outlined the economics of the boycott. He repeated that the heaviest expense was gasoline for the car pools. "It costs about $200 a day to keep the cars running," Johnson wrote. At the first mass meeting, about eighteen hundred dollars was raised. More money rolled in from churches in other cities—New York, Philadelphia, Mobile, Tuscaloosa, Tuskegee—and from other, anonymous friends.

Graetz estimated that he personally carried as many as forty or fifty passengers and drove at least fifty miles around Montgomery each day. When he was offered compensation by one rider, Graetz declined, suggesting that the passenger contribute at the mass meetings to help the entire cause.

On the morning of December 19, Graetz had been driving for two and a half hours when he parked next to a meter near Dean's Drug Store on Monroe Street. Careful not to park in a taxi zone, he waited while a group of five blacks slid into his car. He would carry them from downtown about four miles south to Normandale, Montgomery's first shopping center, where Loveman's was the anchor department store.

As he started to pull away from the curb, a short, squat man in a brown uniform approached the car and held up his hands, motioning for Graetz to stop. After identifying himself as Sheriff Mac Sim Butler, the officer asked, "What are you doing? Running a taxi service?"

"These are friends," Graetz answered.

Butler leaned forward, looked into the car, and said that he'd seen Graetz picking up the people in a taxi zone. "Follow me to the county jail," Butler ordered.

Graetz followed him three blocks south to the courthouse and jail, where Butler led him to a room marked Deputy Sheriff. After Butler closed the door, leaving him alone, Graetz knelt in prayer.

After a short while, another uniformed man whom Graetz assumed was a deputy came into the room and began lecturing the minister on religion, politics, and patriotism. "We like things the way they are here," the man told him. "We don't want anybody trying to change them."

Butler returned to the room and told Graetz that he had attempted to charge him with illegally running a taxi service, but that the judge didn't allow it.

After being held for half an hour, Graetz was released.

The December 22 issue of *Jet* carried a story by Inez Jesse Baskin that described Graetz's courageous stand with the black boycotters. To Baskin, Graetz was "one of the kindest, gentlest men I've ever met. When you look into his eyes, it's like you are seeing into the vision of an angel. He believes deeply in everything he does. If there ever was a saint on this earth, it's Reverend Graetz." Baskin's article further extended the reach of the news about the Montgomery bus boycott to a national audience.

Like Tom Johnson's profile of Reverend King, Johnson's story about Graetz was picked up by numerous big city newspapers, including the Memphis *Commercial Appeal*. Given the newspaper's broad circulation, it was not long before Graetz received a good deal of hate mail, as well as contributions to the cause from around the country.

In the hours after the initial story about his detainment ran in the *Advertiser*, Graetz received dozens of phone calls. One came at 2:15 A.M. Graetz jotted down a note about the call: "White man who seemed to be drunk demanded that I come and give him taxi service like what has been furnished to the dark-complected people. Suggested we set up a car pool for white people so [they] can save the fifteen-cent fare. Refused to give name."

In the days that followed, Graetz received many more calls. Most were angry. Some were from blacks who thanked him for his service. One caller threatened that something might happen to him and his family unless he got out of town by nightfall. Two hours later, three other calls came from the same person in quick succession. Graetz called the police, and several detectives came to the church. When the phone rang again, Graetz quickly passed it to one of the officers, who grinned and said, "I heard him, all right."

Later, Graetz was called by Police Commissioner Sellers, who had learned of the threats. Sellers told him, "You know, I don't agree with what you believe, but I do believe that every man has the right to his own beliefs." Sellers assured Graetz that police cars would watch the parsonage all night to discourage any violence. He told Graetz that he didn't believe boycotting was the way to accomplish any of the goals the blacks sought. He also stated he thought the boycott was failing to accomplish anything. When Graetz told him that blacks wanted to change the way the buses were run in a nonviolent, peaceful manner, Sellers said he did not think it was peaceful at all. He added that many of those who were not riding the buses were boycotting under duress and threat of violence.

Graetz said that he was "thoroughly surprised" by this revelation. He stated that he'd never seen nor heard of blacks being pressured not to ride buses. There had been plenty of preaching in black churches, but no instances of threatened violence that he knew of. He promised Sellers that he would investigate and try to determine if people had indeed been threatened. Prior to that night, Graetz had already asked many ministers if they knew whether any intimidation tactics were being used on blacks to force their compliance with the boycott. He'd drawn negative replies from all of them.

Graetz continued to receive threats. A letter to Graetz from a "white man" in Union Springs, a small town about thirty miles southeast of Montgomery, stated, "May you have for a son-in-law the blackest Negro that ever originated from the wilds of Africa." The writer had underlined the wish three times.

One evening a telephone caller said, "Pastor, if I was you, I wouldn't call myself a pastor. You're a no-good sonofabitch."

Soon Graetz and his family would become not merely participants in peaceful protests, but victims of white violence.

But in the meantime, a woman identifying herself as "an old white lady" and a member of "an old family [who knows] all the city officials" called and offered her Oldsmobile for use in the boycott car pool.

7

The White Establishment Uses the Law

ON THE FIRST DAY of February 1956, Fred Gray and his law partner, Charles Langford, filed a suit in U.S. Circuit Court in Montgomery on behalf of five black women, asking that Alabama and Montgomery segregation laws be declared unconstitutional. Bringing the suit were Aurelia S. Browder, Susie McDonald, Jeanetta Reese, and two minors, Claudette Colvin and Mary Louise Smith, both of whom had been arrested previously and charged with violating the segregationist statute. As minors, they were represented by their fathers, Q. P. Colvin and Frank Smith. Named defendants were Mayor Gayle, Commissioners Sellers and Parks, Police Chief Ruppenthal, Montgomery City Lines, Inc., and bus drivers James Blake and Robert Cleere. The lawsuit asked the federal court to declare and define the legal rights of the parties involved in the boycott controversy; to declare segregation sections of the code null and void; and to declare acts of threats, intimidation, and harassment performed by the defendants to compel the plaintiffs to use bus facilities in violation of the Fourteenth Amendment to the U.S. Constitution. The suit also asked that the defendants be enjoined from enforcing state and city statutes on the grounds that those statues were unconstitutional, and that they be prevented from interfering with colored persons or from using force, threats, or other intimidation regarding the use of private transportation facilities.

Filed as a class action lawsuit, the suit charged that the defendants conspired to interfere with the civil and constitutional rights of the plaintiffs by using "force, threats, violence, intimidation, and harassments."

Behind the scenes, Clifford Durr had worked closely with the two attorneys of record to put together the complicated document. He respected Fred Gray and Charles Langford. They respected him and his vast knowledge of the law. Often they listened while he explained legal complexities, making them seem uncompromisingly simple.

Cliff Durr had come home to what he'd hoped would be his semiretirement. He practiced law in a small office in Montgomery. Having served honorably in the New Deal programs, he had spoken out against the Loyalty Oath, which he thought violated government workers' civil rights. Now he wanted peace and quiet. Back in his beloved South, he didn't plan to speak out against the system. Surely he didn't want to get involved with anything as complex and time-consuming as the taking on of the South's Jim Crow system on behalf of the civil rights movement.

A slight-built man with birdlike bones, thinning gray hair, and gold-rimmed glasses, Durr spoke softly through thin lips, from which an unfiltered cigarette frequently dangled. Often when he talked, the cigarette dipped and bobbed, sifting ashes onto his shirt, where they would remain until he stood and casually brushed them off. By the mid-1950s he was an aging liberal with a strong conscience and a clear understanding of his place in the community, both as a lawyer and as a man. He had made a long journey from his schoolboy days of wondering what it would have been like to lead a Confederate cavalry charge.

A graduate of Starke University School for Boys in Montgomery, Clifford Judkins Durr was the scion of an old Alabama family. His father, John Wesley Durr, and his mother, Lucy Judkins, both had ancestors who fought for the Confederacy. Both were devout Presbyterians.

In his senior year at the University of Alabama, he was elected class president. Durr was not only handsome; he also displayed brilliant skills as a scholar. After earning a Phi Beta Kappa key, in December 1919, he was named a Rhodes Scholar. At Queens College, Oxford, he studied jurisprudence.

Returning to Montgomery in 1922, Durr was eager to fall into the Southern way of life. He joined Rushton, Crenshaw, one of the most impressive and conservative law firms in the town, at a salary of twenty-five dollars a month. His father urged him to be frugal. He could live and take his meals at home.

After a year, a family dispute caused Durr to leave the law firm and move to Milwaukee. Two years later, he was offered a position with a large corporate law firm in Birmingham—Martin, Thompson, Foster, and Turner—with a starting salary of one hundred fifty dollars a month.

The Magic City, as Birmingham was called, had grown up quickly since its founding in the late 1800s. Iron ore was mined in the surrounding hills and brought into the town, where it was processed in steel mills owned by absentee Yankee industrialists. By 1920 Birmingham had a bustling population of nearly three hundred thousand. Even then, tension was heavy between Catholics and Protestants, management and labor, blacks and whites. Connecting government and the new industries, the downtown mills and the surrounding farmlands, the rural country and urban development was the Alabama Power Company, which furnished electricity to most of Alabama. The powerful monopoly was also the leading client of Martin, Thompson, Foster, and Turner.

In the spring of 1925 Cliff Durr met Virginia Foster, the beautiful youngest daughter of the Reverend Dr. Sterling Foster. Foster had been the minister of one of the largest churches in Birmingham, South Highland Presbyterian, until he admitted from the pulpit that he no longer believed in the literal truth of the Holy Bible. He explained that he had studied the story of Jonah being swallowed by a whale, and that he found it a made-up parable rather than literal truth. As a result, he was fired, and he lived in shame.

Born in Birmingham, Virginia was as much Old South as Cliff. Her father's family had been plantation owners in Bullock County, near Union Springs, about thirty miles southeast of Montgomery, which she visited frequently as a child.

In 1921 Virginia persuaded her father to send her to Wellesley College. On the first night in the dining room, she discovered a black girl sitting at her table. Virginia promptly rose and marched out of the room. Upstairs, she confronted the head of the house, a New England spinster. Virginia explained that she was a good Southern girl who had been brought up in a Southern household. Now she was being asked to go against her upbringing. "I'm from Alabama, and my father would have a fit," she said. She was informed that Wellesley had rules: a student had to eat at the assigned table for a month; she would obey the rules or go home. Virginia decided to stay, ate at the table, and began enjoying the young woman's company. Virginia's Southern values had been challenged, and she realized her world was changing. Throughout her life, Virginia would revisit that time, replaying the scene, and her resolve would stiffen, giving her courage to stand firm in her increasingly liberal views.

Attending a required course in Bible history, she learned that her father had been correct about Jonah's being swallowed alive by the whale. When she learned about other myths in the Bible, it allowed her to see her father's bravery more clearly, knowing now that he was strong in his refusal to buckle under hypocritical pressure.

Back home in Birmingham, where her sister Josephine had married Birmingham lawyer Hugo Black, Virginia met Cliff Durr at the Independent Presbyterian Church. A year later they were married in the same church.

Virginia began to notice the world around her. She drove Red Cross workers into the countryside, where they certified families for relief. She saw the hardworking, poor coal miners whose bodies were wrecked from black lung and tuberculosis. She saw their children, with their bulging eyes and swollen bellies, so different from her own well-fed babies.

She read social history and economic theories, and on weekends she took her husband out into the poor sections where she'd witnessed terrible poverty. They talked about these things, and Cliff followed her example, reading the texts that she'd set to memory.

In 1933, comfortably situated economically, Cliff Durr watched as the senior partner of his firm, Logan Martin, fired several employees without reason. Disturbed, Durr questioned Martin. Why fire these people for no reason other than the firm's being squeezed by hard times? In a partners' meeting, Durr suggested that they take pay cuts in their own salaries rather than fire employees for no reason. Martin not only refused the request, he became irate that the most junior partner would make such a request at all. That evening Cliff explained the situation to Virginia, who suggested that he resign. The next day he quit.

Without a job, he and Virginia decided to go to the country, to a small fishing cabin they owned near Clanton, south of Birmingham. They could spend a week in solitude, discuss their prospects, and make a decision.

After several days, Virginia's brother-in-law, U.S. senator Hugo Black, who would later become an outstanding justice on the U.S. Supreme Court, sent a message asking Cliff to call him in Washington. The Reconstruction Finance Corporation (RFC) was looking for lawyers. Black had recommended Durr.

In Washington, Cliff was offered a job with the RFC and a comfortable salary of $6,375 a year. They could stay with Virginia's sister and brother-in-law until they found a place of their own.

The RFC was an organization founded by President Herbert Hoover to fight the dire economic straits of the nation's banking system. It provided low–interest rate loans to banks across the United States. However, as the Great Depression tightened its squeeze on money, more and more banks shut down. President Franklin Delano Roosevelt passed the Emergency Banking Act to strengthen the efforts.

During off hours Durr was an active member of the Southern Policy Committee. Meeting over dinner, congressmen and lawyers discussed economic, political, and social conditions that persisted in the South. Their report, *The South: Economic Problem Number One*, dissected problems and recommended changes. Durr wrote an introduction for President Roosevelt's signature.

The Durrs found a comfortable old home on Seminary Hill, named for the Virginia Episcopal Theological Seminary located there. They enjoyed entertaining on weekends. Folk singer Pete Seeger showed up and strummed his banjo and sang ballads. Fellow Alabamans Anita and Aubrey Williams became close friends. Lady Bird and Lyndon Johnson were regulars.

With the help of first lady Eleanor Roosevelt, Virginia Durr fought to establish stronger child labor regulations and to outlaw the poll tax, which she believed was antidemocratic. In Durr's opinion, it worked to disenfranchise blacks. In Alabama the poll tax was retroactive from age twenty-one, each year's tax added on top of the previous year's, so that by the time a person was forty, he or she had to pay $28.50—a princely sum to a poor farmer during the Depression.

When she heard stories about downtrodden sharecroppers strapped to an economic system that had replaced slavery, Durr became vehement. She heard about Joseph S. Gelders, a Jewish man from Alabama who had been snatched by vigilantes in Birmingham, taken to the country, beaten senseless, and left for dead. The next time she was in Birmingham, she visited him. He suggested they sit in a park because his office was wired by the FBI.

One of Joe Gelders's passions was his effort to organize sharecroppers. In that position, he met Edgar Daniel Nixon in Montgomery, and it was Gelders who told Virginia Durr about the black leader who was trying to help his people.

Early in 1941, at the request of U.S. representative Lister Hill, President Roosevelt chose Durr to become a member of the Federal Communications Commission (FCC). There, Durr soon became known for his dissension by voting against network conglomerates that were gobbling up small radio stations. With the advent of FM radio, Durr fought for frequencies to be set aside for education. When television came into the picture, he championed the idea of designating certain channels for noncommercial use. He became known as the Father of Public Television, and one of the country's first statewide networks of public radio and television stations was organized in Alabama. In December 1944 the *New Republic* magazine stated that Durr was "fighting quietly and steadily for the people's interests," and that he was widely known "as a high[ly] principled, courageous fighter against advertising control of radio" and "for balanced presentation of controversial issues on the air."

At the FCC Durr came into contact with the House Un-American Activities Committee (HUAC). In November 1942

HUAC chairman Representative Martin Dies, a Democrat from Texas who had been an outspoken critic of Roosevelt and the New Deal, turned over to the press a letter accusing an FCC employee of close association with Communist organizations. James Lawrence Fly, chairman of the FCC, called the charges ridiculous and asked Durr to investigate them.

After a thorough investigation, Durr found not only that the employee had no Communist ties, but also that he was actually a member of several conservative groups whose members included Henry L. Stimson, secretary of state under Herbert Hoover; William Allen White, the Republican publisher of the *Emporia Gazette;* and Chief Justice Charles Evans Hughes. Still, Dies insisted that the man be fired.

Soon Durr learned from a neighbor that FBI agents had been snooping around Seminary Hill. After an unnamed person complained to the FBI about Durr, J. Edgar Hoover ordered an investigation. He sent the results to Fly, who showed them to Durr. Durr seethed. He saw the action as the beginning of a pattern: an anonymous source could make a blind complaint, which would set in motion an investigation. Innuendo and gossip would then become a part of the pattern to destroy an individual, going against every tenet of the American legal system. It was the kind of situation that could totally destroy a person, and the destruction would be done by a coward whose name and identity would never be known.

Although Durr was cleared in the report, that did little to quash his anger. As he read it, he saw that Virginia's activities were questioned, especially those of her attendance at the Southern Conference on Human Welfare and her meeting with Joe Gelders in Birmingham.

On March 27, 1947, President Harry Truman decreed by executive order that every federal employee be required to take an oath declaring his or her loyalty to the country. The order also opened up all employees to be investigated for un-

American activities through personal associations and memberships in organizations, including religious institutions. Years later Durr recalled, "I had met with my old and trusted friend Harry Truman several days before he made his decree. I told him I'd heard rumors that he was going to do this. Sitting back in his chair in the Oval Office, he chuckled. 'Oh, Cliff, I'm not going to do any such a thing. I'm just putting some word out around town. You know how rumors spread around this place. I'm just floating a trial balloon.' I nodded. I told him I believed that he'd do the right thing. I reiterated my belief that we could not begin destroying the Constitution with such underhanded dealings. He said he agreed. Several mornings later, when I opened the *Washington Post*, I read the story about his order. It boiled through my veins. It was the most hypocritical action I had ever seen by a public official. I knew that Harry Truman knew better, but someone had gotten to him. It was terribly diabolical."

To Durr, the order presumed guilt without providing for a trial in which a defendant would be allowed to face his or her accusers. In his estimation, the order thwarted the U.S. Constitution and circumvented the rule of law. A democracy, Durr told the National Citizens Conference on Civil Liberties in 1948, is "based upon faith in people—in their innate intelligence and decency—upon a belief in their ability to shape out a good destiny for themselves between the hammer and anvil of conflicting ideas, provided they are given full freedom to know and to discuss, to inquire and to explore, to experiment and to compare, to associate and to exchange their views one with another, and to protest when the occasion arises. This was the gamble which the founders of our government made with destiny. It was not the gamble of fearful men. It will not be won by fearful men."

Following his conscience, Durr refused to accept an appointment to another term on the FCC, and he went into private practice. On his first day in his office in downtown Washington, a former federal employee named Roy Patterson knocked on his door seeking counsel. Patterson explained that he had kept statistics for the Department of Labor before being fired for "disloyalty." A disabled veteran, Patterson had been wounded in combat and decorated for his action. In the 1930s he not only joined several peace groups that were later suspected of being Communist, he also became a member of the Washington Book Shop cooperative, which sold numerous leftist-leaning books along with mainstream literature. (Although she didn't know Patterson, Virginia Durr was also a member of the co-op.) However, when Cliff examined the man's employment record, he discovered that Patterson had been an outstanding employee. Questioning his client closely, Durr learned that Patterson, a native of rural Texas, had once viewed blacks as inferior, just as Durr had. As he came into contact with more educated blacks, however, he found them interesting and enlightening. At the Book Shop, he told Durr, he found that he could sit down, have a cup of coffee with an educated black, and have an open discussion about various subjects they both enjoyed.

Durr appealed to the Loyalty Review Board and asked for a public hearing. His request was denied. Durr then leaked the story to a friendly reporter at the *Washington Post*. After the story was published, the board held a hearing and found that Patterson was not disloyal. Patterson's former employer was ordered to reinstate him to his former position.

As a result of his success and his courage, Durr became the mouthpiece for dozens of clients who had been fired by the federal government for suspected Communist affiliations. In one instance, Durr represented a black librarian who had been fired by the U.S. Air Force after being accused of collecting subversive papers. At a hearing, Durr showed that the "subversive papers" actually consisted of a speech by FBI Director J. Edgar

Hoover, and that the woman's female accusers were extremely bitter over his client being promoted ahead of them. The hearing officers found for Durr's client.

After several years, Durr had little to show financially for his hard work and courageous stands. Soon, although Virginia was dead set against returning to the South, the Durrs came home to Alabama. In March 1952 Cliff opened a law office, and Virginia became his secretary. It was a quiet return, which was the way Cliff wanted it.

While Cliff knew he would never make much money with a small practice in the sleepy old town of Montgomery, he felt good about the South: he thought it was changing for the better, and he hoped that its leadership would bend with the times. Virginia, however, felt more isolated, lonely, and without the friendship of people who felt as strongly as she did about society and politics. Then, in March 1954, she received a subpoena to appear before the Subcommittee on Internal Security of the U.S. Senate's Committee on the Judiciary to testify about her knowledge of the Southern Conference Education Fund, which Aubrey Williams headed. Cliff had turned down Williams, who'd received a similar subpoena, as a client; suffering from angina, he'd said that he would not be able to concentrate strongly enough. But when Virginia was summoned to New Orleans, Cliff said he would defend both Williams and his wife. Hearing Cliff's decision, his old friend, John Peter Kohn, a deeply conservative and highly respected attorney, showed up on the Durrs' doorstep wearing a seersucker suit and standing tall and ramrod straight—the perfect picture of a Southern gentleman lawyer. He said, "Cliff, you will not represent Virginia. You're too close. It would be like representing yourself." And when Cliff said they didn't have the money to pay his expenses, much less his fees, John Kohn said, "I'll hear nothing of it. You're my friend. Your wife is in trouble. I will be there for you. And I don't want to hear a word about any expenses or fees. Is that understood?"

Back in the 1930s Virginia had been a member of the Southern Conference Educational Fund, an organization that had sprung out of the old Southern Conference for Human Welfare that she had attended in Birmingham years earlier, when she met Joe Gelders and E. D. Nixon.

By 1954 the Subcommittee on Internal Security had become the Southern version of Senator Joseph McCarthy's red-hunting HUAC. Senator James Eastland, of Mississippi, planned to lead his band of witch hunters through the South, armed with the testimony of paid informant Paul Crouch, an organizer for the Communist Party. On the stand, Crouch swore that he had known the Durrs in Washington, where Virginia had been a member of the Communist Party and where she had introduced Eleanor Roosevelt and her brother-in-law, Supreme Court Justice Hugo Black, to Joe Gelders, whom he identified as "one of the top Soviet Communist agents in America."

When Virginia took the stand, John Kohn asked that she be allowed to enter a statement into the record. Eastland refused, whereupon Kohn stated that "all of Southern womanhood is in question by this committee." After she stated her name and said that her husband was Clifford Durr, she said that she was not at that moment, nor had she ever been, a member of the Communist Party. Stepping down from the stand, Virginia reached into her purse and took out her compact. For a moment she powdered her nose, while news photographers' cameras flashed.

When Aubrey Williams took the stand, Clifford Durr objected to the very notion of such a hearing. Eastland replied that his objection was not allowed. Williams answered questions about the Southern Conference Education Fund, explaining that it had been formed to bring about proper education for all needy children in the South. He said that he had never met Crouch and had never been a Communist.

Crouch, recalled to the stand, testified that he had had many meetings with Williams, who was "a secret member of the Communist Party." Surprisingly, Durr was given the opportunity to cross-examine the witness. As Durr probed, Crouch told about his own Communist affiliations. Durr remembered, "By the time I finished with him, he could remember nothing. He didn't know when he became a Communist. He didn't know when he stopped being a Communist. He didn't even know *if* he stopped being a Communist. He *did* tell about being on the federal payroll, and all he did for the government was testify in similar hearings across the nation."

The government attorney interrupted, trying to save his witness. He asked Crouch if Durr was a Communist. "I know he was a Communist," the witness stated. "But I don't know if he's still one or not."

Laughter tittered through the room. Eastland, who chuckled, said, "I'm going to strike that remark."

Durr said, "His testimony is under oath. Let's leave it in, under oath," and Eastland agreed.

Moments later, Durr asked Crouch to give dates and places. "When did you see me with 'national Communist leaders,' as you've stated?" Crouch could not remember exact dates or places.

Durr continued his line of questioning until the witness blurted, "I know Joe Gelders told me you were 'a reliable comrade.'"

Dismissing Crouch, Durr turned to Eastland. Durr wanted to take the stand. "I have been accused by this man." Durr gestured toward Crouch. "I should at least be given the opportunity to clear the air here and now."

Again, to Durr's surprise, Eastland agreed.

Durr denied that he had ever been a Communist and stated that he had no intention of ever becoming a Communist. He called Crouch's testimony "a complete and absolute falsehood."

After Eastland announced that his next hearing would be held in Birmingham, people began to disperse. When Cliff Durr neared his accuser, he leaped over the jury rail, grabbed at Crouch, and said, "You dirty dog! I'll kill you for lying about my wife!" Marshals separated them. Durr, exhausted, was led to a bench, where Virginia comforted him.

The next day newspapers around the country, including the *New York Times*, carried the photograph of Durr face-to-face with his accuser.

Journalists who had covered the hearing told the *Montgomery Advertiser* that they were divided as to who displayed the greatest threat to America: half thought it was Eastland, and the other half voted for Crouch.

On the editorial page of the *Advertiser*, editor Grover Hall, Jr., who seldom defended the Durrs or any other liberal, wrote, "There is a matter of Southern honor involved here. A Southern gentleman and lady have been publicly branded with the most opprobrious term of the hour. They have denied it under oath. This is the type of character lynching which Southern Senators should deeply resent."

Years later, Virginia told writer Studs Terkel, "Cliff would wake up every morning and say, 'Thank God I'm in Alabama. Back here, I'm home. I know who the sons of bitches are and where the attacks are comin' from.' As soon as he was able to open his law office, we got right in the middle of the whole civil rights fight. Martin Luther King. E. D. Nixon. We got Mrs. Parks out of jail. It was thrilling and exciting."

In 1955 young black attorney Fred Gray sought legal help from Cliff. When Claudette Colvin was arrested and charged with violating segregation statutes, Durr joined hands with the young man and agreed to help. After the case proved not to hold up for appeal, Durr told Gray not to worry, to have patience; a new case would come his way soon. In December, when he got a call from E. D. Nixon about Rosa Parks being arrested, Durr knew the case was happening, even as he and Virginia rode downtown with Nixon to get Parks out of jail.

And when Fred Gray asked him to help with suing the city in federal court, Durr felt obliged to do so.

When Mayor Gayle learned about the suit, he was furious. The black lawyers had beaten the politicians and the city's attorneys to the punch. He telephoned Commissioner Sellers, who marched down the hall of police headquarters to the office of Chief Ruppenthal. Sellers angrily ordered the chief to call his best two detectives. Moments later, Jack Shows and K. W. Jones entered the office. Sellers banged his fist against the desk on which that morning's *Advertiser* lay, displaying the article about the lawsuit. He told the plainclothes officers, "Find out everything you can about these niggers."

In less than twenty-four hours, Shows and Jones brought one of the plaintiffs, Jeanetta Reese, a sixty-four-year-old woman who worked as a maid for a white family, into the mayor's office, where Commissioner Sellers sat to the side. As it turned out, the woman's employer said she was surprised to see Mrs. Reese's name in the newspaper. "I'm surprised, too," she told her employer. "You know I don't want nothing to do with this mess."

After the suit was filed, Reese's husband received a phone call threatening Reese to get out of town. Reese told Mayor Gayle, Commissioner Sellers, and the detectives that she had gone to Gray's office to deliver insurance papers and that she had no idea what she was signing. Her husband's sister had died recently, and she wanted the attorney to "straighten out the matter of collecting on the policy."

While in his office, she said, Gray asked, "What do you think about the buses?"

"It looks awful. It looks like they could get together," she told him.

Asked if she received fair treatment on the buses, she answered, "No, I have been pushed around and passed up a lot of times."

Reese told the officials that Gray asked her if she would say that anywhere. "And I told him, 'Sure, I'll say it anywhere that I didn't get (fair) treatment.' And then he asked me to sign some papers [but] I didn't know what they were.

"He asked me if I was sure I wanted to sign and I said, 'Yeah, I'll sign. They treat us like horses.' So I hauled off and signed. He didn't say anything about a suit."

Gray insisted that Reese knew from the beginning all of the details of the suit. Still, she withdrew her name. The other four remained in the case.

———

Angered by the suit and distraught by the overwhelming success of the boycott, the white politicians decided they had to strike back. The best and most effective way was to get rid of this smart young attorney, Fred Gray, whom they discovered had been classified 4-D by the local draft board because he'd claimed to be a "practicing minister." Gray had preached regularly at the Holt Street Church of Christ.

Alabama Selective Service director James W. Jones told the *Alabama Journal* on February 8, less than a week after Gray filed the suit in federal court, that Gray had been reclassified as 1-A. If Gray didn't agree with the classification, he had ten days to file notice of appeal to the Middle District of Alabama Appeal Board.

Not satisfied with just getting rid of Gray, members of the local white establishment racked their brains about how to defeat the boycotters. While they publicly expressed sentiments that the boycott was failing, they could see the obvious toll it was taking on the white community. Not only was the bus company losing money, but some irate citizens were already taking up arms, breaking the law in the dark of night. If that continued, the actions might demand martial law—or worse.

The bad publicity increased. When King's house was bombed, the news exploded across radio, television, newspapers, and magazines. Every time an act of violence occurred, it made headlines.

Local television reporter Frank McGee, anchor on the NBC affiliate WSFA, was featured on the national network almost as much as he appeared on the local six o'clock news. Journalists from across the nation and the world were in and out of Montgomery, reporting favorably on the success of the boycott. And its leaders, especially Dr. King, were becoming headline favorites, interviewed by every major newspaper from the *Los Angeles Times* to the *Times* in London. In early February King, giving a guest sermon at a black church in Chicago, said that the boycott "is part of something that's happening all over the world. The oppressed peoples of the world are rising up. They are revolting against colonialism, imperialism, and other systems of oppression."

Alabama Associated Press correspondent Rex Thomas's byline appeared regularly in newspapers worldwide, carrying news of the boycott. And the roving southern reporter for the *New York Times*, John "Pop" Popham, was in Montgomery more than he was in his home base of Chattanooga, Tennessee. Governor Folsom joked that he had a spare room for Popham anytime the reporter wished to stay at the Governor's Mansion.

Mayor Gayle, city commissioners Sellers and Parks, city attorney D. Eugene Loe, and Circuit Solicitor William F. Thetford stayed up late at night, discussed strategy, and came up with a plan. They knew they could not create a new ordinance or law to alleviate the problem. Such a law would be clearly unconstitutional, and it would be stricken down almost as fast as they could write it and pass it.

Instead, they found a state law dating back to October 1921 that outlawed boycotting and blacklisting. Faced with the lingering strike of several thousand black and white members of the United Mine Workers Union in Jefferson and Walker counties in north Alabama that had resulted in boycotts, dynamiting, and several murders, Governor Thomas E. Kilby had called the legislature into special session on October 4, 1921, and asked that it strengthen the law in the state criminal code that had been passed in 1907. Addressing the joint session of the House and the Senate, he stated that stronger laws were needed to promptly and properly deal with the strike. Conditions were so critical, the governor declared, that it appeared almost imperative that martial law be declared in the coal-mining districts of the state. Had the statutes been adequate, he continued, the civil authorities would have been able to deal with the labor trouble and much if not all of the loss of life and property, and the enormous expenses of the state would have been avoided.

And now, more than thirty years later, Gayle, Sellers, and the other white public officials felt powerless in the face of the peaceful demonstrations. Back in 1921, Kilby had championed the get-tough-with-labor amendment that would stop what he called "outside agitators." Using these same words, Sellers had addressed a White Citizens Council meeting a week earlier and spoken about the bus boycotters. In Kilby's words, it was a conspiracy to cause great suffering and inconvenience to the public and was "little less than treason against the government."

The 1921 law declared that "two or more persons who, without a just cause or legal excuse for so doing, enter into any combination, conspiracy, agreement, arrangement, or understanding for the purpose of hindering, delaying, or preventing any other persons, firms, corporation or association of persons from carrying on any lawful business shall be guilty of a misdemeanor."

A week later, Montgomery circuit judge Eugene B. Carter charged a special grand jury, advising the jurors that the organized boycotting of lawful businesses was against the law in Alabama. Persons found guilty of unlawful boycotting could be punished with a jail term of six months, a thousand-dollar fine, or both.

Judge Carter observed that Montgomery County had seldom been confronted with boycotts of any kind in the past and had never experienced a boycott of city buses. He told the eighteen white men that their responsibility as grand jurors was to investigate acts of boycotting and to determine if the law had been broken. "If it is illegal," he said, "it must be stopped. You are the supreme inquisitorial body." He explained that the law applied to situations in which persons were involuntarily forced, through leadership or conspiracy, to boycott business organizations, that the simple failure of an individual or a group to patronize a business did not constitute a boycott. However, he said, persons who were responsible for inciting or organizing others to resist doing business could be prosecuted under the law.

"Montgomery has been a city that both races have had the pleasure of living in. I say to both black and white, let's continue to live as neighbors," Judge Carter said. "The doctrine of hate has no place here and particularly has no place in our churches. It seems strange that in this day, and in this free country—a country in which law interferes so little with the liberty of the individual—it should be necessary to announce from the bench that every man may carry on his business as he pleases, may do what he will with his own, so long as he does nothing unlawful, and acts with due regard to the rights of others."

Judge Carter added, "Justice should be dished out of the same spoon, regardless of who violates the law—whether he be doctor, lawyer, rich, or powerful. If anyone feels the laws are wrongful, we have the courts to go to for the settlement of differences."

The jury convened under the supervision of Solicitor Thetford, who began presenting evidence immediately.

Thetford told reporter Tom Johnson that many states had laws against organized boycotting. He pointed out that Justice William C. Thomas, of the Alabama Supreme Court, had written an opinion on the law in 1943, after a Jefferson County man had been found guilty of disturbing the good relations between an insurance company and its stockholders. Thomas ruled that when an "unlawful agreement in the nature of a conspiracy" was made, "all conspirators are subject to trial for conspiracy." In his opinion, he stated that legitimate businesses were protected from malicious boycotts by the statute. "Under both Alabama and federal constitutions, it is recognized that a person's business is 'property' and, if lawfully conducted, is entitled to protection from unlawful interference," Thomas wrote.

Laws prohibiting boycotts were nothing new. They had been a part of the English common law for hundreds of years. The word "boycott" was derived from a Captain Boycott, who in the nineteenth century was an agent of Lord Earne in the wild Irish district of Connemara. A potato farmer, Boycott charged the servants who lived on his land a certain amount of rent. However, these servants fled, and Boycott's life was threatened, his property was attacked, and his crops lay unattended to by the tenants. Boycott and his wife had to work the fields themselves while their former tenants did their dirty play at night. Finally, his friends the Orangemen of the north sent armed workers to help Captain Boycott. According to legend, Boycott's harvests were brought in and his potatoes were dug by the armed Ulster laborers.

In his "City Limits" column Joe Azbell wrote, "The power of the grand jury—such as the Montgomery County panel now in session—compares with the force of lightning. It has almost unlimited striking range as long as it can make a connection between a person and a crime." But he also pointed out that the Alabama law implied that persons who have just cause for boycotting a firm may do so legally.

It soon became common knowledge that the grand jury was on the verge of issuing as many as a hundred indictments to black leaders who were involved in the boycott. From Willie's Pool Parlor on Montgomery Street to Jason's Barber Shop on Bell Street, the gossip was heavy.

But first, as if it were not enough to have attorney Fred Gray reclassified as 1-A, putting him in jeopardy of being drafted by the army at any time, the grand jury issued a partial report indicting Gray and charging that he made an unlawful appearance as an attorney for Jeanetta Reese, who claimed she had not hired him.

Gray was booked at Montgomery County Jail after the grand jury charged him with a misdemeanor under the Alabama code that stated: "Attorney appearing without authority—any attorney appearing for a person without being employed must, on conviction, be fined not less than $500 and shall be [deemed] incompetent in any court in this state."

Gray was fingerprinted, photographed, and held in custody for thirty minutes before he was released on a three-hundred-dollar bond.

Later Dr. King stated in Atlanta, where he was filling a speaking engagement, that the charges were "a subtle and insidious attempt to have Gray disbarred and hinder the cause of integration." He said that "all 50,000 Negroes of Montgomery . . . as well as numerous white Montgomerians of good will" were behind Gray, and that, "when this issue comes before fair-minded men in the courts," a speedy acquittal would result.

On the day before the grand jury was scheduled to report to the court, Montgomery's political powers put out one last request for compromise. The mayor, city commissioners, and several white businesspeople, including representatives of the bus company, offered a plan, which was discussed in a black Methodist church in a meeting that was closed to newsmen. This plan was never revealed in detail, but it did not address all of the requests that had been made by King and the MIA. The leaders felt duped. An hour before deadline, the Reverend Ralph Abernathy, chairman of the negotiating committee, said that the offer was refused. He announced the vote against acceptance: 3,998 to 2.

The white power structure didn't know that U.S. district judge Frank Minis Johnson, Jr., a thirty-seven-year-old from north Alabama, whom President Eisenhower had appointed only a few months earlier, had already written to Joseph Hutchenson, chief judge of the U.S. Fifth Circuit, of which Alabama was a part, asking him to appoint a three-judge panel to hear *Browder v. Gayle*, the case that Gray had filed. The federal court had taken jurisdiction of the case as quickly as it was filed. But it would take the three-judge panel to decide the constitutionality of the local law. Without it, the court's decision would not carry full weight, Johnson pointed out.

On the eve of the arrests of the black leaders, Aubrey Williams, a tall, gaunt, ruggedly handsome man who resembled movie star Henry Fonda, dropped by E. D. Nixon's office on Monroe Street. He asked how things were going with the boycott, which he supported. He was one of several white people who regularly attended the mass meetings.

Like his friend Nixon, Aubrey Williams knew what it meant to work for a living as a child. Like his friend Cliff Durr, he was born into the unyielding toughness of the Presbyterian church.

Born in rural north Alabama, he experienced personal disaster early when his father drank up all the family money and left them stone broke. After moving to Birmingham, Aubrey worked at age twelve for the Loveman, Joseph, and Loeb department store as a package wrapper, making three dollars and fifty cents a week. He took most of his pay home to his mother, but he always managed to save a few cents every week.

During his working childhood, Williams witnessed poverty on the streets of downtown Birmingham and in the rural mining camps north of town. He won a scholarship to a year at a small Presbyterian college in Tennessee, signed on as a wartime ambulance driver and was shipped to Paris, and later joined the French Foreign Legion and witnessed death and destruction as a combat infantryman. After attending graduate school in France, Williams returned to the United States and became a leader of social workers in Wisconsin.

On May 1, 1933, during Franklin Delano Roosevelt's first month as president, Williams was called to the nation's capitol by Harry Hopkins, whom FDR had appointed to oversee and initiate new government programs. Williams soon became Hopkins's right-hand man, and he was later made deputy director of the Works Project Administration and director of the National Youth Administration. It was during these days that he first met and enjoyed the company of E. D. Nixon, whose straight talk and unyielding eye contact made Williams feel comfortable. The two talked and talked about what each was doing in his own backyard.

Williams became embroiled in one controversy after another in Washington. In the early 1940s he moved to Montgomery and became editor and publisher of *Southern Farmer*, a magazine owned by his wealthy friend, Marshall Field.

Throughout these years, Williams's friendship with E. D. Nixon became stronger and deeper. After Mattie Johnson called Nixon and told him about Thomas Edward Brooks being shot and killed on the bus, Nixon sat down one day and told the story to Williams. As Nixon spoke, he thought Williams was going to cry. Williams put his hand out, touched Nixon's hand, and said, "Nixon, we've got to stop these things from happening. We've got to stop it. No matter what it takes."

And on the night before the arrests in Montgomery, Williams dug into his pocket and withdrew a sheaf of hundred-dollar bills. He placed them in Nixon's hands. "I know this isn't enough, but it ought to help with the bails tomorrow. If you need more, call me and I'll come up with it."

Later, when he looked back on those days, E. D. Nixon remembered, "He'd tell us to hold our heads high and be proud of ourselves. You don't know what it means to have a white man that Negroes can trust, and we trusted Aubrey Williams. That man got so much respect, it rubs off on you."

The arrests started. They came fast and furious, and were conducted with military precision–like efficiency. Just as Joe Azbell had found his way inside the churches during the boycotters' mass meetings, Azbell was the only reporter allowed inside the county jail when the arrests were taking place.

In the next morning's *Advertiser*, Azbell wrote about the events in his typical hard-hitting, staccato style, drawing out every detail he could find and pushing the drama he saw unfolding. Later he would say, "I knew this was my big chance to explore something that was history. Many journalists think they are reporting history. I *knew* it."

Azbell began his article: "It was like an army recruit line, and as speedy. Two deputies were handed a batch of warrants. They drove off. In fifteen minutes they were back."

All told, ninety-eight black leaders were arrested, booked, and charged with violating the Alabama statute against boycotting. Later, three were dropped as defendants.

At a desk inside the county courthouse, a deputy sheriff checked the arrest warrant against a four-page list. Confirming the warrant, the deputy said, "You're one." Then he wrote down the person's name, age, weight, and height. As Azbell saw it, "That was the booking."

From the makeshift booking desk, the defendants passed the normal booking desk, walked through a swinging gate, detoured down a dark hall, and went into an ill-lighted room, where two young policemen were taking fingerprints and pictures. The room was crowded with cameras and printing apparatus. Five or six defendants waited in line. As each was fingerprinted, a police officer poured alcohol from a bottle onto the defendant's inked hands and passed him or her a paper towel. As Azbell wrote, it was as efficient as an army recruit line.

The other police officers fixed a number onto a frame, hung it around the defendant's neck, looked through the lens of the camera, and photographed the subject.

Each defendant was then handed three fingerprint cards and pointed toward an adjoining room, where a deputy sheriff, seated at a desk, took down information: age, weight, characteristics, teeth markings, next of kin, occupation, and date and place of birth.

The defendants then squeezed their way back through the crowded fingerprint room, down the hall, and back to the main booking desk. Throughout the day, there were always three or four people standing at the booking desk, ready to sign bonds for those who'd been arrested.

Once the three-hundred-dollar bonds were signed, the released defendants filed outside. Few left. Most waited for others to arrive. When they came, they clasped hands and exchanged greetings.

The atmosphere outside was like that of an old home week. Those who'd been charged with the crime of boycotting laughed and joked, slapped each other on the back, spoke casually, and shook hands as though they belonged to a fraternal order. Azbell had seen hundreds of criminals in city and county jails, army stockades, and federal penitentiaries. To him, these men and women didn't act like criminals. None walked with a bowed head. None dragged their feet. They held their heads high. They stepped spryly down the halls. Smiles were fixed on their faces. They spoke joyfully.

"Man, you're late," one said. "I've been here an hour."

Another smiled and nodded.

As a car approached the jail, Azbell heard one of the defendants say, "Well, here comes my preacher."

After a while, when the procedure became routine, those who had already been booked escorted their arriving friends into the rooms without deputies. Defendants pointed the new ones down the hallway and told them where to go and what to do. By noon, more than half of those who'd been arrested had volunteered to help.

Azbell wrote, "Early in the morning, several Negroes appeared at the jail ready to sign bonds for the arrested Negroes. They did sign the bonds—but as the indictment warrants were issued, it was discovered that some of those signing bonds were to be arrested themselves on the boycotting charges."

After that discovery, Sheriff Mac Sim Butler ordered the indictment list checked before a person could sign a bond.

While E. D. Nixon was being processed, his friend Aubrey Williams entered the courthouse and offered to sign Nixon's bond. The two spoke quietly to the side, then Williams told Azbell, "I think these people are right and just in what they are doing." The reporter noted that Williams was the only white to appear at the courthouse that day to help the black protesters. Abernathy told Azbell that the people who'd been arrested were "law-abiding citizens."

As he was being booked, the Reverend L. R. Bennett, dressed in a black minister's coat and clerical collar, held a Bible in his hand.

Azbell asked, "Why did you bring your Bible?"

"I'm gonna make a speech today. I'm the Brotherhood Week speaker at a gathering," he said.

Dr. M. C. Cleveland, an elderly minister, told Azbell, "This is the first time I have ever been arrested for anything in seventy-two years. This is a new experience, but I suppose at my age you are used to new experiences."

Azbell wrote that police files showed that 90 percent of those arrested "were Alabama-born Negroes. Their birth places for the most part were small Alabama towns. Most were born on farms."

The majority were thirty-five to fifty years old; none were under twenty-three. One of the youngest was the Reverend Martin Luther King, Jr.

Among them were a half dozen women, including Rosa Parks and Jo Ann Robinson.

Late that afternoon, in his office on the northeast corner of the *Advertiser* building on Washington Avenue, Grover Cleveland Hall, Jr., threw back his head and told Azbell and others gathered around his desk, "This is the dumbest thing that that bunch of half-assed politicians has ever done. Don't they know that every newspaper, radio, and television station in the world will make it their duty to lambaste hell out of this action? They can't possibly win!

"The trials will drag on for weeks, maybe months, and every piece of dirty laundry that the city has ever soiled will be hung out to dry by every snot-nosed journalist from Hoboken to Honolulu.

"It's just plain dumb!" he declared.

In his own account of the arrests, Azbell was careful in his choice of words. His description of the carefree boycotters, telling jokes and loitering outside the jailhouse, infuriated many of the whites who perused the story the following morning. However, Cliff Durr found the details especially interesting. For weeks since Rosa Parks had been arrested, the white leaders had been pointing to the boycott and saying it was planned by "outside agitators." Some went so far as to say it was part of "the Communist-Jewish conspiracy." When they staged their meetings of the White Citizens Council, leaders ranted and raved about the agitators and the conspiracy.

However, according to Azbell's report, those who had been arrested and charged with the crime of boycotting were mostly older men who'd been born in Alabama and who lived most of their lives in Alabama. The protesters were local people who were tired of being treated like second-rate citizens.

The grand jury report stated that there had been a growing tension between the races in Montgomery. The bus boycott was simply one manifestation of this tension. Obviously written by white men, the report pointed out that "distrust, dislike, and hatred are being taught in a community which for more than a generation has enjoyed exemplary race relations. Small incidents have been magnified out of their true importance and ugly rumors are being spread among both races. It is axiomatic that distrust produces distrust and hate breeds hate.

"It is the feeling of this grand jury that if we continue on our present course of race relations, violence is inevitable. The leaders of both races are urged to take a long and thoughtful look into the future."

The grand jury failed to look into a mirror to see the white community it represented. Instead of searching for the sins and evils created by the white status quo, trying to dig the poison from a festering wound, it chose instead to point its finger stubbornly at what it perceived as the outside enemy. Those eighteen white men refused to look back at that sweltering August afternoon in Cloverdale when Thomas Edward Brooks fell under the weight of a police officer's bullet because he did not yield to a Jim Crow law created by all-white lawmakers.

The grand jury wrote, "Our segregation laws and the NAACP attack on segregation are the primary cause of the unrest and increasing tension between whites and Negroes in Montgomery. In this state we are committed to segregation by custom and by law; we intend to maintain it. The settlement of differences over school attendance, public transportation, and other public facilities must be made within those laws which reflect our way of life. During the past hundred years, no racial group has progressed so rapidly as the Negro, and no minority group has received so much in material aid and encouragement as the Negro. All of us recognize that change and progress are inevitable; however, every part of the country and every racial group must approach its own unique problems with the determination to face facts and make decisions which are in the best interest of all, now and in the years to come."

The words of the grand jury were a slap in the face of every black person and clear-thinking white person in Alabama—and America. These words previewed those that would ring out over Montgomery, Alabama—and the United States—some eight years later, when George C. Wallace would make his inauguration speech on the steps of the state capitol, shaking his fist and shouting, "Segregation now! Segregation tomorrow! Segregation forever!" In fact, on the same page of the *Advertiser* that carried the text of the jury's report was a small story about the Dale County grand jury praising circuit judge George Wallace and his stand to protect his court and his grand juries from investigation by the federal government. Wallace was already laying the groundwork for the political stand he'd take against the U.S. Civil Rights Commission a few years down the road.

The editorial page of the *Washington Post* stated, "The municipal authorities of Montgomery chose Washington's birthday—
they might even more appropriately have chosen Lincoln's
birthday—to ease their sense of frustration with a monumen-
tal display of folly. Their sense of frustration is easy to understand. Negroes in Montgomery have refused over the past
eleven weeks to ride in buses where they were humiliated by
segregation and by frequent discourtesy on the part of bus
drivers. The effect of their refusal has been serious from the
point of view of the bus line's economic status—and serious also
from the point of view of a white community determined to
perpetuate a pattern of race relations which gradually is being
swept aside by the logic of justice and the force of economic
change."

The *Post* continued that the most frustrating thing about
the protest was that it was "impeccably lawful, orderly, dignified—and effective. It strikes at an important pocketbook
nerve of the community."

On the evening following the arrests, Cliff and Virginia Durr
sat in the living room of their modest apartment on Felder
Avenue and listened to their friend Aubrey Williams describe
what he'd witnessed at the jail. "It was obvious to me," Cliff
said later, "that these black people displayed pride and dignity
while the white establishment showed cowardice under the
color of the law." To Virginia, Cliff said, "I was angry and infuriated. It was awful. Just plain awful."

8

King on Trial

LESS THAN A MONTH after the mass arrests, on March 19 at
11 A.M., Circuit Judge Eugene Carter called the court to order.
He asked, "Which case are you going to try first?"

The largest courtroom in the old courthouse on Washington Street was filled with spectators, witnesses, and representatives of the press. Circuit solicitor William Thetford, a
mature, seasoned prosecutor, was flanked by his two assistants,
Robert B. Stewart, a veteran attorney best known at the time
for having been Hank Williams's personal lawyer, and young
Maury D. Smith, who would become well known as a tenacious
and hardworking lawyer in the solicitor's office and, later, in
private practice. Thetford answered, "The King case." It was
styled *The State of Alabama v. M. L. King, Jr.*

Heading the defense was Arthur D. Shores, a distinguished
black lawyer from Birmingham who was already at the forefront of civil rights litigation. Dressed in a black pinstriped
three-piece suit, he was tall, and touches of gray ribboned his
wavy hair and a perfectly trimmed thin mustache. Shores, a former high school principal, was known throughout the South as

a first-rate attorney, and he had been the first black lawyer in Alabama to accompany his black clients into court. Previously, black attorneys had associated with white lawyers, who would actually take the clients to court. Since before World War II, Shores had been by far the busiest NAACP attorney in the South. Flanking Shores were Fred Gray and Charles Langford, the bright young local black lawyers. Also at the defendant's table were Peter A. Hall and Orzell Billingsley, Jr., who were already making names for themselves as black Birmingham attorneys.

Two weeks earlier, on March 2, the defense attorneys had begun laying their legal groundwork, stating in demurrers that the allegations asserted in the indictment were "vague and indefinite," that the statute itself was unconstitutional under both the Alabama State Constitution and the U.S. Constitution, that the law abridged the freedom of speech clause in violation of rights and liberties guaranteed by the First and Fourteenth Amendments of the U.S. Constitution, and that it also violated citizens' right to assemble freely. In this matter, Gray and Langford had followed the advice of Clifford Durr, who researched and wrote much of the pretrial filings while the young lawyers huddled to plan strategy with their older counterparts from Birmingham.

On the morning the trial began, Judge Carter issued an order overruling the demurrers to the indictment.

Thetford asked that the rule requiring all witnesses to be sequestered outside the courtroom (witnesses are not allowed to hear the testimony of another witness) be evoked. Then Thetford asked that an exception be made for Joe Azbell, who would appear as a witness and who would also be covering the trial for the morning newspaper. The defense agreed. After all, Azbell had written exactly what they had wanted him to write in previous stories. They had no reason to believe he wouldn't continue. Bunny Honicker, a reporter for the *Journal*, the afternoon newspaper, had also been called as a witness. Thetford asked that he, too, be given the same privilege. Lawyer Shores refused. Honicker's articles had not been as favorable to the demonstrators.

Through the testimony of their witnesses and a smattering of documented evidence, the prosecution planned to put together the pieces of a legal jigsaw puzzle—one that Thetford hoped would provide a clear picture of Dr. King as the leader of a conspiracy to break the boycott law. Shores and his fellow attorneys planned to throw up every defense they could muster to block Thetford from completing that picture. Every trial is filled with minute details—bits and pieces designed to prove minor points—and this one would be no different. If the defense was successful, the outcome of this trial could and would change a society and embrace a people with the courage to move forward into a world they had never known.

Called first to the witness stand was James H. Bagley, transportation superintendent and general manager of the Montgomery City Lines, Inc., which had operated buses out of its headquarters at 701 North McDonough Street for the past twenty years.

Thetford began by showing, through Bagley's testimony, how the boycott had first started. Bagley told about meeting with Dr. King at City Hall at the invitation of Mayor Gayle. At the meeting were the mayor, Bagley, Commissioners Sellers and Park, and Jack Crenshaw, an attorney representing the bus company. Also present were Dr. King, attorney Gray, Reverends Thrasher and Abernathy, and Jo Ann Robinson. It was during this meeting, Bagley said, that King made plain the demands of black citizens: that bus drivers be more courteous to riders, that seating arrangements be changed, "that colored people sit from the rear to the front and white people from the front to the rear," that no seats be reserved for anyone, and that the company "hire some colored drivers on routes which were predominantly [taken by] colored people."

When Thetford showed the witness a copy of a resolution passed by MIA membership, attorneys for King objected. It was not dated. Nor was it signed by King. Therefore, the attorneys argued, it should not be introduced as evidence. Judge Carter sustained the objection on the grounds that the resolution was not adequately connected to the defendant.

Thetford tried again to introduce the document. Again, a defense attorney objected. Again, Judge Carter stated, "Unless you connect it up, and [if] they object to it, it can't go in." Lawyer Hall said, "We do object to it." And Judge Carter reiterated, "It has to be connected in some way with the defendant. At this stage of the case, it hasn't been."

Thetford insisted, "Every conspirator would be liable for the acts of a fellow conspirator."

Judge Carter replied, "A conspiracy hasn't been proved yet."

Trying to prove criminal intent on the part of the blacks, Thetford asked Bagley repeatedly if King ever told him why blacks were no longer riding the buses. Each time, King's attorneys objected.

Finally, the judge overruled the objection. Bagley said, "That is the reason they wasn't riding, on account of what they was requesting; that they were tired of being treated with discourtesy, and also as being treated as second-class passengers when they was paying the same fare as any other passenger, or something to that effect."

Again, King's attorneys objected. The judge sustained the objection, "unless connected with King. Not what any white people said. I am assuming this is a conspiracy among colored people."

Thetford asked, "Did any colored representative say that?"

Bagley answered, "Yes."

Lawyer Hall again objected "to that particular question and answer in connection with Reverend King, unless he shows where, by whom, and under what circumstances. King wouldn't be responsible for what a colored member of the committee said."

Judge Carter stated, "This is an alleged conspiracy. Of course, a conspiracy under the law doesn't have to be proved by direct testimony. The Supreme Court has so held."

With the judge's statement allowing the testimony, Thetford had finally won a small point of law. Still, the defense team knew that they had kept King himself away from a direct hit—at least temporarily.

Next, the State called the Reverend A. W. Wilson, pastor of the Holt Street Baptist Church and a member of MIA's executive committee. Through his testimony, assistant solicitor Stewart would attempt to connect King to the boycott action.

In response to Stewart's questions, Wilson stated that he had met with numerous members of the MIA, that the meeting at his church on December 5, 1955, was "over-running" with people, but that his memory was not what it used to be. He could not recall who presided over the meeting or even whether Dr. King was present.

At a meeting with the mayor and others, Wilson said, King had presented a copy of the MIA resolution to a representative of the bus company. Over objections by Billingsley, Judge Carter allowed the resolution to be entered as evidence. Again, the State won a small but important point. The resolution made it clear that black bus riders had major problems with the way the buses were operated. They provided motivation for starting a boycott. And they had been presented at the meeting by King himself.

The State then called Erna Ashley Dungee, the financial secretary of the MIA, to the stand. As secretary of Mt. Zion AME Church, where the Montgomery Interdenominational

Ministerial Alliance had met on the afternoon of December 5, Mrs. Dungee was present when the MIA was organized, as well as when she was later elected to her office in the organization. She signed checks along with E. D. Nixon and Reverend King. She was shown numerous deposit slips and canceled checks. Over and over again, King's attorneys objected. Each time, the judge overruled. Adding up the deposits, Dungee counted $30,713.80.

While each tiny detail did little by itself to damage Dr. King's case, the overall testimony provided evidence that the MIA was operating for a purpose and that King was one of its principal leaders.

After she was shown checks and was asked what the money went for, she answered, "Generally for gasoline."

Stewart asked, "About how many stations do you have on your list?"

Dungee answered, "We have eight."

Stewart asked, "Do you know what that gasoline was used for?"

Dungee said, "Naturally, the gasoline was apparently used in driving, driving and taking people."

Stewart delved, "Taking what kind of people?"

Dungee said, "Well, people like colored people, I imagine."

Stewart asked, "Colored people who don't want to ride the buses?"

Dungee answered, "That is going further than I was going to say."

On his feet, attorney Billingsley objected.

The judge told her to answer yes or no.

Stewart pushed the point: "Isn't it?" Dungee answered, "No. People who want to ride."

The witness was shown a series of checks to the eight service stations, each station had been paid a total of $300 to $400, and each check had been signed by her, Nixon, and King.

After more than two hours of similar testimony, the prosecution pushed a new point with a larger check. In asking about a check for $5,017.50, endorsed only by King, prosecutors indicated that the money had gone to the minister's account in Georgia. However, the witness said that it was a "transfer of funds" from the Alabama National Bank in Montgomery to the Citizens Trust Bank in Atlanta, and that it wasn't for Reverend King personally.

The court adjourned at 5:33 P.M.

Reconvening at 9:00 A.M. on Tuesday, March 20, the prosecution pursued the money trail they had started the day before. They wanted to show that King was the chief MIA perpetrator of the boycott.

Stuart W. Patton, Jr., an assistant cashier at Alabama National Bank, identified ledger sheets for the MIA from December 1955 to March 13, 1956.

Then Dungee was recalled. Again, she began identifying checks, stating that some were used to pay for transportation.

Lawyer Shores asked if she approved payments or checks, or if she just signed them. "I sign checks. I write them and sign them." It was obvious from the testimony that, as financial secretary, she had only elementary duties. She was certainly not a part of an overall conspiracy. It seemed that the money trail ended with her.

The State then called the Reverend U. J. Fields, the pastor of the Bell Street Baptist Church. He was shown the minutes of the organizational meeting of the MIA, which indicated that officers had been elected, resolutions had been passed, and the determination was made that the protest would continue. However, Fields did not recall actually hearing or seeing such action.

Stewart asked, "What action was taken at the mass meeting?"

Fields remembered, "I think it was described by one newspaper report [as being] a happily singing group."

Frustrated, Stewart asked, "You were there on the platform.
Tell me just about what took place as you recall it. What affirmative action was taken?"

Fields answered, "Seemed like what I call a sort of spiritual
edification."

Stewart probed, "Do you recall any discussion of the bus
protest or bus boycott?"

Fields said, "I don't recall any."

Stewart inquired, "Tell me why Rosa Parks was present?"

Fields said, "I couldn't say, but I think this thing, she had
been arrested, I believe. Called her up before the citizens, just
wanted the citizens to see a woman of her character."

Once again, the State failed to connect the mass meeting,
King, the MIA, and the boycott.

The State called Rufus Lewis, who identified himself as a
member of MIA's executive and transportation committees. He
and other members, he said, had asked for volunteers "to transport people to various destinations." Asked how many people
used MIA transportation, he answered "about two hundred"
daily.

Stewart asked, "Did you have a regular pay schedule of any
kind?"

Lewis answered, "Yes."

Stewart asked, "What was it?"

He said it was "four dollars a day to people who did transport or used their car all day from approximately six o'clock in
the morning until six o'clock at night."

Lewis outlined the transportation system his committee
had organized. The system called for forty-three dispatch stations, a mimeographed list of people and pickup stations, and
twice-a-week mass meetings at various churches around the
city, where people could sign up for rides and volunteer their
time and services.

Asked if he discussed the details with King, he answered, "I don't recall discussing that with Reverend King." But he did make reports to the MIA.

In his cross-examination, lawyer Shores asked, "Has your committee ever kept Negroes from riding buses?"

Lewis stated, "No."

Shores asked, "Just left it up to the people?"

Lewis answered, "Yes."

During redirect, Stewart asked if Lewis had heard people being urged not to ride buses at the mass meetings. He answered, "Yes."

As in most trials, much of the testimony was repetitious. Attorneys on both sides wished to underline a particular point or emphasize a statement they thought might add weight to their side of the legal equation.

Throughout the morning, service station owners and operators were questioned. Each told about being paid for gasoline by the MIA. City detective K. W. Jones testified that he'd seen various cars hauling black people to different locations. He identified these as part of a carpool operation. Jones said that he had interviewed individuals at different pickup locations and had questioned them about their activities. On cross-examination, he said he had been ordered to investigate the boycott by his superiors in the police department. He said that his investigation was not a part of the city officials' plan to intimidate boycotters.

In the prosecution's attempt to show that the boycott was not nonviolent, as King insisted, but that it was instead organized violence against the city buses, five different Montgomery City Lines drivers were called to the stand by the State. All told the court that the buses they were driving in early December had been fired on. J. B. Gardner, another driver, said that someone had thrown "a rock, brick, or something" at his bus, breaking a glass. In a separate incident, he said, as he crossed Union Street on Columbus at 10:28 P.M., someone had fired a gun twice at his bus, hitting the crosspiece next to a window. And C. A. Bedsole, who had been a bus driver before he went to work for Hall Brothers Dairy, said that he'd been driving through Washington Park on December 8 when one of three young black men threw a brick and hit his bus.

The State next called Willie C. Carter, a black man who worked at Maxwell Air Force Base. Carter said that he had been threatened "a little more than a month ago" by a black man named Willie Dee. "He picked me up on May Street. In other words, I was coming to the field on the bus, see, and some of my friends saw me. One of those guys worked where I was. At that time I was working around the Sinclair station. I was going into the place and one of my friends was in the car with him. I was going to catch the bus. So that man, he said he wanted to see me."

Asked what Willie Dee had said to him, Carter answered, "Well, he didn't have very much to say. He said, 'You know, the boys going to whip you about riding the bus.' So I didn't know what to say. So he said, 'If you stay off, the boys won't whip you.' And I says, 'I don't think they will whip me.' He said, 'Don't you tell me they won't whip you.'

"I said, 'Maybe I can beat them to it and they won't whip me.' He said, 'You need your neck broke. I want to get a good look at you anyhow, see what you look like.' I didn't know why he just went ahead and talked like that. And finally he told me, 'You all stay off the bus.'"

Continuing the same line of testimony, Ernest Smith, who worked at the county courthouse, said that he had been told by another black to stop riding buses, but he never stopped. "I went to step up on the bus and a man standing there just pulled me back and said I wasn't going to get on. I got down and turned around and knocked him down. I got back on the bus, and when it turned the corner he still was laying down there," he said.

Lawyer Shores asked him to repeat his name, his address, where he worked, and how long he'd worked there. Then he asked when exactly the man had attempted to pull him off the bus.

Smith answered, "A week after it happened, after the boycott started."

Shores asked, "After what happened?"

Smith said, "A week after the boycott started."

In a classic attempt to confuse the witness, who had interjected the word "boycott" into his testimony, Shores began a series of quick questions.

Shores asked, "Do you know when it started?"

Smith said, "No."

Shores asked, "In your best judgment, did it start in 1956, or 1955, 1954, or when?"

Smith said, "Nineteen, what you say?"

Shores asked, "Started in 1954?"

Smith said, "It started after this boycott. I think it was about a week after this. I don't know what date or nothing."

Shores asked, "Was it the year before last? Last year? Or this year?"

Smith said, "It was last year."

Shores asked, "Was it in the spring of the year? The fall of the year?"

Smith said, "Kind of in the spring like."

Although the point seemed nebulous, the defense attorney had finally shown that the witness obviously had no idea when the boycott had started, making his testimony of little importance.

To show that the white politician's accusation of "goon squads" operating to keep other blacks from riding buses had been correct, the State called a black woman named Beatrice

Jackson. She said that after she'd ridden home on a bus one evening, at about six o'clock "this man came up to me and said, 'I
caught you riding, and if I catch you again I am going to have
to cut your damn throat.' I said, 'No, you won't.' He said, 'If I
catch you riding again I am going to cut your damn throat.' I
said, 'If you don't let me alone, I am going to phone it to the
mayor.'"

The State called Joe Azbell. He reiterated his *Advertiser* article of December 5, in which he'd reported seeing no blacks riding the buses. In Washington Park, he said, a black had told
him, "We are not riding the buses."

Azbell said that he could not tell if any particular person
had presided over the first mass meeting at Holt Street Baptist
Church, that the speeches he'd heard there involved questions
such as, "Did they desire to choose to get all of their democratic rights as American citizens. They introduced Rosa Parks
and explained that she was an outstanding citizen of the community and she had been denied her rights by being arrested."

Asked if any affirmative action had been taken at the meeting, Azbell answered that a resolution was introduced and read.

During cross-examination, Shores asked if Azbell had ever
been intimidated or seen any violence at any meeting.

Azbell answered, "I have never been intimidated in any of
them. I have been to about six of them. I have been asked one
time to leave, but I wasn't intimidated."

Shores asked, "Did the speakers or any person there urge
any violence or intimidation?"

Azbell explained that after King's house was bombed, "there
was a crowd of Negroes about to get out of hand, and Reverend
King came from his house on the porch, he came out to the
steps and asked the crowd not to become violent, not to get
unruly, don't get out of hand, don't ever use weapons, continue

the things that we are doing, give up any idea of retaliation or any idea of intimidation."

At this point in the trial, Thetford and his team wanted to show that the white power structure had done everything in its power to solve the problems on the buses.

Henry Parker, the white pastor of the First Baptist Church of Montgomery, testified that Mayor Gayle had appointed him to a biracial committee to attempt to reach a settlement. After two lengthy meetings, with King and Gray as the principal spokesmen for the black community, no satisfactory solution had been found.

Mayor Gayle testified about Montgomery City Lines having had the bus franchise since 1935; about receiving, from an unknown person, the resolution asking for changes in the bus situation; and about meeting with Reverend King, who presented the requests to the city commission and the bus company.

At a meeting on January 9, Reverend King said he had a small group of blacks who would like to meet with the commission, the mayor told the court. "They met with the commission that afternoon at three thirty. Lawyer Gray then presented the resolution, read it first and then submitted it to the commission, and they had, however, modified the seating arrangement," he said.

Mayor Gayle said that, after another meeting, on January 21 with three black ministers at the chamber of commerce, he and the other commissioners had been satisfied that they had reached an agreement. The solution, he said, "was read to those three ministers three times." For a reason he said they thought best, they decided not to make the preachers' names public, with the exception of Reverend Benjamin F. Mosely, who'd rejected the proposal.

On another occasion, Gayle said, he'd met with Governor Folsom and told him what he, the city commission, and the three ministers had agreed on. The governor had asked his director of the Department of Public Safety, Bill Lyerly, to find Reverend King and get him on the phone. Lyerly did, Mayor Gayle said, and King had "said that it is agreeable to him."

After King denied that he had made such an agreement, Gayle said, he'd cut off all communications with King and the MIA.

When the State rested, Thetford and his team believed they had dotted all the i's and crossed all the t's, especially with the mayor's testimony. They believed they had proved their case against King.

Gray made a detailed, seven-part motion to dismiss the State's evidence on the grounds that it did not prove criminal conspiracy, made no showing that the defendant conspired with anyone to commit a criminal act, failed to establish a prima facie case, and showed that the statute itself was unconstitutional. Judge Carter overruled the motion.

Now it was time for the defense to show that leaders of the black community had made all the moves toward resolving the bus problem but had received no cooperation from the city or the bus company. Shores also believed that the leaders' testimonies would prove that the protesters had just cause and a legal excuse to boycott.

The first witness for the defense, Thelma Williams Glass, a member of the Women's Political Council, testified that WPC committees had met on numerous occasions with the Montgomery City Commission and the bus company, asking for remedies to the enormous problems that plagued the buses.

Glass painted the grim picture of the bus-riding world in Montgomery. "Negroes have to stand over empty seats when no whites are riding. Negroes pay fares at the front, get off, and go to the rear door to board the bus. When fares are paid at the front, passengers should get on at the front. There is danger of a passenger being struck without the driver knowing it. There have been instances where persons have paid their fares and the bus has driven off and left them standing on the street. Buses stop at every corner in sections where whites live, but in sections occupied by Negroes they stop at every other block. Since all pay the same fare, the buses should stop at every corner in all communities. Those are the specific things the committee asked for in November of 1953."

In March 1954, the committee had outlined similar problems with the bus system.

During cross-examination, Glass denied being a member of the MIA and said that she had attended none of the mass meetings because "I work late."

Asked by the judge if any of the requests made by the WPC had been given consideration, she said that buses now stopped at every block in all of the communities.

Judge Carter asked, "How about the arrangement on the buses?"

Glass answered, "That is still going on, unfortunately."

The next witness, Sadie Brooks, was a member of the City Federation, a fifty-eight-year-old women's group that had originated with the Negro Association for the Advancement of Colored Women (NAACW) in 1898. As a member of this group, she'd visited the city commission first in 1952 to complain about problems with the bus system. She'd met with them again in 1954 to discuss the same problems. Brooks said that nothing had ever been done to remedy the situation.

Rufus Lewis was recalled to the stand. He testified that, as a member of the Citizens Coordinating Committee, he had gone with others in 1952 to complain about problems with the city's bus system, and that the same problems were discussed again in a 1955 meeting. Little had been done to alleviate the problems.

Then a chorus of witnesses told of the dramatic situations they faced every day while riding city buses.

Georgia Jordan, of 405 Dericote Street, said she'd stopped riding buses in October 1955. On a Friday afternoon between three and five o'clock, she was standing on the corner of Court and Montgomery streets. When the Oak Park bus had rolled to a stop, she'd climbed aboard.

"The bus was pretty near full of colored people, only two white people on the bus. I put my money in the cash box and then he told me to get off. He shouted I had to get on in back. I told him I was already on the bus and I couldn't see why I had to get off. A lot of colored people were in the middle aisle almost halfway to the front. Couldn't he let me stand there? Other people were down there, colored, not white passengers. He said, 'I told you to get off and go around and get in the back door.' I have a rather high temper and I figured, I have never been in any trouble whatsoever in my life. I was always taught that two wrongs don't make a right."

She exited the front door and went around the side of the bus to get in the back door. When she reached the back door and started to get on the bus, the driver shut the door in her face and pulled off. "So I decided right then and there I wasn't going to ride the buses anymore," she said. When Billingsley asked what the driver had said, Jordan answered, "Nigger, get out that door and go around to the back door."

Jordan testified that she had been mistreated and called names a number of times by white drivers.

Once, she said, she'd seen Mrs. Willie Mae Caffey board a bus without having ten cents in change. She had only a dollar bill, and she gave it to the driver and asked for a transfer. He asked why she didn't have the change. She answered that she just didn't have anything but a dollar. She said, "Please give me the transfer and change," but he didn't say another word until they arrived downtown, when he finally gave her the transfer and change for a dollar.

At another time, Jordan said, she'd seen an old woman go to the front door to get on a bus that was nearly full. The bus driver was mean and surly, and when the woman asked him if she could get on through the front door, he said she would have to go around and climb in at the rear. She told him she couldn't get up the steps, that they were too high. He said she couldn't board through the front door. He said, "You damn niggers are all alike; you don't want to do what you are told. If I had my way, I would kill off every nigger person."

Richard Jordan, of 872 East Grove Street, had lived in Montgomery for twenty-six years and had ridden city buses twice a day for more than twenty years. However, he had not ridden a bus since the day after Thanksgiving, 1955. Jordan said that he was a member of the Negro race, a member of the Montgomery Improvement Association, a registered voter and taxpayer, and a member of the Dexter Avenue Baptist Church. He said his first bad experience aboard a bus had been in 1937. Lawyer Stewart objected, and Judge Carter said that a 1937 incident was "too remote."

Jordan continued with his testimony. In 1946, he said, when his wife was expecting a baby, the couple had no other choice but to ride the buses. They didn't own a car. After seeing her doctor, they'd walked to the corner of Lee and Montgomery streets, boarded a bus, and ridden to the corner of Dexter Avenue and Perry Street. His wife had been complaining that she was feeling poorly. At one o'clock in the afternoon a number of white women who worked at the state capitol crowded onto the bus and left two seats open. Jordan and his wife had sat in those. The bus driver had looked back and said, "Nigger, give up that seat back there." Jordan's wife began to shiver and started to cry. Several of the white women tried to help, but the driver told Jordan and his wife to get up. "I wanted to do something, but I knew if I did I'd be in trouble," Jordan testified. Instead, the couple had gotten up, stood in the aisle, and ridden home.

Gladys Moore, of 927 Adams Street, told the court that she had ridden buses twice a day for fourteen years until December 5, 1955. She testified that once, she had been going home on the Highland Avenue bus when the driver turned and said, "Don't you upset me with the racket." Moore stood still. As far as she could tell, there was no disorder in the back of the bus. Nevertheless, the driver stopped the bus and looked back again. The black riders were talking in their normal, everyday tones. The driver shouted, "You niggers, come on and get your fare and get off." Some took their fare and got off, but she stayed on the bus. She said she just wanted to get home.

Billingsley asked, "Will you spell that word he used?"

Moore replied, "N-i-g-g-e-r-s."

During cross-examination, Moore was asked why she'd stopped riding buses after December 5. She replied, "I stopped because we had been treated so bad down through the years that we decided we wouldn't ride the buses no more."

As far as Gray, Langford, Shores, Hall, and Billingsley were concerned, it was the perfect reply. They were convinced that the repetitious testimony had showed without a doubt that all of the previous riders had just cause and legal excuse to boycott.

The refrain continued, recounting the confrontations between black bus riders and the white drivers.

To illustrate the extent of the abuse heaped upon black riders, the defense called witness after witness, each of whom had had his or her own experience with the city's buses, in quick order: Leola Bell of 577 Stone Street, Frances Rutledge of 741 Travis Street, Lula Mae Hopper of 401 Underwood Street, Loena Perkins of 214 North Dorothy Street, Irene Dorsey of 1011 Central Avenue, Dorothy Louise Johnson of 566 Oak

Street, Janie Pace of 617 Columbus Street, Aretta Burney of 871 Clay Street, Rosa Lee Murray of 2154 Hill Street, Geneva Johnson of 1501 Mt. Meigs Road, Odessa Williams of 1010 Bragg Street, Odelliah Garnier of 627 Columbia Avenue, Bessie Sanderson Logan of 719 Orum Street, R. A. Parks of 634 Cleveland Court, Inez Ricks of 462 Greyhound Street, Mary Harris of 917 South Union Street, Willie Elmore of 919 South Union Street, William James of 448 Godfrey Street, Willie Chisholm of 810 Patterson Street, Joseph Alford of 656 Elmwood Street, R. T. Smiley of 896 North Union Circle, Mary Banks of 510 South Holt Street, and Louise Osborne of 1312 Peach Street—all of whom lived in Montgomery. They told how they had been mistreated by drivers working for Montgomery City Lines.

Then Estella Brooks, who gave her address as 633 Cleveland Avenue, took the stand. She was twenty-six years old. Six years earlier, she said, she'd been living with her in-laws in west Montgomery.

Billingsley asked, "I ask you during your lifetime in the City of Montgomery whether or not you have had occasions to ride these buses in the city, operated by Montgomery City Lines?"

Nervous, but gazing directly into the lawyer's face, Brooks answered, "Yes, I have."

Billingsley asked, "Do you ride these buses frequently, or just sometimes, or what manner?"

Brooks's voice quivered slightly as she stated, "I haven't rode the buses since they killed my husband, since 1950."

Billingsley asked, "What month?"

"Twelfth of August."

Billingsley asked, "For what reason did you stop riding the buses?"

"Because the bus driver was the cause of my husband's death," Brooks said, her voice low and unsteady.

The solicitor objected.

Judge Carter leaned toward the witness. Nodding, he said in a gentle, almost fatherly voice, "Tell the court what happened."

Looking up at the judge, Brooks also nodded. "He just got on before the bus driver told him, he asked for his dime back, and he (the driver) wouldn't give his dime back."

Billingsley asked, "What happened then?"

Brooks said, "The police killed him."

Billingsley asked, "Did the bus driver call the police?"

Brooks said, "The bus driver called the police and the police came up and shot him."

Billingsley asked, "And shot him?"

Brooks: "Yes, sir."

Billingsley continued, "I ask you whether or not you have had any other experiences on the buses?"

Brooks said, "No, I haven't. I keep off of them."

During cross-examination, the solicitor asked, "Were you there when your husband was shot?"

Brooks answered, "No."

Thetford then moved to exclude her testimony.

Judge Carter agreed to do so, if she had not been present when the incident occurred.

Billingsley asked, "Was your husband shot?"

Brooks answered, "Yes, sir."

Judge Carter ruled, "The testimony would have to be confined to what she knows herself."

Billingsley urged, "But he was killed?"

Brooks answered, "August 12, 1950."

The solicitor objected strenuously.

The judge ruled in favor of his objection.

The young widow of Thomas Edward Brooks stepped down from the witness stand. As it turned out, her testimony about the death of her husband almost six years earlier would not even be considered in the case. Nevertheless, it had been stated in open court. She was pleased that she had at least had her few moments to tell what had happened.

On the afternoon of Thursday, March 22, Reverend Graetz took the stand. Through his testimony, the defense team wanted to put a question in the judge's mind about King's position in the black community and to reiterate that King did not force anyone to stay off the buses. Graetz said he had attended several meetings of the MIA, that he'd heard Reverend King speak on several occasions, and that he had heard him tell those gathered, "We are your representatives, and we will have to do what you want us to do. It is up to you whether you want to ride the buses or not."

Reverend King never threatened anyone, Graetz stated. "As a matter of fact, right from the very beginning, Dr. King and others constantly urged, 'If someone wants to ride the buses, let them ride; we are not suggesting to threaten them, coerce them, or intimidate them, or anything else.'"

Under cross-examination by Stewart, Graetz said that he'd been present at the mass meeting in which a resolution outlining grievances against the bus company was read and approved overwhelmingly by the people. He testified that he and King had spoken privately about a compromise, but King had said he always wanted to ask the people first. It was their choice.

Finally, Dr. King was called to the stand. Dressed neatly in a dark suit and tie, the young minister strode with dignity to the front of the courtroom, raised his right hand, and was sworn in by the judge.

The MIA, he said, had been organized "to improve the general status of Montgomery, to improve race relations, and to uplift the general tenor of the community."

He said he had never urged his audiences, either in his church or at any meetings, to refrain from riding buses. "My exposition has always been, 'Let your conscience be your guide; if you want to ride, that is all right.'"

Asked if he had urged violence, he stated emphatically, "My motivation has been the exact converse of that. I urged nonvi-olence at all points."

When proposals to solve the bus situation had been presented, he said, he had always taken them to the members of the MIA and "they were always rejected by the people."

Shores laid out the situation between King and the mayor. Gayle had said that a proposal had been accepted, then later rejected, by King. Shores asked, "Did you receive any proposal from the mayor with respect to the settlement of this controversy over the telephone? And later rejected?"

King answered, "No, I did not. I have never received a proposal that I accepted. I have always contended I could only take it up with the people, and that is what I said to Mayor Gayle when he offered the proposal over the phone. I would take it up with the people, and that is as far as I would go. He was to call me back on Friday to discuss it, but he never called back."

During cross-examination, Thetford took King through the formation of the MIA and its organizational meeting, and he repeatedly asked if King had not called for a bus boycott on December 5. King answered that he had not. He said that the boycott had been "a spontaneous happening."

After King's testimony, the State rebutted with the testimonies of seven bus drivers, including that of O. O. Martin, who had been president of the Bus Drivers Union. All tried to refute the testimonies of the numerous black riders who claimed to have experienced racist incidents while riding city buses.

At 3:00 P.M. the State rested.

Hall made a motion for judgment on the grounds that the State's evidence "is legally insufficient to substantiate a con-

viction," that the defendant "is shown by conclusive and undisputed evidence that he is not guilty," and that a conviction
"would be illegal and void" because "it would deprive him of
due process of law and equal protection" guaranteed him by the
Constitution. Judge Carter overruled the motion.

Judge Carter asked, "What says the defendant?"

Shores stated, "We have no further testimony."

Without hesitating, Judge Carter announced, "The Court
is of the opinion the defendant is guilty of illegal boycott, and
I find him guilty and fix his fine at five hundred dollars."

Thetford stated, "The State has agreed with the defendants,
through their several lawyers, that the other cases, which we
might refer to as the boycott cases, will be continued pending
appeal of this case."

Judge Carter said he thought that was fair. "They have a
perfect right to take this appeal to the Supreme Court to find
out if my ruling is right or wrong, and, on account of the many
witnesses, the amount of time, and all, I believe that is perhaps
the better procedure."

By now, everyone concerned with the case knew that it
would take more than a year in the courtroom and millions of
dollars to the state alone if all ninety-five cases were tried.

As King walked onto the steps of the county courthouse,
flanked by his attorneys, he found himself facing a crowd. People from all over Montgomery and visitors who had traveled to
hear and see the trial had gathered. They covered the steps
down to Washington Street. They applauded enthusiastically.
As King held his hands high, a smile creasing his lips, bulbs
from a dozen cameras flashed and the people shouted, "King!
King! Behold the King!"

Before that afternoon, the most spontaneous outpouring of
black people that E. D. Nixon had ever seen was the one in front
of City Hall after the judge found Rosa Parks guilty. Now, four
months later, more people than ever had come to Washington

Street, and they stood in the twilight and shouted for their leader. As they displayed their defiance over the court's ruling, tears came to Nixon's eyes. Nixon watched the young man standing there in front of the people. A ray of sunlight struck King's forehead and made it shine.

During the four-day trial, seventy-seven witnesses had testified. Court reporter Hallowell Lewis prepared a five-hundred-page transcript for the King attorneys to use on appeal. The court records included fifty-one prosecution exhibits.

Judge Carter said that the King trial had drawn more press, radio, and television coverage than any other trial during his tenure as criminal judge in Alabama's Fifteenth Judicial Circuit.

The immediate aftermath of the trial brought ripples of emotions from across the nation. In Washington, D.C., journalists tried to draw from President Dwight Eisenhower an opinion of the Alabama situation from a national viewpoint. Eisenhower was asked by Robert G. Spivak, of the *New York Post*, "Mr. President, with regards to the situation in Alabama, how do you feel about Negroes being brought to trial for refusing to ride the Montgomery buses?"

Eisenhower answered, "You are asking me, I think, to be more of a lawyer than I certainly am. But, as I understand it, there is a state law about boycotts, and it is under that kind of thing that these people are being brought to trial.

"I believe that it is incumbent on all the South to show some progress. That is what the Supreme Court asked for. And they turned it over to local district courts.

"I believe that we should not stagnate, but again I plead for understanding, for really sympathetic consideration of the problem that is far larger, both in its emotional and even in its physical aspects, than most of us realize."

In the same press conference, Anthony Lewis, of the *New York Times*, asked, "Mr. President, do you have any plans to mobilize religious and other leaders of the South to your point of view of moderation and progress on segregation?"

Eisenhower stated, "Well, that is one thing that Billy Graham teaches not only abroad, he teaches it among ourselves and, frankly, I believe that the pulpits do have a very great responsibility here.

"This is a very tough one, and people have to search their own hearts if we are going to get a decent answer and keep going ahead. Now, let's don't try to think of this as a tremendous fight that is going to separate Americans and get ourselves into a nasty mess. Let's try to think of it of how can we progress and keep it going and not stop it. Now that, I believe, the pulpits can help on."

Edward P. Morgan, of the American Broadcasting Company, asked, "Mr. President, a number of prominent Southern conservative Democrats supported you actively in 1952, and many of these since have indicated their defiance of the Supreme Court's decision on segregation. In view of what you said just a moment ago, would you accept their support in '56?"

Eisenhower answered, "I don't believe they expressed defiance. I believe they expressed their belief that it was in error, and they have talked about using legal means to circumvent or to get it, whatever the expression they have used. I do not believe that anyone, the ones that I know, have used the words 'defy the Supreme Court,' because when we carry the point, when we carry this to the ultimate, remember that the Constitution, as interpreted by the Supreme Court, is our basic law. The one thing is, though, the basic law appears to change, as I pointed out last week. It was one thing in 1896, and it is a very greatly different thing now.

"There are emotions, very deep emotions, connected with this problem. Consequently, these people, they have, of course, their free choice as to what they want to do. As far as I am concerned, I am for moderation, but I am for progress; that is exactly what I am for in this thing."

In the days following the trial, the father of the White Citizens Council, Senator Sam Engelhardt, introduced in the Alabama Legislature a new bill that strengthened segregation on buses and railroads. The bill, which was passed into law, empowered railroad and bus companies to make and enforce what Engelhardt called "reasonable rules and regulations for seating of passengers to maintain peace and good order or to preserve property."

Engelhardt told the press that existing laws requiring segregation in public transportation didn't spell out clearly enough the carriers' right to make their own regulations.

Reacting to the segregationist atmosphere, Alabama legislator Charles McKay drafted new legislation to make it unlawful for white and black players or spectators to play or sit together at "any game of cards, dice, dominoes, checkers, baseball, softball, basketball, football, track, or in swimming pools, lakes or ponds, or on any beaches." According to the bill, which was quickly passed by both houses, it was now illegal to have mixed public gatherings unless the participants were segregated. Theaters and restaurants could cater to both races, but the races would have to be seated in different sections and would have to use separate entrances. For those who were found guilty of breaking the law, fines from one hundred dollars to five hundred dollars and jail sentences from fifteen to one hundred eighty days could be imposed.

The Alabama House of Representatives voted unanimously on a resolution asking the U.S. Supreme Court to modify its recent school integration decision "so as to permit the white and colored people of the South to live together in peace and harmony."

In New York, Congressman Adam Clayton Powell, speaking at the Community Church, warned that he was planning a "prayer meeting for national deliverance." In a telegram to E. K. Fitzpatrick, the president of National City Lines, Inc., of Chicago, Powell asked that the company reexamine the Montgomery bus situation or face the possibility of people boycotting buses in other cities as well. National City Lines operated forty lines, thirty-three of which were located in the North.

In Boston, Massachusetts, lawmakers voted unanimously to send an "expression of sympathy" to the "colored citizens of Alabama who are seeking by nonviolent means to bring equality to all Americans."

Dr. King's photo was featured on the cover of *Jet* magazine, which called him "Alabama's Modern Moses."

A *New York Times* "Man in the News" profile stated that King's oratory style "overwhelms the listener with the depth of his convictions" that "all men are basically good."

Within the next few weeks, King traveled across the North, speaking to tens of thousands of people, raising thousands of dollars to assist the boycott, and meeting alone with Harry Belafonte at Adam Clayton Powell's Community Church in Harlem. When King told Belafonte, "I need your help," the famous entertainer was highly impressed. He told King he would do what he could to help the cause. Later Belafonte would appear at numerous functions and concerts to raise money for what became the civil rights movement.

In San Francisco, at the forty-seventh NAACP national convention, delegates from all states squeezed close to King after his dynamic talk, eagerly shook his hand, and wished him well.

From Canada, where he had gone to address a convention of black morticians, E. D. Nixon called King to inform him that A. Philip Randolph had gotten an invitation for King to testify before the platform committee of the Democratic National Convention in Chicago. Because he was now more conscious of protocol among black leaders than ever before, King told Nixon that he would make the appearance only if Roy Wilkins, then the president of the NAACP, gave his approval. Nixon, who knew all of the leaders on a first-name basis, telephoned Wilkins and briefly outlined the situation, telling Wilkins that he thought it would be a good thing for the Democratic party and for King. Wilkins said, "I agree with you, Brother Nixon. He ought to be there, although it will take some of the spotlight off me." Nixon then went back to King, opening the door for him to tell the Democrats that civil rights was "one of the supreme moral issues" of modern times.

In Gary, Indiana, at the First Baptist Church, the Reverend J. W. Bonner told a crowd of fifteen hundred that the "new Negro" did not get angry, mad, or distraught when he was treated badly. "In Montgomery, we will continue to stand together despite what may come, and if one of us is persecuted—all of us will suffer together.

"The new Negro in the South is restless and tired of being pushed around and driven. He is tired of waiting for everybody to decide when he is ready for the full citizenship he deserves. He thinks he can help them make up their minds if he is given a chance to demonstrate his talents and abilities and to adjust himself to a new society."

After his talk, Bonner raised thirty-five hundred dollars for the MIA.

In Chattanooga, Tennessee, the Reverend Abernathy told a congregation at West Side Baptist Church that the blacks of Montgomery had been "treated like dogs" by the city's bus drivers. "We used to be scared of white people," he said, "but we're not scared anymore. We have fought for this democracy, and our buddies have died for it.

"We recognize that behind the iron curtain of Russia we could not protest, but in America it is our right to protest."

At a rally of more than twenty-five hundred people at the Concord Baptist Church in Brooklyn, which was sponsored by the Business and Professional Women's Club, King said, "We in Montgomery have discovered a method that can be used by the Negroes in their fight for political and economical equality. We fight injustice with passive resistance. And it works!"

The crowd rose to their feet, cheering.

"A little brown man in India—Mahatma Gandhi—used it to topple the British military machine. Gandhi was able to break loose from the political and economical domination by the British and brought the British Empire to its knees. Let's now use this method in the United States."

As the boycott continued successfully, Mobile, Alabama, columnist Ted Pearson was one of a number of Southern journalists who kept heaping the racist coals onto the fire of public opinion.

His column in early March began, "MONTGOMERY—A colored bellboy in a hotel shifted his eyes from side to side as he spoke.

"'I don't know much about boycotts, boss,' he said. 'But I'll tell you this. They's a bunch of our folks who'd go right back to riding them buses tomorrow, but they's scared to.

"'The preachers say we gotta keep on 'cause this thing's done got so big, we just can't quit!'

"This simple appraisal of the race situation in Montgomery today is not an isolated one. You hear the same sort of expression all over. In a state that has suddenly emerged as the focal point of tension between the white and colored races, the bus boycott in the city that gave birth to the Confederacy has been persistently built up by its instigators as something more than a mere protest against segregation on the common carrier."

The Alabama Legislature "jumped headlong Thursday into the burning issue of racial relations," Pearson wrote in the *Mobile Register* in April. "A move was launched to conduct a 'full inquiry' to determine if there is any connection between Communist activities and the National Association for the Advancement of Colored People."

A bill to allow Congress to appropriate federal funds to move blacks out of the South "to areas where they are wanted and needed and can be assimilated" was passed in one House and awaited a vote in the other.

Congressman T. K. Selman, of Walker County, Alabama, sponsored a resolution calling for the establishment of a five-member committee "to make full inquiry into the activities of Communists and Communist-front organizations in this state with a view to determining whether the NAACP or any affiliated organization in this state is substantially directed, dominated, or controlled by Communists." The House passed the measure 75–0.

In Montgomery, Circuit Judge Carter made public a Western Union telegram he'd received from an industrialist who had planned to build a 150,000-square-foot plant in Alabama. Sol Diamond, the vice president and treasurer of Diamond Brothers, told the judge that his company canceled its building plans after King was convicted.

In Federal Court

ON THE FIRST DAY of February, when Fred Gray filed *Browder v. Gayle*, Frank M. Johnson, Jr., the young district judge who had been appointed to the position in mid-November, wrote to Joseph Hutcheson, the chief judge of the Fifth Circuit, asking that Hutcheson appoint a three-judge panel to hear the case. Upon reading Johnson's request, Hutcheson shot back a quick reply: "It doesn't take a three-judge panel to hear a matter of local law." The thirty-seven-year-old Johnson, who had cut his teeth as an assistant U.S. attorney for the northern district of Alabama, where, among other cases, he had prosecuted a defendant who was charged with slavery, sat down and fired off another letter to Hutcheson, stating that Alabama's laws on segregation were the centerpiece guiding the bus situation in Montgomery. He felt it sufficiently important that the case be given constitutional status. But Hutcheson would not be moved. He "begged to differ" with Johnson, whom he told to try the case by himself. This time Johnson wrote a three-page, single-spaced, detailed letter, stating emphatically that the U.S. Constitution was in question. Hutcheson finally relented and called for circuit judge Richard Rives and district judge Seybourne Lynne to hear the case with Johnson.

Sixty-one-year-old Richard T. Rives was a native of Montgomery. A member of the first graduating class of Sidney Lanier High in 1911, he'd graduated head of his class and won a scholarship to Tulane University. After a year at Tulane, he came back to his home town and read law. Two years later, at age nineteen, Rives passed the state bar exam and joined the firm of Hill, Hill, Whiting, and Rives.

A member of the Alabama National Guard, Sergeant Rives was sent to lead a patrol on the Mexican border after revolutionary general Pancho Villa attacked Columbia, New Mexico. During World War I Rives served a short stint in France, then returned to the law firm. In 1951 he was recommended to the federal bench by U.S. Senators Lister Hill and John Sparkman, and he was appointed to the bench by President Harry Truman. Rives was steeped in the traditional Deep South culture. His great-great-grandfather on his mother's side was the first Baptist minister to preach in Montgomery. After the Civil War his family lost its Montgomery County plantation. Rives was brought up listening to stories of the just cause of the Confederacy, but he prided himself on his keen sense of both justice and the supremacy of the rule of law.

Seybourne H. Lynne was forty-three years old. Born in Decatur, Alabama, on the Tennessee River, he'd received his undergraduate degree from Auburn University in 1927 and his law degree from the University of Alabama in 1930. His family dated back three hundred years to pre–Revolutionary War days in Alabama. His maternal grandfather, C. C. Harris, had served as a state representative in the first Congress to admit Southerners after the Civil War. Harris had been a colonel in the Confederate army. Lynne himself entered the U.S. Army in 1942 as a captain. Three years later he was discharged as a lieutenant colonel. Lynne practiced law in Decatur from 1930 to

1934, when he became Morgan County's court judge, and in 1941 he was named circuit judge. Following World War II, he was appointed to the federal bench in 1946 by President Truman. Like Rives, Lynne had heard the stories, handed down from generation to generation, about the Cause of the Confederacy.

Frank M. Johnson, Jr., was the youngest member of the panel. Born in Winston County, which had once been the Free State of Winston—the county had attempted to secede from Alabama when the state seceded from the Union in 1861—Johnson was extraordinarily proud of his heritage. Young Johnson's great-grandfather, James Wallace Johnson, had been the first Republican sheriff in Alabama following the Civil War. He was such an advocate for law and order that he was known as "Straight-edge Johnson." Young Frank attended the University of Alabama, where he was close friends with fellow law student George C. Wallace, who in 1956 was circuit judge of three counties southeast of Montgomery. Johnson earned his law degree from the university in 1942. Drafted into the infantry in 1943, he was shipped to Europe, where he was twice wounded and awarded the Bronze Star for bravery in action. After he'd recuperated from his second wound, he was stationed in England as an army lawyer. By the time he was discharged in June 1946, Johnson had risen from the rank of buck private to that of captain. Back home in Alabama, he worked as an assistant district attorney for north Alabama until President Eisenhower appointed him to the federal bench in November 1955.

In early February, shortly after Fred Gray was indicted by the Montgomery County grand jury for representing a client without her knowledge, he saw Judge Johnson in his office. After pointedly asking Gray how things were going, Johnson told him, "You know, whatever offense there was, if any, it was committed after the lawsuit was filed on the second floor of this courthouse, of which the United States government has exclusive jurisdiction."

Gray appreciated Judge Johnson's comment, and he thought he might be able to use the interesting statement as an argument in a motion to dismiss the charge. As it turned out, it was not necessary. Before the hearing on the matter got under way in circuit court, solicitor Thetford moved to dismiss the indictment on the grounds that the court did not have the jurisdiction to hear the case, saying that he would refer the matter to the U.S. Attorney. Gray never heard another word from the court about it.

Before the *Browder v. Gayle* case could be heard in federal court, however, city attorneys did some quick legal maneuvering of their own.

After Congressman Powell threatened to take the boycott to a national level, officials with National City Lines put their heads together and decided to ask Mayor Gayle and the city commission to allow them to relax the seating rules on the buses. In order to do so, the city ordinances would have to be changed.

Gayle, Sellers, and Parks balked. Under no circumstances would they change the segregation laws. As far as they were concerned, the federal court had no standing, and federal judges did not have the authority to tell them how to run their city. With this in mind, city attorneys went into state court to ask Judge Walter B. Jones to declare constitutional the city's laws requiring segregation on public transportation.

Jones was the older of the county's two circuit judges. Although he was the subject of vicious courthouse gossip about his weekend escapades with young male defendants at his country place in a neighboring county, Jones was nevertheless known for his ultraconservative outlook on the law, and he was firmly embedded in the white establishment of the city, county, and state. His father, Thomas Goode Jones, had carried the white flag of truce to the courthouse at Appomattox, where he sat with Robert E. Lee while the famous general surrendered the South to General Ulysses Grant. Judge Walter B. Jones enjoyed telling the story about his father's duty to the Confederacy to anyone who would listen.

It did not surprise MIA attorney Fred Gray when Judge Jones, after hearing the evidence, ruled from the bench that segregation was the law of the land in Montgomery, asking in his ruling: "Where in the United States Constitution is there one word, one sentence, one paragraph that says . . . the sovereign states cannot make reasonable rules pertaining to the separation of the races in public transportation?"

A year later, Judge Jones would write a column in the *Advertiser* stating, "I speak for the White Race, my race, because today it is being unjustly assailed all over the world. It is being subjected to assaults here by radical newspapers and magazines, Communists and the Federal Judiciary. Columnists and photographers have been sent to the South to take back to the people of the North untrue and slanted takes about the South." He concluded, "Their real and final goal is intermarriage and mongrelization of the American people. We shall never submit to the demands of integrationists. The white race shall forever remain white."

In the meantime, lawyers for both sides filed pretrial motions and briefs with the federal court. Researching and writing for the plaintiffs, Clifford Durr thoroughly dissected *Brown v. Board of Education*, showing that the Supreme Court decision regarding public education applied to public transportation as well. The city's attorneys—and the state attorney general defending the state's position that the Alabama Public Service

Commission had authority over public transportation—argued that *Brown* had no bearing on *Browder.*

Regardless of the legal arguments, the judges were bound by law to hear the evidence as it would be presented by the witnesses before they could draw a conclusion.

On May 11, 1956, on a bright morning in Montgomery, E. D. Nixon pulled up in front of the federal courthouse and parked on Church Street. He sat behind the steering wheel for a long minute, watching as his brethren, dressed in dark suits and ties, and sisters, in their Sunday-go-to-meeting best dresses, arrived and filed through the front doors. Nixon said later that he was "mighty proud, watching my peoples going to court like they was going to church. You could read a happiness on their faces, like they knew already that they were about to see the start of something very special. It was like that a lot of days, like it was a job to get up in the morning, even though we all knew there were some mean white folks out there waiting for us sometime. Still, we knowed that something was about to happen, we just didn't quite know what it was. But there was a feeling of comfort going into the federal courthouse, which was very different from going through the front doors of the county courthouse down on Washington Street just a block or so. We felt like we was protected here."

In the courtroom on the third floor, NAACP lawyers Fred Gray and Charles Langford, of Montgomery, and Charles Carter, of New York, sat in front of the mahogany railing. At a table to their right sat Montgomery city attorney Walter Knabe, a short, slender, athletic-looking man with close-cut sandy hair and a tennis-tanned complexion. Next to him was Alabama Attorney General John Patterson, a short, dark-haired young man whose father, Albert, had won the Democratic nomination for attorney general on the promise that he would clean up corruption in the east Alabama town of Phenix City. Known as the Sin City of the South, Phenix had achieved notoriety as a haven for gambling and prostitution on the Alabama-Georgia border. Shortly after his political victory, Albert Patterson had been killed by an assassin's bullet, and his son John, a bright young attorney, had taken his place on the ticket, which was tantamount in those days to being elected. Republicans seldom even ran for office in Alabama before the 1960s.

Entering before the blue-draped, silver star–studded backdrop, the three judges took their places at exactly 9:00 A.M. Silver-haired Judge Rives sat in the middle. He was flanked by the dour, salt-and-pepper-haired Lynne and the equally dour, rawboned, and sharp-eyed Johnson. After reading the complaint, Judge Rives eyed Gray. "Call your first witness."

In federal court, Gray and his fellow attorneys started once again the series of tales of woe about terrible happenings on the city buses. However, unlike in Montgomery County circuit court, here they were confined to presenting the plaintiffs and how they had been wronged. Gray knew that he was asking the court to reach far beyond its usual scope. In asking the lower court to overturn *Plessy v. Ferguson*, the nineteenth-century Supreme Court case that established the legal concept of separate but equal and provided a hard foundation for Jim Crow segregation both in public education and public transportation, the attorneys were seeking something that had never before been done. No lower court had ever found against the highest court in the land. The very essence of the case showed hardcore audacity, at the very least.

Gray called the named plaintiff, Aurelia Browder, a thirty-four-year-old nurse's aide, mother of four children, and part-time student at Alabama State College. The young widow, who lived at 1012 Highland Avenue, was a longtime resident of Montgomery. She testified that she had been riding city buses for years but had stopped on December 5 because she wanted to cooperate with her fellow black riders in an attempt to persuade city politicians and bus company officers to change segregated seating requirements and to offer a more courteous service.

She pointed out that on April 29, 1955, she was riding a downtown bus when the driver ordered her and two other black women to get up from their seats and stand in the aisle so that a white man and a white woman could sit.

After Gray asked a number of pointed questions, Browder answered that she would ride city buses again, if she could sit in any open seat on the bus.

Judge Rives gave Knabe the sign to cross-examine the witness.

Knabe glanced through his notes while rolling a pencil between his fingers.

In answer to his questions, Browder once again said she'd stopped riding buses because she was seeking better treatment. When Knabe asked if King had told blacks not to ride the buses, Browder stated that it was the riders who decided not to ride the buses, not King.

Knabe tried to put words into the witness's mouth, but Browder refused to be bullied by his tactics. He said, "You did not stop on account of segregation, but you stopped riding before the segregation issue was ever raised. That is correct, isn't it?" And Browder answered, "It is the segregation laws of Alabama that causes all of it."

The next plaintiff to take the stand was seventy-seven-year-old Susie McDonald, who had lived all of her life in Montgomery and who had ridden buses regularly before December 5. She, too, said she'd stopped riding because black people had asked repeatedly for changes to the system and were repeatedly denied those changes. The elderly woman said that she had often been made to rise from her seat and give it to a white person who had boarded the bus on which she was riding, no matter what his or her age, simply because that person was a different color.

When Knabe asked if she'd actually stopped riding the buses because of agitation among the blacks, McDonald answered, "I reached my own judgment. I stopped because I thought it was right and because we were mistreated."

McDonald stated, "We didn't want no social equality. We wanted what we asked for. We wanted recognition." Knabe nodded, stiffened, and said, "I see. In other words, you did not want equality of any type, but you merely wanted recognition?" When she agreed, Knabe nodded again. He was satisfied with her answer.

Gray asked if she would ride the buses if segregation were abolished. When Knabe objected, Judge Rives, appearing irritated, said, "She has said she will. Overruled."

The third plaintiff, nineteen-year-old Mary Louise Smith, another lifelong resident of the city, testified that she, too, had quit riding city buses on December 5. She told about her arrest on the Highland Avenue bus on October 21, 1955, when she'd refused to give up her seat to a white woman. She'd been taken to jail, where she was kept for about two hours and charged five dollars plus court costs. Smith answered that she would ride buses if they were not segregated.

Knabe asked a series of short questions designed to jar her story about fighting against segregation. He asked if she had ever thought about segregation when she'd stopped riding, then if she had ever mentioned segregation to city officials. Smith continued to stay on track, saying that segregation was never far from her mind.

Finally, the city's attorney asked if Reverend King represented her, and she replied that "we appointed him our leader" but "we represent ourselves."

Next came sixteen-year-old Claudette Colvin, who explained the details of her March 2, 1955, arrest, when she'd been dragged from the bus.

During cross-examination Knabe asked, "You and other Negroes have changed your ideas since December 5, have you not?"

Colvin replied, "No, sir. We haven't changed our ideas. It has been in me ever since I was born."

As he had with the previous witnesses, Knabe attempted to guide her testimony to tell about the selection of King as leader, but Colvin, like the others, said that it was King who took the requests of all of the black people to city commission meetings. He did not necessarily represent them all.

When Knabe asked why, exactly, she'd quit riding buses after December 5, Colvin said, "Because we were treated wrong, dirty, and nasty."

When the audience nodded and murmured agreement, Judge Rives warned them to keep quiet or face extraction from the courtroom.

Attorney Langford called Mayor Gayle, one of the defendants, as a hostile witness.

Langford asked what instructions Gayle had given city police with respect to enforcing segregation. Gayle answered that he and other city commissioners told officers to enforce all laws and ordinances.

When Langford pressed specifically about segregation, Gayle insisted that it "is one of the laws. I believe in segregation, and I believe in enforcing the city ordinance concerning it."

Wanting to clarify the record, he said, Langford asked again if it was the mayor's instructions to arrest persons who violate segregation laws. Gayle answered, "That is right. That is the law, and that is the way we enforce the laws."

During cross-examination, Knabe once again carried Gayle through the times he'd met with King and others about the bus problem. Then he asked if there had been violence in Montgomery after the boycott started. Gayle stated that "there is a danger of bloodshed or something like that unless we can strictly enforce the segregation laws."

During redirect, Langford asked, "Mayor, how did you know there was going to be bloodshed if segregation laws were not enforced? Have you taken a survey?"

Gayle responded, "It is my responsibility to look after the welfare and comfort of the people—and if I anticipate anything, I try to avoid it before it gets here. We don't wait until it happens."

When Langford suggested that no violence had occurred during the six months since the boycott had started, Gayle stated, "Well, they had shooting in the buses, knocked the windows out, and beating up the colored women and quite a number of things like that."

Gayle stated that, from his experience, he knew that there would be violence if integration on the buses were permitted, adding, "It would be dangerous."

Langford rose to his feet. "Mayor, do you know how many incidents of shooting, beating, and knifing have been introduced?"

Gayle answered, "No."

Langford said, "Well, if I told you that only two Negroes said they had been molested, would you accept that? Only two out of the twenty thousand or more Negroes in Montgomery?"

Gayle said, "I know some have called me and said they wanted to get back on the buses but they were afraid of a 'goon squad' who would hurt them."

Langford asked, "But you don't know for sure how many incidents there have been?"

Gayle replied, "Not for sure."

Other similar witnesses appeared. City Commissioner Clyde Sellers predicted that "if segregation barriers are lifted, violence will be the order of the day."

Leaning slightly forward, Judge Rives looked directly into Sellers's face and asked, "Can you command one man to surrender his constitutional rights—if they are his constitutional rights—to prevent another man from committing a crime?"

The question, of course, was rhetorical, but it foreshadowed what might be ahead for the segregation laws regarding public transportation.

By late afternoon, both sides rested.

The three judges retired to the chambers of the youngest, Judge Johnson. As Johnson was lifting his robe over his head, Judge Rives, following tradition, asked for a vote. "Well, Frank, you're the junior judge here. You vote first. What do you think?"

Johnson, who had not uttered a word throughout the entire hearing while he listened to the testimony and the verbal wonderings of the two more experienced jurists, regarded the question thoughtfully. He knew the reason behind the tradition of the senior judges first seeking the judgment of the youngest judge: by announcing his decision first, he would not be influenced by the decisions of the senior judges.

After thinking it over for several minutes, Johnson said, "As far as I'm concerned, state-imposed segregation on public facilities violates the Constitution. I'm going to rule with the plaintiffs here."

Judge Lynne shook his head, but he didn't speak. Johnson figured that Lynne thought he was reacting too fast.

Judge Rives looked Johnson straight in the eye and said, "I feel the same way."

Judge Lynne shook his head again. "I don't reach it that way," he said. "As far as I'm concerned, the court has already spoken on this issue in *Plessy*. It's the law, and we're bound by it until it's changed."

Johnson couldn't reconcile in his mind how, on one hand, the court could put the stamp of approval on segregation, as it had in *Plessy*, while, on the other hand, it mandated desegregation of the races in public schools, as it had in the *Brown* case.

In Johnson's mind, it was true that *Brown v. Board of Education* had confined the scope of its ruling to desegregation in schools alone, not to desegregation in other areas of public life. In addition, the Supreme Court's ruling was made with specific respect to children; it stated emphatically that segregation had a psychological impact on black children. But while it confined itself to the school issue, as far as Judges Johnson and Rives were concerned, the ruling set a trend, which the Supreme Court expected the courts of the land to follow. While it did not address transportation directly, the two judges concluded that the Supreme Court, in *Brown*, had issued a doctrine showing that *Plessy* was no longer valid.

Judge Lynne, however, believed that the Supreme Court had not intended the ruling in *Brown* to be applied to other areas. As far as he was concerned, the *Brown* decision was confined simply to public schools. Lynne figured he stood on solid legal ground with a Supreme Court decision to back up his opinion.

For Johnson, "it wasn't a difficult case to decide. There were no conflicting constitutional questions at issue. The long and short of it was that there was a state law that said Negroes— simply because they were Negroes—had to ride in the back of a bus, and [the law] had been extended to say they had to get up when white folks wanted their seat. Now, Judge Walter Jones had asked the question: 'Where in the Constitution is there one word, one sentence, one paragraph' that says you couldn't segregate folks in public transportation? My question was: 'Where in the Constitution is there anything that says you can segregate them?' It just isn't there. To the contrary, it specifically says you can't abridge the freedom of the individual. The boycott case was a simple case of legal and human rights being denied."

If Johnson and Rives ruled in favor of the plaintiffs, they would, in effect, overturn the *Plessy* case of 1896. That would make it a highly unusual decision, and one that would surely be taken all the way to the U.S. Supreme Court for a final decree. In essence, it would make new law.

Years later, Johnson found it necessary to "point out for the record that my vote in favor of the plaintiffs in the case was not based on any personal feeling that segregation was wrong: it was based on the law, that the state imposing segregation violated my interpretation of the Constitution of the United States. It wasn't for a judge to decide on the morality question, but rather the law."

On June 19, 1956, the U.S. Court for the Middle District of Alabama handed down its decision in favor of the plaintiffs in the *Browder* case, with Johnson and Rives writing the majority opinion and Lynne dissenting. The order read, "We hold that the statutes and ordinances requiring segregation of the white and colored races on the motor buses of a common carrier of passengers in the city of Montgomery and its police jurisdiction . . . violates the due process and equal protection of the law . . . under the Fourteenth Amendment of the Constitution of the United States.

"The 'separate but equal' doctrine set forth by the Supreme Court in 1896 in the case of *Plessy v. Ferguson* can no longer be applied.

"There is no rational basis upon which the 'separate but equal' doctrine can validly be applied to public transportation in the city of Montgomery. In their private affairs, in the conduct of their private business, it is clear that the people themselves have the liberty to select their own associates and the persons with whom they will do business, unimpaired by the Fourteenth Amendment. Indeed, we think that such liberty is guaranteed by the due process clause of that amendment. There is, however, a difference, a constitutional difference, between voluntary adherence to custom and the perpetuation and enforcement of that custom by law. . . . We cannot, in good conscience, perform our duty as judges by blindly following the precedent of *Plessy v. Ferguson* of 'separate but equal.'"

In his dissent Judge Lynne wrote, "Only a profound philosophical disagreement with the majority that the 'separate but equal' doctrine can no longer be safely followed as a constitutional statement of the law would prompt this, my first dissent."

The order would not take effect for two weeks. Mayor Gayle said simply that it would be appealed to the Supreme Court.

Throughout the South, white politicians, editorialists, and people on the street reacted. They were angry. They railed against a federal court telling them how to run their lives. Many stated they would not allow a tiny minority of jurists to ruin the Southern way of life. But in New York, Congressman Adam Clayton Powell praised the judges for their courage.

And in Montgomery, King, Nixon, Gray, Parks, Robinson, and the boycotters felt they had won a great victory. As they had so many times that year, they held a meeting at the Holt Street Baptist Church, where King praised the court and the people who had led the protest.

A Long, Hot Summer

WHILE KING, ABERNATHY, Nixon, and the other black leaders were happy with the federal court's decision, they knew that their people had a long way to go before they could exercise their freedom without fear.

While in special session that spring, the Alabama Legislature, in one of its many moves to halt the civil rights movement, passed a resolution creating a five-member committee "to make a full inquiry into the activities of Communists and Communist-front organizations in this state with a view to determine whether the NAACP or any affiliated organization in this state is substantially directed, dominated, or controlled by Communists."

Following the legislature's lead, on June 1, 1956, Attorney General Patterson went into Montgomery Circuit Court and asked Judge Jones for a court order prohibiting the NAACP from operating in the state. Patterson said that such an injunction would protect the property and civil rights of Alabama citizens. Without an attorney present to represent the black group, Judge Walter B. Jones issued the order for the NAACP to stop raising funds, collecting dues, or soliciting new members. The order stated emphatically that the NAACP was "organizing, supporting, and financing an illegal boycott by Negro residents of Montgomery."

Later, Patterson filed a petition with the court, asking for a court order to have all NAACP chapters in Alabama produce financial reports, copies of charters, lists of members, contributors, and people who were authorized to solicit memberships or funds, information regarding bank transactions, and lists of properties owned. He also asked for all correspondence, telegrams, memoranda, and other records involved in a Montgomery federal court suit to test bus segregation laws. Judge Jones agreed with Patterson and signed an order demanding that these records be turned over to the court before a July 17 hearing.

When the NAACP did not comply with the order, Judge Jones levied a fine of one hundred thousand dollars for contempt of court. Until the organization paid the fine and produced all of the data requested by the attorney general's filing, it would be enjoined from doing business in the state.

In early August, attorneys for the NAACP appealed to the Alabama Supreme Court, where they charged that Jones had made ten errors in his finding. One error, attorneys alleged, was that Jones had violated the NAACP's rights to due process of law and equal protection under the Fourteenth Amendment to the U.S. Constitution. Attorneys representing the NAACP were Robert L. Carter, Fred Gray, and Arthur Shores.

After the state supreme court refused to lift the ban, assistant special council Carter told the Associated Press that he did not know whether he would ask for a rehearing by the state court or go directly to the U.S. Supreme Court. Shortly thereafter, Gray filed two petitions with the state court: one asked for a rehearing, and the other asked for review of the original hearing.

In E. D. Nixon's view, the white power structure had finally found a way to get to the black leaders. When the ninety-eight men and women had been arrested in February, they had actually been jubilant and joyful. Nixon remembered that day in the county courthouse as one of the "mountaintop experiences" of the first year of the civil rights movement. But Attorney General Patterson took them by surprise in Judge Jones's courtroom; it was a legal ambush they had not seen coming, and it hit the black leadership a roundhouse blow. It was not a knockout punch, however. They were down, they felt, but not out. In Nixon's estimation, it was "a pretty dirty trick, going to court without even telling any of us first. But that was the way they wanted to work it and [they] found 'em a judge in Jones." Throughout the time, Nixon stayed in touch with Roy Wilkins, who assured the Montgomery NAACP leader they would eventually win in court.

After the state's highest court turned them down, Gray carried the matter to the U.S. Supreme Court. The lawsuit set in motion a legal battle that continued for eight years. On four different occasions the case was sent to the U.S. Supreme Court: twice through the state court system and twice through the federal court system. Finally, on October 9, 1964, the Supreme Court overruled the Alabama courts, and the NAACP was allowed once again to qualify to do business in Alabama. The decision ended one of the longest legal struggles in the history of the nation's oldest civil rights organization.

Ultimately, the lawsuit gave the NAACP and similar organizations the legal right to assert and protect the rights of its members, and it allowed them to refuse to give names and addresses to the attorney general or to any other law enforcement agency that might use the information for intimidation and other harassment purposes. To Gray and Nixon, it was very important that the NAACP continue to protect the rights of

African Americans, especially in Alabama and other Southern states.

Word of the underhanded courtroom antics of the Alabama attorney general spread rapidly and widely. On a national level, King was developing even more star power than he'd had before. A speaking tour through the Midwest brought headlines and television coverage. This also gave Nixon the power to raise more funds. On his train runs through the North, he called on numerous institutions and rich individuals, who contributed tens of thousands of dollars to the cause.

After the sun went down, night riders roamed the streets of Montgomery, looking for ways to upset the blacks. Many of the white men who'd gathered together behind the service station in late January found themselves behind the station once again. The stench of used oil from nearby drums tinged the sweltering air as the men stood in their sweat-stained T-shirts, drank beer, and ranted about the events that had recently taken place.

As L. T. Green explained more than forty years after the summer of 1956, while cruising the same neighborhoods that he and other angry men had terrorized, the men were even more frustrated than they had been seven months earlier. As far as Green and his buddies were concerned, old Tacky Gayle had promised he was going keep the blacks in their place, and they had believed him. Gayle and Sellers and all the others did a lot of talking in their prestigious positions as mayor and commissioner, getting on television and saying they were going to stand up for the white people. Now they'd gone to court and came out and said everything was all right. They'd told the good old boys to mind their own business. They'd even come around and spoken to them privately, warning them to stay off the streets and to keep things quiet, that they'd take care of the situation and everything would be just fine and dandy, that the men's lives would go on just as they had before. But pretty soon, as the blacks continued to operate their car pools and, Green and friends felt, laugh behind their backs, these white men didn't believe the politicians. "It looked to us like Martin Luther Coon and the Communists from up North had already taken over," Green said.

The good old boys continued to attend meetings of the White Citizens Council, and they listened as Engelhardt, Givhan, Gayle, and Sellers said that they were prepared to do something that would make life right, once again, for their white constituents. As far as Green was concerned, however, the white leaders just made a lot of speeches, shook their fists in the air, and strutted around like a bunch of Nazis. To Green, it was all just so much hot air.

Terry Leon Hall, sitting in a Montgomery breakfast café in 2003, reiterated Green's words. The white men believed they'd been backed into a corner. They felt helpless against the obvious stranglehold the nonviolent protest was having on the community. Hall, Green, and others felt they had to do something to break the stronghold. When they saw blacks standing around on street corners downtown, piling into cars driven by white volunteers, riding down the street singing their happy songs, they became infuriated. They met behind the service station, stood around, drank beer, and talked. They talked about what they'd seen during the day, each painting angry pictures of uppity blacks feeling the power of their movement. When they saw King speak so eloquently on television to crowds in New York or Chicago or Los Angeles, the very sound of his voice angered the white middle- and lower-class Southern men down to the core. Terry Leon Hall told the others, "Let's quit throwing a little ol' piece of a bomb; let's blow up the whole damn outfit at one time." But, Hall said, the others wouldn't listen to him "until one night when one guy started talking about the white preacher who was helping 'em out with his sissified grin and his smooth-talking ways. That got us going. It was toward the end of August, hot as blazes, and we were ready to do something that'd get all of their attention."

On the night of August 25, several sticks of dynamite exploded near the front porch of the Cleveland Avenue home of Reverend Graetz. Luckily, no one was home. The family had left six days earlier on vacation to Highlander Folk School in Monteagle, Tennessee. The explosion blew out glass panes in the front windows of the house, and it was so powerful that it shattered glass in windows of several nearby houses. A neighbor said that it sounded like thunder and felt like the earth was shaking.

On the Saturday morning that the family was to leave Monteagle, Graetz was called from his cabin to the main office, where a telephone call was waiting. Ted Poston, a reporter for the *New York Post* who had been covering the boycott since its early days, told him his house had been bombed. After breakfast, the family packed their belongings and headed home to the damaged dwelling.

That afternoon's *Alabama Journal* carried a story in which Mayor Gayle accused the bus boycotters of the bombing. "This latest 'bombing' follows the usual pattern," Gayle said. "It's a strange coincidence that when interest appears to be lagging in the boycott something like this happens. It's interesting to note that Reverend Graetz and his family were out of town and the explosion was set off at least twenty feet away from the house at 1110 Cleveland Avenue so that no extensive damage was done. We are inclined to wonder if out-of-state contributions to the boycott have been dropping off. Perhaps this is just a publicity stunt to build up interest of the Negroes in their campaign." That afternoon, Graetz called the *Advertiser* and told a reporter that the mayor's words were "foolishness." He said that the destruction had been caused by either the "same group" that had been responsible for bombings earlier in the year "or by like-minded persons since it all follows a similar pattern." While Graetz, his wife, and his children inspected the damage, Rosa Parks, who had accompanied them on their trip to Highlander, picked up broken glass and swept the kitchen floor.

While inspecting the Graetz home before the family arrived, city detectives had confiscated his personal records. They also took the minister's private telephone directory, in which he kept numbers of close friends, including a secret number for the local FBI that had been given to him only a few weeks earlier by an agent friend. When Graetz told the agent that his records had been taken, the agent said that now, perhaps, the local police would realize that the FBI was working with them, and that they would "be a little more careful."

Several days after the blast at the Graetzes' home, E. D. Nixon was on his front porch "with a 33 Winchester on my knee when they came up the street and shined the lights on our house. When they saw me standing there, they knew I had something. When they saw me, they cut back and sold out up the street. But if I hadn't been standing on that porch, they'd-a bombed my house a second time."

According to Nixon, "In the middle of all this hard time, I got a call one time from a white man that I'd-a done some work for for a dollar a day. He called and said, 'Nixon, I don't want you and Mrs. Nixon staying in your house for a while. Get your pajama suit and come on over to my house.' He lived over on South Perry Street. I said, 'Man, if they find out I'm over at your house, they'll bomb your house, then they'll kill me and my wife and you and your wife.' You see, there were some real nice white peoples who would do things like that."

As soon as he heard about the bomb exploding at Reverend Graetz's house, Clifford Durr telephoned the minister and invited him, his wife, and his children to stay with them on Felder Avenue. Graetz laughed nervously and said that everything was fine, that they would be safe because the police were watching their place around the clock.

Virginia Durr, who had offered her home more than once to E. D. and Arlet Nixon, called them and insisted that they move into the Durrs' apartment. Nixon remembered, "The Durrs were always afraid for us. They told us if we ever got afraid, to come over to their place on Court Street. But we didn't do that. We didn't want to put them in jeopardy. They were really nice people and had us over to their house for dinner. We'd sit around after and talk, me and Mr. Durr would smoke, and talk. He was a good talker, told stories about President Roosevelt and Mrs. Roosevelt, and I liked to hear him. And Mrs. Durr would chime in and speak about Mrs. Roosevelt, who was a personal friend of hers."

To Nixon, Clifford Durr was more than a lawyer who assisted them in their legal plight; like Fred Gray, he was a friend who gave advice and offered a positive philosophy during hard times. Nixon would sit and listen while Durr smoked his unfiltered cigarettes and told him about the New Deal days in Washington. To Nixon, Durr was a great hero, and he wished that all of his people could hear and learn from the man.

In the last week of August, when daytime temperatures ran upward of a hundred degrees and nighttime tempers ran short and snappy, Attorney General Patterson and an attorney for the city filed appeals of the *Browder* case with the U.S. Supreme Court. The high court was asked to reverse the three-judge panel's decision that the city's segregation laws were unconstitutional.

Attorneys for the city commission questioned the authority of the special court to act in the case. "The judgment of the

special court departs from principles of federal court procedure long considered essential to a proper accommodation of
state and federal courts," the notice of appeal read. In the very
beginning, the attorneys believed, the federal court should have
dismissed the complaint filed by the black attorneys on behalf
of black bus riders, "or, at least, stayed it" pending action filed
by blacks in a similar suit in Alabama state courts.

Patterson's appeal questioned the court's decision on the
constitutionality of the laws. It also argued that the court's
order prohibiting the Alabama Public Service Commission
from enforcing bus segregation went beyond the jurisdiction
of the three-judge court. "The evidence is undisputed that the
Alabama Public Service Commission has never attempted to
enforce the statutes and ordinances relating to segregation on
buses operated by Montgomery City Lines, Inc. Equitable
relief can never be against persons to prevent them from doing
that which they have never threatened to do and have no power
to do," the attorney general wrote.

The Supreme Court was in summer recess when the appeal
was filed. It would decide whether or not it would hear the case
after October 1.

Writing in *U.S. News & World Report*, Grover Hall, Jr., allowed,
"Bus seating is no longer the real *casus belli*, but only a symbol
of the war. The whites—that includes me—are persuaded that
they cannot allow themselves to be overwhelmed on this terrain, ill-chosen for strategic and tactical defense though it is,
lest they be routed in the schools, which is the citadel."

Desegregation of bus seats, according to Hall, "was a poor
area for the whites to make a stand, because the old system was
unjust and because the system in other comparable Southern
cities clearly shows that at one time—now past—adjustment
could have been made without disorder. Furthermore, there is

not a single segregated elevator left in Montgomery: horizontal segregation (as opposed to) vertical segregation. The pregnant difference is that elevators were made 'first come–first serve' without advertisement as a critical battle in the universal desegregation war."

Parties to both sides of the question, Hall wrote, were being fed misinformation and outright lies about the basic situation. "I submit that mainly due to a failure of the U.S. press, this country hasn't achieved a rational, factual basis for grappling with the problem. You employ a quite imprecise analogy if you point to the abolitionist North and the antebellum South, for the latter-day circumstance is that a third of the Negroes are already in the North, with a mighty stream following. Yet, the national mind is still thinking of the problem as a Southern one."

Hall surmised that "the United States doesn't even know the location of its race problem" and that, therefore, "the geography of Jim Crow is unknown."

Although it had been a long, hot, frustrating summer, black leaders in Montgomery noticed a change in their people. Something had happened to them, Jo Ann Robinson noted. One could see it in the poorest of the poor, the most ignorant field hand or house servant, the shoeshine operator or the grease-smudged mechanic. One could watch a black man or woman walk down the sidewalk and behold a person who carries himself or herself straighter, holds his or her head higher, for "he is little more of a man and she a woman because they feel a little more like a man or a woman," Robinson told a New York journalist.

The black people on the Montgomery streets, continued Robinson, "no longer lack courage; they're no longer afraid. They're free for the first time in their lives and they know they've won their own freedom. This goes not only for the lowest domestic but for the highest Negro professional also."

Political science professor J. E. Pierce remarked, "What you're seeing here is probably the closest approach to a classless society that has ever been created in any community in America. The whites have forced the Montgomery Negro to recognize one thing—that they are Negroes first and then domestics, doctors' wives, scholars, or lawyers second.

"But for the first time the Negro is accepting with pride, not shame, the fact that all Negroes look alike to white people. Through their unity, their car pools, their determination to share and share alike, they have found each other—as Negroes. . . . [They] walk a little straighter . . . head a little higher.

"This new dignity is not accidental. And it is no accident that they call each other 'ladies' and 'gentlemen' on every possible occasion. For the first time in their lives, they feel like ladies and gentlemen from the bottom to the top."

"A Glorious Daybreak"

IN LATE OCTOBER the white establishment in Montgomery joined hands with a most unlikely ally—staff members of a labor union magazine, the *Alabama Labor News*—in a new maneuver to stop the car pool that had successfully operated for ten months.

Jack D. Brock, the editor of the labor publication, told the *Advertiser* that he and other staff members were ready to swear out warrants against the car pool operators. They were represented by attorney John Peter Kohn, the same outspoken lawyer who had given his services free of charge when Virginia Durr had been brought before Senator Jim Eastland's committee in New Orleans.

A ramrod-straight, board-thin scion of an old Montgomery family who was given to wearing Panama hats and seersucker suits in the summertime and a fedora with tailored tweeds in the winter, Kohn marched to the beat of his own drummer. In his later years, Kohn wrote a scathing satire of his community called *The Cradle*, which he published privately. Of his representation of Virginia Durr, he said, "I was defending Southern womanhood. Virginia is a lady. Besides, I've always liked and admired Clifford Durr."

Kohn loved a good fight in the courtroom, and he declared without reservation that he would use "a double-barrel legal approach" to halt the station wagons and cars that he saw as a "sabotage of franchise transportation in this city" and an effort to do "by subterfuge what the commission had denied them the right to do." Kohn's reference was to the commission's earlier action refusing to grant the protesters a franchise to operate their own bus line.

The city commission and the labor group met for three hours behind closed doors. Mayor Gayle and the commissioners then issued a statement: "The city's latest activity in this connection [to maintaining segregation] has been the assembling of evidence for action against the operations of so-called carpools. The commission is glad for individuals to take such action as they see fit in their own best interest; however, regardless of whether such action is taken or not, the city will follow its plans of bringing action for an injunction to stop all activities which the city considers illegal at this time."

Kohn, who considered himself a son of the Old South, stated that the car pool operation was an "emasculation" of city and state laws. It was supported, he said, "by people who hate the South and don't understand it."

Within the next decade, Kohn would align himself with George C. Wallace. He and Grover Hall, Jr., would put the finishing touches on Wallace's inauguration speech, written by former Ku Klux Klansman Asa Carter, in which Wallace would declare, "Segregation now! Segregation tomorrow! Segregation forever!" A close adviser to the governor, Kohn would be appointed to the Alabama Supreme Court when Wallace's wife, Governor Lurleen Wallace, lay on her deathbed in 1968. When Wallace's second wife, Cornelia, filed for divorce, Kohn represented her and became an outspoken critic of his old friend.

As evidence of legal authority for immediate action, Kohn cited a section of the Code of Alabama that "any firm, association, or corporation using the streets of any city for the construction or operation of any public utility cannot do so without first obtaining permission of the city commission."

The city commission added, "We intend to maintain the way of life which has existed here in Montgomery since its origin, so far as we are legally able."

King answered that his car pool organizers and drivers would wait for the city to act. "We feel that we're within our legal rights," King told the press. "As for now, we're just going to sit tight and wait to see what the city does" and continue what he called a "jitney service or car-for-hire system."

A day later, on another legal front, after the commission passed a resolution ordering its legal staff to "file such proceedings as it may deem necessary" to stop the carpool, city attorney Walter Knabe said his office was looking into a legal means to halt the carpool operation.

King stated, "As far as we are concerned, the carpool will continue to exist. We feel that the cause for which we are struggling is just and the methods we are using are constructive, deep-rooted in the long tradition of our Christian faith. In the face of a threatening injunction, the Negro community is determined to struggle and sacrifice until the walls of injustice are finally crushed by the battering rams of surging justice. We are simply offering free rides to the Negro citizenry of Montgomery through the services of our church."

Then attorneys Gray and Langford beat the city to court, filing papers in U.S. District Court asking for a federal injunction to block any interference with the carpool. The lawyers charged in their request that the city was conspiring to interfere with the civil and constitutional rights of Montgomery blacks who had refused to ride city buses since the previous December 5, and they contended that the motor pool was legal and that it was operated on a voluntary basis without charge to riders. Because the drivers did not charge a fee, the attorneys maintained, the pool was not competing with taxis or city buses.

In early November, however, the city filed a request in Montgomery County Circuit Court for an injunction to break up what they termed an "illegal transportation setup" organized by the black protesters.

Immediately, Gray filed an objection. He argued that Judge Carter did not have jurisdiction to rule on the request, on the grounds that the federal court, not the state court, had the case.

Knabe contested Gray's argument, saying that, although it was true that one court could not take jurisdiction from another, the suits that were pending in state and federal courts involved different individuals and were actually separate actions.

Regarding the segregation matter, Knabe maintained that the state court had jurisdiction over that issue long before it was taken into federal court.

Overruling Gray's objection, Carter agreed with Knabe, "This is a state matter. The federal courts do not have jurisdiction."

The judge called for testimony to begin, although a hearing was scheduled to begin the next day in U.S. District Court before Judge Johnson.

MIA attorney Peter Hall wondered aloud, "If the carpool is illegal, as the city contends, why haven't the drivers and dispatchers been arrested and tried in city court? They would have had the Negroes in jail long ago if it were illegal." If the motor pool was illegal, as the city attorney claimed, Hall pointed out, the city would have a remedy in its own courts and would not be entitled to an injunction to stop it.

Later that morning, after a witness for the city testified that the carpool was a "public nuisance" and a "private enterprise" that was not properly licensed, a rumble of whispers rippled through the press section of the audience. After the city rested its case, Judge Carter called a recess.

Gray was handed a note by WSFA-TV newsman Frank McGee that read, "I need to see you immediately outside the courtroom." Gray pushed through the crowd and found McGee in the hallway. The reporter said he had just received word that the U.S. Supreme Court had affirmed the federal court's ruling in *Browder v. Gayle*. Elated, Gray said he would meet McGee later at the Washington Street entrance for an on-camera reaction. At the moment, however, he had to go back into the courtroom for the business at hand.

Inside the courtroom, Associated Press correspondent Rex Thomas handed Reverend King a bulletin that stated: "WASHINGTON (AP)—The Supreme Court today upheld a decision holding unconstitutional Alabama and Montgomery, Ala., laws requiring racial segregation on buses.

"The decision by a special three-judge U.S. District Court in Montgomery was appealed by the city's board of commissioners and by the Alabama Public Service Commission. Each filed separately.

"Today's Supreme Court action was unanimous."

King said to Thomas, "This is a glorious daybreak to end a long night of enforced segregation."

When he saw Gray reenter the courtroom with a broad grin on his face, King felt jubilant, but he knew they had to wait to celebrate the victory. At the moment, they had to continue their fight to keep the city from outlawing the car pool.

Gray attempted to interject the high court's ruling into the hearing before Carter, but the judge ruled it inadmissible. This was a hearing simply on the question of whether or not the MIA was operating a legal or an illegal car pool; the ruling on segregation, Carter stated, "has nothing to do with it." At the end of the hearing that afternoon, Judge Carter wasted no time.

He enjoined the Montgomery Improvement Association and its members from continuing the car pool. The judge told Gray and other MIA attorneys that the ban would begin at midnight.

The register in chancery, George H. Jones, Jr., told the press that restraining orders would go out from his office immediately the following morning, and that sheriff's deputies would serve them on the MIA, fourteen black churches, and twenty-seven individuals.

Feeling glorious in light of the Supreme Court ruling, the attorneys nevertheless had to prepare for the next morning's hearing in Judge Johnson's court, at which Gray would ask Johnson to set aside Carter's injunction.

While Gray immersed himself in legal homework, King and Abernathy put the word out to black ministers across Montgomery: there would be mass meetings tonight.

The Associated Press's Rex Thomas interviewed seventy-eight-year-old plaintiff Susie McDonald, who told him, "We were badly treated on the buses but now they've given us justice."

Across Dixie, however, white officials disagreed wholeheartedly. Alabama's senior senator, Lister Hill, replied that "every lawful means to set aside the ruling" of the Supreme Court should be put into effect. Georgia's senator-elect, Herman Talmadge, said that Congress should limit the power of the Supreme Court. Georgia governor Marvin Griffin said that his state would do everything in its power to oppose the application of the decision.

That night, two mass meetings were held in Montgomery. The first, at Hutchinson Street Baptist Church, accommodated about four thousand people, and the second, at the site of the first mass meeting eleven months earlier, filled the Holt Street Baptist Church with more than four thousand men, women, and children. At both locations, cheering crowds poured out onto the sidewalk and into the street for several blocks. When King entered each church, his head held high and proud, the people stood and applauded. They shouted praise. At both meetings, Reverend King asked for the attendees' approval of a recommendation made by the executive board of the MIA to stop the boycott and return to the buses on a nonsegregated basis.

After he spoke, the crowds cheered loudly. Many shouted, "Amen!" Many called out, "God bless you, Reverend King!"

As the Reverend S. S. Seay read the invocation, his white hair glowing like a halo—"Wherever the Klans may march, no matter what the White Citizens Councils may want to do, we are not afraid because God is on our side"—tears rolled down his cheeks.

Reverend King told the crowd that, while it was true that the Court's ruling in Washington was a procedural matter, it was a matter that might be used by white reactionary Southern leaders "to plunge us into needless harassment and meaningless litigation."

Until the high court's ruling actually came to Montgomery to be enforced by the local authorities, King said, which might take three or four days, the people should continue to walk or share rides with friends.

Then he hit once again on his recurring theme of nonviolence.

"We must take this not as a victory over the white man, but with dignity. Don't go back to the buses and push people around," King warned.

"I wish I could say that when we go back to the buses on an integrated basis that no white person will insult you—or that violent factions will not break out. But I can't say that—because I don't know.

"If someone pushes you, don't push him back. I know that is a hard thing not to do. Our western philosophy teaches us that in the end there can only be violence. But we must refuse to hit back. We must have the courage to refuse to hit back."

Again, the crowd cheered as loud as they could.

The next morning in federal court, Fred Gray asked Judge Johnson for an order to permit the MIA to continue the motor pool although the long boycott appeared near an end. City attorney Knabe asked Johnson to dismiss the request on the grounds that the Supreme Court decision had removed the necessity of the boycott and the car pool. He also said this was a state matter outside the jurisdiction of the federal court. Knabe pointed out that, in their petition, the Negroes had said they would ride the buses again once the buses become desegregated.

Then Gray asked Johnson to make Judge Carter a defendant in the case, since he had issued an injunction the previous day against the car pool. Judge Johnson denied that request.

On the other matters, he withheld his ruling until he heard testimony.

The first to take the stand was King, who said under cross-examination that "there is no basic need" to continue the car pool after the Supreme Court ruling. However, he said that the bus boycott had not formally been abandoned.

After Carter's injunction against the car pool, he said, black citizens of Montgomery walked to work this morning. They had not yet returned to the buses.

Throughout the day, city attorneys showed through testimony from King, Abernathy, and others that the car pool was financed by contributions from black churches and that some drivers were paid for their services. However, black lawyers told the court that the boycotters had the right to use the car pool as long as the riders did not pay for their transportation.

At the end of the day, the matter was still not settled. Judge Johnson took the case under advisement. Black boycotters, taking refuge behind the words of a ruling they had only read in the newspapers and heard on radio and television, were frustrated to be in the midst of the legal limbo.

Day after day, the frustration showed in the cadence of their walk.

Nixon realized that "it had been a long year. When we heard the words that the Court ruled in our favor, we were happy. Everybody cheered. King had risen to the top. He was the grand hero of the hour. But the peoples felt heavy-hearted and dog-tired. They lifted their feet when they were going to work in the morning, but they dragged them along the ground when they came home at night. Some tended to move toward the shot houses for some likker at the end of the day. And into the night, they got drunked up and swore they'd do bad things to the white so-and-sos who were now keeping 'em off the buses. Then it fell into King's hands to do what he could to help all the peoples stay in tune with his nonviolent march. It's hard to do sometimes, when folks feel downtrodden and whupped up on."

To keep his promise of nonviolence, King sat down with the MIA executive committee and created the Institute on Non-Violence and Social Change to be held December 3–9. The event would include a huge celebration of the anniversary of the beginning of the boycott on December 5. With the motto "Freedom and dignity with love," the Institute would close on its final day with a mammoth religious service. The principal speaker would be Dr. J. H. Jackson, the president of the National Baptist Convention, the world's largest black church organization.

Named chairman of the institute was MIA vice president Reverend Abernathy, who explained, "We are planning to involve the entire national community by discussing in the South, in interracial groups, the major issues that affect Negro-white relations in our nation."

Workshops for Southern blacks would instruct the participants in voter registration, principles of nonviolent action, and "the problems of survival in the face of economic pressure and boycott," King said.

White leaders who would attend included the author Lillian Smith, of Clayton, Georgia; the Reverend Glenn Smiley, field secretary of the Fellowship of Reconciliation in New York City; and the Reverend Homer A. Jack, pastor of the Unitarian Church in Evanston, Illinois.

Those who walked every day felt the soles of their shoes becoming heavier and heavier. They waited for what Nixon called "the real word" to arrive from the Supreme Court. In the meantime, King continued to preach nonviolence, knowing that every cold, wintry morning made it tougher and tougher for the people who had to walk to be patient and to show tolerance.

In the major cities of Virginia and Arkansas, Richmond and Little Rock, municipal buses were integrated. In Georgia, where whites sat in seats from the front to the rear and blacks sat in seats from the rear toward the front, Governor Marvin Griffin promised that "there will be no breach in the pattern of segregation in Georgia as long as I am governor." In Mississippi, Governor J. P. Coleman said his state would "continue to separate the races on public conveyances. Our attitude about this decision will be the same as about the school segregation cases." The attorney general of Florida, Richard Ervin, said that as long as segregation laws were on the books of his state they would be enforced.

Sam Engelhardt, executive director of the White Citizens Council, declared that if the Supreme Court "insists on disrupting our social order, including destroying the peaceful coexistence that has existed here for years, it must make preparations to enforce this order."

In Washington, the clerk of the Supreme Court said that formal notice of the ruling would be issued in about a month.

Under the Court's rules, notice of a decision was not sent out until at least twenty-five days after a decision was announced. In the bus segregation case, a certified copy of the high court's judgment would first be sent to the three judges who'd made the original decision. This waiting period was designed to give the losing party time to ask for a rehearing.

It was more time than King wanted to give. He had hoped for a final declaration within days. Now he would have to attempt to keep the waters of unrest calm for the next month. He knew it would be a difficult job, but he was determined to keep all demonstrations nonviolent.

Within several days, Mayor Gayle stated that the city government did not accept integration as inevitable and that it would "do all legal things necessary to continue enforcement of our segregation laws and ordinances of all kinds" while insuring "public safety, to protect the peoples of both races, and to promote order in our city." Police Commissioner Sellers made a separate statement, asking that citizens be calm and "coolheaded. This is not the time for hotheads, oratory, loud talk, or threats," he added.

In Washington, U.S. Attorney General Herbert Brownell summoned thirty-four federal attorneys from fourteen Southern states to attend a conference he would conduct on how to enforce the ruling of the Supreme Court. At the conference in mid-November, he said, the attorneys "will consider and decide upon measures most appropriate to secure observance of the United States Constitution and laws by carriers and all others who may hereafter require segregation of white and colored passengers on common carriers."

Brownell instructed the attorneys to bring with them copies of any local or state law relating to racial segregation.

He added that the Court's decision invalidated Alabama's and Montgomery's statutes on the subject, stating, "It is now clear that any such law, statute, ordinance, or regulation must be regarded as dead letter.

"It is also clear that the enforcement or observance of any such discriminatory measure by any common carrier of passengers will constitute in the future and in the light of the unmistakable declaration of the federal courts a willful deprivation by the carrier of the constitutional rights, privileges, and immunities of those discriminated against in the United States. Anyone who commands, induces, procures, counsels, aids, or abets the carrier in the commission of any such crime is equally guilty," he concluded.

The day after Brownell made his statement, Alabama Public Service Commissioner C. C. "Jack" Owen told the press that he was working on an order to circumvent the Court's ruling. "Under the commission's broad rule-making powers," he said, "I think we can work up an order without using the words 'white' and 'colored' in any of our regulations." He refused to comment on Brownell's conference.

Given the extra days before the official word came down, the Montgomery City Commission announced that it would ask for a rehearing before the Supreme Court. In the meantime, the buses continued to operate on a segregated basis.

On the last weekend in November, some five thousand members of the Ku Klux Klan, which had enjoyed a resurgence in membership throughout the year across the nation, rode into Montgomery, crowded onto the steps in front of the capitol draped in their snowy gowns and pointy hoods, and raised their fists and their voices. Men, women, and even children who donned their miniature gowns and hoods listened to Grand Dragon Bobby Shelton, from Tuscaloosa, rant and rave. "The Yankee Communists are controlling the niggers of Alabama, Georgia, Mississippi, and Florida with their underhanded promises and their almighty dollar," Shelton told them.

That night, in a field outside the city limits, off Old Selma Road, the KKK continued its demonstration, lighting a forty-foot-high cross whose flames licked against the black night as the Klansmen screamed their racist epithets.

On the third day of December, as he had announced two weeks earlier, King stood before the opening audience of the Institute on Non-Violence and Social Change. Standing at the pulpit of the Holt Street Baptist Church, where he'd looked down on an overflowing crowd during the first mass meeting of the boycott, he outlined the successes of the past year.

The sanctuary was filled with even more people than King had anticipated. Many who sat in the front row and behind him on the stage were famous dignitaries—author Lillian Smith, Congressman Powell, singer Mahalia Jackson, and nationally known church leaders. Now every black star in America and the world wanted to share their names with the movement. And King himself was the biggest star of all.

He titled his keynote address "Facing the challenge of a new age." During the past year, he told the crowd, six lessons had been learned. "We have discovered that we can stick together for a common sense. Our leaders do not have to sell out. Threats and violence do not necessarily intimidate those who are sufficiently aroused and nonviolent. Our church is becoming militant, stressing a social gospel as well as a gospel of personal salvation. We have gained a new sense of dignity and destiny. We have discovered a new and powerful weapon—nonviolent resistance."

Today, he said, "We are living in one of the momentous periods of human history. Nobody has been able to convince me that the vast majority of white people in this community, or the whole state of Alabama, are willing to use violence to maintain segregation. It is only the fringe element—the hoodlum element—which constitutes a numerical minority, that would resort to the use of violence.

"We must continue to believe that the most ardent segregationist can be transformed into the most constructive integrationist." However, he told them, "Segregation is still a fact in America. We still confront it in the South in its glaring and conspicuous forms. We still confront it in the North in its hidden and subtle forms.

"Let nobody fool you. All of the loud noises you hear today from the legislative halls of the South in terms of 'interposition' and of outlawing the NAACP are merely the death groans from a dying system."

To raise the spirits of those who had been walking every day and who might walk for another month or so with little relief, he told them, "Whatever your life's work is, do it well. A man should do his job so well that the living, the dead, and the unborn could do it no better. If it falls your lot to be a street sweeper, sweep streets like Michelangelo painted pictures, like Shakespeare wrote poetry, like Beethoven composed music; sweep streets so well that all the hosts of heaven and Earth will have to pause and say, 'Here lived a great street sweeper, who swept his job well.'"

He told them: "Our defense is to meet every act of violence toward the individual Negro with the fact that there are thousands of others who will present themselves in his place as potential victims. Every time one schoolteacher is fired for standing courageously for justice, it must be faced with the fact that there are four thousand more to be fired. If the oppressors bomb the home of one Negro for his courage, this must be met with the fact that they must be required to bomb the homes of fifty thousand more Negroes. This dynamic unity, this amazing self-respect, this willingness to suffer, and this refusal to hit back will soon cause the oppressor to become ashamed of his own methods." And he told them, "when this day finally comes, 'The morning stars will sing together and the sons of God will shout for joy.'"

During the week, a black columnist from Washington named Carl Rowan extolled the virtues of King and his movement. On December 9, the morning of the final day of the Institute on Non-Violence and Social Change, King's predecessor at Dexter Avenue Baptist Church, the fiery old preacher Vernon Johns, took over the pulpit there to commemorate the seventy-ninth anniversary of the church's breaking off from First Baptist to form its own congregation. That afternoon, Abernathy welcomed an overflowing crowd at his church. After more than an hour of spiritual music from various choirs, with the world-famous gospel singer Mahalia Jackson singing "Precious Lord, Take My Hand," King introduced Dr. J. H. Jackson, the head of the National Baptist Convention, who offered his hand to the young minister as a welcome into the highest ranks of Negro Baptists in the land. It was a holy moment for King.

Although King, Abernathy, Nixon, and the others knew that it was only a matter of days before the Supreme Court's order would arrive in Montgomery, for them every day was a new challenge to keep nonviolence at the forefront of the movement.

After the Supreme Court refused the city's request for a rehearing, the leaders knew that the day was near when they could step aboard an integrated bus. But when they stepped, what would happen?

Once again, King sat down with his executive board of the MIA. It was time that they gathered the troops and taught their people real nonviolence. Until that day came when they would be allowed to board a desegregated bus, King and the other leaders would conduct hours of intense training for their people on being nonviolent in the face of real violence. It was one thing to say the word; it was another to face it in real life.

The first training session was held in the basement conference room of Dexter Avenue Baptist Church. Chairs were placed in two rows separated by an aisle down the middle to resemble as closely as possible the layout of a bus.

A group of King's constituents stood against one wall and watched while he stepped around the first row, as though he were boarding a bus.

He pretended to drop his coin into an imaginary token taker.

When he sat down in the first chair, the man who was playing the role of bus driver turned and snarled, "Get on back, nigger!"

The benevolent minister folded his dark hands in his lap and gazed into the angry driver's face. He smiled a smile that shone from within.

Every eye in his audience of several dozen stared at him, waiting.

When the bus driver grabbed him by the shoulder and twisted him angrily into the aisle, King, moving as easily as he could, stood and stepped away. And when the driver moved back to his seat, King stepped forward and sat once again in his original seat.

When King finally turned to the watchers, he said in a soft voice, "You must keep smiling. When you step aboard the bus, smile. Put a smile in your heart. Let it glow from within. That is the only way you will be able to manage the hurt."

"Abuse," he told them, "can be overcome with a joyful heart."

On Sunday he told his congregation, "Just because we have won in court, life will not suddenly become easy. The travails will not vanish. The hills will not suddenly flatten. The valleys will not suddenly rise. The road you travel will not be paved with gold. Not yet! Heaven does not exist on this earth. If it did, there would be no promised land."

On weekdays, morning and afternoon sessions on anger and abuse management were taught in churches across Montgomery. Many black men, women, and children attended.

On December 20, copies of the Supreme Court's writs of injunction were carried by deputy marshals from the U.S. courthouse to Montgomery City Hall, where they were delivered to the offices of the mayor and his commissioners. Similar papers were carried to the state offices of the Alabama Public Service Commission.

A short time earlier, anticipating the finality of the court's order, the MIA executive committee had sent a letter to city officials telling them that "as soon as the district court issues the formal decree, we shall be returning to the buses. Although we are hopeful that no violent incidents will occur, we must recognize that possibility. There is that element of violent-minded people, of both races, of which we must be mindful.

"Past experience reveals that the only places where violence has occurred in connection with the buses have been at the ends of lines and on very dark streets, and the hours after dark are potentially more dangerous than the daytime.

"We, therefore, request that you use every precaution to prevent possible violence, and that you will insure that the above-mentioned danger zones will be patrolled with extra caution."

That night, another mass meeting was called. Once again, it was held at the Holt Street Baptist Church. Once again, the people were ecstatic. The word was out: the black people of Montgomery had overcome. No longer was the old spiritual that had become their anthem simply words to be sung. By their fortitude, they had made the song a reality. They had won over the powerful white establishment that had ruled by Jim Crow laws for nearly a century. Their leader, Dr. King, spoke in a quiet voice of moderation and restraint: "For more than twelve months now, we, the Negro citizens of Montgomery, have been engaged in a nonviolent protest against injustices and indignities experienced on city buses. We came to see that, in the long run, it is more honorable to walk in dignity than ride in humiliation. So in a quiet, dignified manner, we decided to substitute tired feet for tired souls—and walk the streets of Montgomery until the sagging walls of injustice had been crushed by the battering rams of surging justice."

The thousands of blacks who'd gathered together that evening jumped to their feet, slapped their hands together, and shouted, "Amen!"

King waited. He had waited for a long year. He and his people had waited for years and years. Now they could see the glimmer of hope in the distance. He waited until quiet came to the multitude.

"Often our movement has been referred to as a boycott movement. The word 'boycott,' however, does not adequately describe the true spirit of our movement. The word 'boycott' is suggestive of merely an economic squeeze devoid of any positive value. We have never allowed ourselves to get bogged in the negative; we have always sought to accentuate the positive. Our aim has never been to put the bus company out of business, but rather to put justice in business."

As he had done so often during the year, he found just the right words, and his voice lifted with a familiar cadence. "These twelve months have not been easy. Our feet have often been tired. We have struggled against tremendous odds to maintain alternative transportation. There have been moments when roaring waters of disappointment poured upon us in staggering torrents. We can remember days when unfavorable court decisions came down upon us like tidal waves, leaving us treading in the deep and confused waters of despair. But amid all of this we have kept going with the faith that as we struggle, God struggles with us—and that the arc of the moral universe, although long, is bending toward justice."

At least three women in the audience fell to their knees in a spiritual trance, screaming sounds of jubilation, raising their arms above their heads, and throwing their hands from side to side as others bent to offer assistance.

King continued, "We have lived under the agony and darkness of Good Friday with the conviction that one day the heightening glow of Easter would emerge on the horizon. We have seen truth crucified and goodness buried, but we have kept going with the conviction that truth crushed to Earth will rise again.

"Now, our faith seems to be vindicated. This morning the long-awaited mandate from the United States Supreme Court concerning bus segregation came to Montgomery. This mandate expresses, in terms that are crystal clear, that segregation in public transportation is both legally and sociologically invalid. In the light of this mandate and the unanimous vote rendered by the Montgomery Improvement Association about a month ago, the year-old protest against the city buses is officially called off, and the Negro citizens of Montgomery are urged to return to the buses tomorrow morning on a nonsegregated basis."

He ended with a word of caution and a reminder of their "united nonviolent protest."

"We cannot be satisfied with a court 'victory' over our white brothers," he stated. "We must respond to the decision with an understanding of those who have oppressed us and with an appreciation of the new adjustments that the court order poses for them. We must be able to face up honestly to our own shortcomings. We must act in such a way as to make possible a coming together of white people and colored people on the basis of a real harmony of interests and understanding. We seek an integration based on mutual respect."

He told them that this was the time to show "calm dignity and wise restraint. Emotions must not run wild. Violence must not come from any of us. If we become victimized with violent intents, we will have walked in vain—and our twelve months of glorious dignity will be transformed into an eve of gloomy catastrophe.

"As we go back to the buses, let us be loving enough to turn an enemy into a friend. We must now move from protest to reconciliation. It is my firm conviction that God is working in Montgomery. Let all men of goodwill, both Negro and white, continue to work with Him. With this dedication, we will be able to emerge from the bleak and desolate midnight of man's inhumanity to man to the bright and glittering daybreak of freedom and justice."

And the crowd roared, like claps of thunder.

———

Shortly before dawn on the morning of December 21, King, Abernathy, Baskin, Nixon, and Glenn Smiley, the white minister from New York City who had come down to help King with his teaching of nonviolence, boarded a bus. King and Smiley sat side by side toward the front, becoming the first integrated bus riders in the history of the city.

During the day few incidents occurred. An elderly white man declared, "I would rather die and go to hell than sit behind a nigger." A white man slapped a black woman who refused to move from her seat in the front of a bus. Later the woman said that she "could have broken that little fellow's neck all by myself, but I left the mass meeting last night determined to do what Reverend King asked." Several other blacks reported that white men and women had called them names and pushed them roughly when they attempted to sit in the front sections, but overall the first day ended in an atmosphere of calm.

At the end of the day, the blacks of Montgomery bowed their heads in prayer. They had overcome the adversity of being a minority in a land where white men were kings. They had won a simple right guaranteed them under the Constitution of the United States. It had been a long time coming. But now they had the privilege of making it work.

Years later, when he talked about that day, E. D. Nixon closed his eyes. "It's hard on me, remembering that morning. When I climbed out of bed, I sat on the edge a few minutes. Mrs. Nixon reached out and took a-hold of my hand and just held it. For more than a minute, I knowed I was somewhere else. It was like it wadn't happening. Then it hit me. I squeezed her hand back and I didn't bother to hold it in no more. I cried like a baby. When I tried to speak, my lips wouldn't say nothing; they just trembled. I felt like an old miserable fool, but Arlet made me feel like a king. She held me and rocked me, like I *was* a baby. She just said, 'I know, I know, I know.' And finally I nodded my head and still couldn't say nothing.

"When I got on that bus that morning, for a minute or two I thought I'd start babbling all over again, but I didn't. I held it inside me, and it stayed there like a rock—a heavy rock pressing against my heart. And when I saw Rosa climb aboard and look around, her eyes glistening like I knew she, too, had been crying, I thought it was gonna come on me again, but it didn't. Her eyes caught mine, and we knew what we'd done, and we both grinned real big and didn't say nothing. We just rode. It was the best ride I ever had in my life, just riding through downtown and out to the west and back again, going nowhere but feeling like we was heading to heaven."

Epilogue

THE AFTERMATH

The movement won a great victory in federal court. But after the people exercised their hard-earned right to take the first nonsegregated ride on the city buses, an atmosphere of hate and intolerance permeated Montgomery and, once again, the buses became a battleground.

On the same day that segregation on the buses ended, Sam Engelhardt asked the white people of Montgomery to begin their own boycott of the buses. He said the two federal judges, Johnson and Rives, were responsible for overthrowing segregation. He stated that "the real white people of Alabama" should never forget the names of the judges. "Nothing they can ever do would rectify this great wrong they have done to the good people of this state. Already more hate has been generated on this day than any day since the days of the carpetbag legislature.

"We are dedicated to the preservation of segregation by peaceful means. This we are striving to do. One way to accomplish this is for the whites to refrain from riding the buses. I can't help but add that federal judges that crack the door on any integration question will, when faced with other integration questions, open the door further. Have no fear, the right and the white will win."

On a Sunday morning in December 1956, not long after the ruling was carried out, Judge Johnson, his wife, Ruth, and their adopted son, Johnny, entered the large sanctuary of the all-white First Baptist Church. As they moved onto a pew and sat, while the organ played its heavy inspirational melody, people sitting at the opposite end of the smoothly carved bench rose and moved to another row. Even when the church became crowded, no one would sit in the same row—or even near—the Johnsons.

Although Ruth and Johnny decided that they had had enough, and that they would attend another church rather than put up with the un-Christianlike behavior of the First Baptist congregation, Judge Johnson stubbornly kept attending every Sunday. "They may do their best to embarrass me, but as far as I'm concerned, they only embarrass themselves. They may treat me badly, but they will not take my religion from me."

He told close friends, "It's hard for them to ostracize a man who loves fishing."

Hurt perhaps worse than Johnson was Judge Rives, whose son had died of a terminal illness. The boy had told his father about learning to love all people, no matter what the color of their skin. The father, who had adored his son, thought long and hard about what the young man had told him. It was a lesson in life seldom played out in the South that the older man knew and loved. Shortly after the bus boycott decision, Rives visited his son's grave in Montgomery and found that it had been desecrated by vandals. He was heartbroken.

One publication wrote that Rives, a son of the Old South, had "forfeited the right to be buried in Southern soil."

Three days after the first bus ride, Bayard Rustin, the famed black Socialist, flew into Alabama at King's invitation. He arrived at the Birmingham airport on Sunday, December 23, and was driven south to Montgomery to meet with King at the parsonage where, only a few hours earlier, a shotgun blast had broken front windows. King recognized Rustin's power among the upper-crust of worldwide black politics. Rustin would arrange a New York fundraiser; several important speaking engagements; a trip to India, where King would meet with followers of his hero, Gandhi; and a meeting with A. Philip Randolph to solidify relationships between King and Roy Wilkins.

On the day before Christmas, as a fifteen-year-old black girl stepped off a bus, two cars stopped nearby and five or six white men jumped out and beat her. The girl, who was identified as Ollie Mae Collins, told investigating officers D. W. Mixon and F. B. Day that she'd dropped to her knees when the beating started. A white man riding the bus said he'd seen the girl on her knees on the pavement with her arms raised, trying to protect herself. No arrests were made.

A week after the first integrated bus ride, twenty-two-year-old Rosa Jordan was riding a bus at night when an unidentified white man boarded the bus wielding a twenty-two-caliber pistol and fired it. A bullet passed through Jordan's left leg and lodged in her right leg. Ironically, she had been sitting toward the back of the bus. She was carried to Oak Street General Hospital. The bus driver, W. H. Fullilove, said he'd been unaware of the problem until other passengers began shouting, "Stop the bus! A woman's been shot!" After Jordan was hospitalized, the bus continued its regular run. A bullet struck the front of the bus. No one was injured. However, white passengers huddled on the floor while Fullilove drove to police headquarters downtown. No one was arrested for either shooting.

When violence persisted, nighttime bus service was halted by city officials.

On Christmas night in Birmingham, about eighty miles north of Montgomery, the home of black minister Fred Shuttlesworth was bombed. His wife and children suffered minor injuries. To Shuttlesworth, who had preached in churches throughout rural Alabama—Selma, Tuscaloosa, and Jasper—and who now was pastor at Birmingham's Bethel Baptist Church, the bombing was a sign from God for him to step out and lead. He went directly to his people and asked that they fall in step behind him in a boycott of buses that was very similar to the one that had taken place during the previous year in Montgomery. When asked by another black preacher to cancel his organizational meeting because God had sent him his own vision, Shuttlesworth asked, "When did the Lord start sending my messages through you? The Lord has told me to call it on." And that was the beginning of the Alabama Christian Movement for Human Rights. Shuttlesworth was made president, and he stood strongly against the likes of Police Commissioner Eugene "Bull" Connor and Birmingham's white establishment.

In mid-January 1957, within twelve hours after a city bus had been ambushed and fired on by an unknown assailant, a corner of Montgomery's Bell Street Baptist Church was blown away by a blast of dynamite, causing the choir loft behind the pulpit to collapse. On the same night, bombs ripped holes in walls of the Hutchinson Street Baptist Church and the Mount Olive Baptist Church. Other bombs heavily damaged both the First Baptist Church on Ripley Street and the parsonage where Reverend Abernathy and his family lived. And, once again, the home of Reverend Graetz was hit by dynamite; the front door was blown in and front walls were damaged. No one was injured in the bombing.

Governor Folsom offered a two-thousand-dollar reward for the capture and conviction of the bombers.

Grover Hall, of the *Advertiser*, struck with a featured editorial, asking, "Shall Montgomery Surrender?" In the editorial, Hall described the dramatic events from the point of view of Montgomery's white establishment, which, said Hall, was quaking in its boots over the prospect of more violence, even in the black sections of the town.

Hall asked rhetorically, "Is the night air of this genteel old city, the capital of a state and once the capital of a nation, to reverberate with dynamite explosions? Is Montgomery to be a city in which dynamite sticks are tossed onto lawns like the morning paper? Is Montgomery to be a city in which bullets fly between sundown and sunup? Is Montgomery to be a city in which a handful of terrorists overawe the police power of city, county and state—squeezing a trigger and abolishing a bus fleet? Are the powers of government of the City of Montgomery to be surrendered to outlaws?"

When a few ruffians run rampant through the streets, throwing dynamite at dwellings and onto the front stoops of churches, the city is not safe, the editorialist told his audience. He added that, unless the powers that controlled law enforcement and guarded the legal institutions met the challenge of a few violent people, the city could become "a badlands, or at worst, a bloody cockpit."

Rather than make excuses for such violence, Hall wrote, "The soundest preventive action is a stern response to this challenge—right now."

For the moment, he stated, the violence was manageable. However, if the city fathers allowed the outlaws to continue their violence, that violence would grow until it became unmanageable.

"The issue now has passed beyond segregation," he wrote. "The issue now *is whether it is safe to live in Montgomery, Alabama.* Those buses should run with a police protection so obvious and so determined that outlaws will desist or be run down."

If not stopped immediately, he said, the outlaws would become more bold and more numerous.

"We are already paying a grievous toll. The story of Thursday's dynamiting is already broadcast all over the world, blackening this city's name. Such events firm the hand of the South's enemies in Congress. Those who are at this moment seeking enactment of unbearable civil rights legislation welcome such events, for they serve their cause."

In a meeting at the headquarters of the Alabama League of Municipalities in Montgomery in early 1957, mayors of the state's twenty-five largest cities pledged to continue to enforce segregation laws. The executive director of the league, Ed Reid, stated, "We thought it would be a good idea to get the mayors together so they could exchange experiences on segregation problems and would benefit one another. We want the mayors to know where to turn when they need help or advice. They can help each other out when the occasion arises if they know what's going on in other cities."

The mayors of Montgomery, Birmingham, Tuscaloosa, Gadsden, Anniston, and nineteen other cities discussed legal action pending in their cities against segregation laws and talked about potential federal suits. They also discussed possible integration trouble in city recreational areas and schools. However, most of their discussion centered around issues of their buses.

A group of white businessmen met in Montgomery in late January 1957 and outlined plans to start what they called the Rebel Club, a private organization that would purchase buses and allow only members to ride the transportation. In essence, it would be an all-white bus company.

Two city attorneys and a member of the state legislature met with U.S. District Judge Johnson to ask if such a plan would be allowed under Johnson and Rives's ruling that had been upheld by the Supreme Court. After the meeting, neither the attorneys nor the legislator nor Johnson would comment.

By late February, however, the same three federal judges who had heard the *Browder* case listened to the city's request for instructions on the matter. In an interview after arguments, Judge Rives allowed as how he and Johnson "personally deemed the bus line as proposed public and not private, and that it would have to comply with the federal injunction now banning enforcement of racial segregation."

It was their personal opinion, they said, that the city could grant a franchise to the all-white company or club, but that it would be required to see that "the holder of such franchise does not discriminate between white and colored passengers."

Judge Lynne declined to express a personal opinion.

The judges refused to give an advisory ruling, stating that federal courts have no jurisdiction over "abstract, hypothetical, or contingent questions."

Since the first bombing of churches and houses, detective Jack Shows had been on the trail of the culprits. He not only snooped through the white neighborhoods, including the service station on Norman Bridge Road where a group of known white ruffians and Klansmen had gathered periodically for more than a year, but he had also visited with inmates in Kilby Prison, on the northeast edge of Montgomery. Shows knew these convicts personally. He had put many of them behind bars through his diligent investigative work. A member of the police force since he'd returned home from World War II, Shows knew the underbelly of the city's criminal world. It was not long before he began putting together the pieces that he presented to Circuit Solicitor Thetford, who then took his findings to the grand jury.

Indicted were Sonny Kyle Livingston, Jr., and Raymond C. Britt, Jr., on charges of bombing unoccupied buildings. Several days later the grand jury brought indictments against Henry Alexander and James D. York for the dynamiting of occupied residences. Conviction of the latter offense would be punishable by death. Conviction of the former, by ten years' imprisonment.

Britt was indicted for bombing the First Baptist Church on the morning of January 10 and the People's Cab Company on January 27. Britt and Livingston were indicted together for the bombing of the Hutchinson Street Baptist Church, which had also occurred on January 10.

Both Alexander and York were charged with dynamiting the occupied home of Reverend Abernathy. Alexander was also charged with dynamiting a taxi stand and shooting at the driver of a racially integrated city bus.

City prosecutor D. Eugene Loe said that if the grand jury did not indict the other three men arrested in the bombing incidents, he would drop their cases. The men were not indicted. Loe dropped the pending cases.

The day after the last two defendants were arrested and released on bond, a curfew of city buses was lifted by the city commission, who had halted nighttime bus service after the violence escalated. Two weeks later, Montgomery City Lines superintendent Bagley praised city police for protecting the nighttime bus runs. "I would like to pass along to you the thanks of our bus drivers and myself for the splendid protection that you and your police officers have rendered during the past two weeks while trailing our late-run buses. Most all of the drivers have commented on the good remarks made by the passengers toward the police department in making it safe and possible for them to use the bus transportation which they are dependent upon."

For a while, it looked as though segregation would finally be ended quietly and without the dramatic flare of sudden violence. Black people and white people boarded the buses, paid their fares, and rode without incident.

On the night of January 22, twenty-five-year-old Willie Edwards, Jr., was driving a black truck for the supermarket chain Winn-Dixie when he was pulled over by a carload of four white men, who were later identified to city detectives as Ku Klux Klan members. One of these was Raymond C. Britt, Jr., who had been arrested with Sonny Kyle Livingston, Jr., for the bombing of the First Baptist Church. Later, Britt identified the others in the car as Livingston, Henry Alexander, and James York.

Britt stated that, when they'd pulled Edwards from the truck, accusing him of "being smart" with a white woman, he was "crying and sobbing" while the men slapped and beat him.

According to Britt, the four men had taken Edwards to the Tyler-Goodwin Bridge, across the Alabama River in rural north Montgomery, and told him to jump into the water.

Although no arrests were made at the time, the case was reopened nine years later. On February 21, 1976, Livingston, Alexander, and York were arrested and charged in the death of Edwards. Jack Shows, by then an investigator in the office of Attorney General Bill Baxley, said that Livingston had always denied being with the group, but that Britt, who was dying of cancer, told his wife everything that happened. Less than two months after Livingston, Alexander, and York were charged, Circuit Judge Frank Embry quashed the indictments because they failed to show how Edwards died.

In February 1957, the Alabama Court of Appeals upheld the city court's conviction of Rosa Parks for violating the city bus segregation ordinance. Judge Robert B. Harwood wrote that, since the defense attorneys failed to spell out any errors, it became mandatory for the court to uphold the conviction. "Where no errors are assigned in appeals from convictions for violations of municipal ordinances, the judgment appealed from must be affirmed," the judge wrote.

In March 1957, after white officials heard that the MIA was preparing to shift its focus from integrating buses to the city parks, the city commission passed an ordinance outlawing race mixing in all kinds of recreational contests, from baseball to billiards. The ordinance was an attempt to circumvent the U.S. Supreme Court ruling that declared that segregation of public playgrounds was illegal. In November 1955 the Court had ordered the city of Baltimore and the state of Maryland to open their public parks to blacks. It also ordered Atlanta to allow blacks to play on the Bobby Jones Golf Course.

In Montgomery, the city commission passed a law stating, "It shall be unlawful for white and colored persons to play together . . . in any game of cards, dice, dominoes, checkers, pool, billiards, softball, basketball, baseball, football, golf, track, and at swimming pools . . . or in any athletic contest or contests." When violations occurred, the commission simply closed the parks: when black parents took their children to play in Oak Park, the Montgomery Parks and Recreation Board, following orders of the city commission, closed the park and all other public parks in Montgomery.

The most immediate effect of the new law was the cancellation of a pending professional baseball game between the American League's all-white Birmingham Barons and the Kansas City Athletics, which had some black players.

Ernest O'Connor, the president of the Class D Montgomery Rebels of the Alabama-Florida League, had scheduled the exhibition game, but said that he was canceling it in light of the new law. He said he would make no more attempts to bring major-league teams to Montgomery. "The law is the city council's business and none of mine, but I think there's too much ado about these things," he said.

Two of the defendants charged with bombing Abernathy's church, Sonny Kyle Livingston, Jr., and Raymond C. Britt, Jr., were tried in Montgomery Circuit Court by an all-male, all-white jury. Evidence showing that the two defendants had thrown the bombs was presented, as was testimony from city detectives.

After deliberating for one hour and thirty-five minutes, the jury returned a verdict. Peter B. Mastin, III, the foreman, handed the verdict to Judge Eugene Carter, who asked, "How do you find?"

Mastin replied, "We the jury find the defendants not guilty."

Throughout the packed courtroom, men whooped Rebel yells and women cried and applauded.

Livingston told the press, "The Lord was on our side."

Although the black citizens of Montgomery felt the injustice, King spoke once again in a quiet voice and calmed what might easily have been a riot mob. Once again, he told them to find room in their hearts to forgive. Once again, they muttered, "Amen!"

Nearly fifty years later, former detective Jack Shows said that both defendants could have gotten on the stand and testified that they'd thrown the dynamite "and the white men on that jury would have still set them free."

Dr. Martin Luther King, Jr., was hailed throughout the nation as a great leader. He spoke to overflowing crowds from Miami to New York, and from Seattle to Washington, D.C. He traveled to India, Europe, and South America. He was welcomed in capitals throughout the world, became the guest of royalty, and had an audience with the pope.

Less than a decade after the birth of the civil rights movement in Montgomery, King was awarded the Nobel Peace Prize. In his acceptance speech, he spoke of the long and tortuous road between Montgomery, Alabama, and Oslo, Norway. He said he considered the award "profound recognition that nonviolence is the answer to the crucial political and moral questions of our time—the need for man to overcome oppression and violence without resorting to violence and oppression." He spoke of his "abiding faith" in his country and in the future of all mankind. "I refuse to accept the idea that man is mere flotsam and jetsam in the river of life which surrounds him. I refuse to accept the view that mankind is so tragically bound to the starless midnight of racism and war that the bright daylight of peace and brotherhood can never become a reality. I believe that even amid today's mortar bursts and whining bullets, there is still hope for a brighter tomorrow."

In the days that followed the first wave of violent reaction to
the Supreme Court's ruling, little by little, hardly noticed by
midsummer of 1957, more and more blacks stepped aboard the
buses, paid their fares, and sat in the front seats. Fewer and
fewer whites rode the buses, but those who did sat quietly near
the majority of black riders. There were few incidents of
violence.

FIFTY YEARS LATER

On a bright, crisp autumn morning in 2004 in Montgomery,
Johnnie Rebecca Carr, nearing her ninety-fourth birthday, is
dressed for an outing. Not unlike her friend Rosa Parks, her
small build, sweet-sounding voice, and slight but square shoulders do not illustrate the strength with which she has fought
for the rights of her people for more than half a century.

Born Johnnie Rebecca Daniels in rural east Montgomery,
Carr never actually thought about fighting for civil rights until
she was nearly grown. Her first role as an activist came several
months after she turned twenty, when she read in the *Advertiser* that nine young blacks, who were called the Scottsboro
Boys, had been arrested in the small northeastern Alabama
town of Scottsboro. Based on flimsy evidence, the Scottsboro
Boys had been charged with raping two white women on a
train. After a hasty trial, they were found guilty by an all-white
jury and sentenced to death. Johnnie Rebecca Daniels helped
raise money for a defense fund to save the Scottsboro Boys.
Eventually, in the 1970s, their sentences were commuted, and
they were pardoned.

Daniels's first experience as an activist left her wanting to
keep up the work. She became an active member of the NAACP,

working as a part-time secretary and a Youth Council adviser, and she fought battles with city hall.

On this morning in November, Carr, resplendent in a royal blue suit, sassy matching beret, and bright red blouse, rises to face the One Montgomery Breakfast Club to tell the group about the bus boycott and the birth of the civil rights movement that she witnessed fifty years ago.

As president of the MIA since 1967, Carr still sees a need for the organization that has had only five presidents—Martin Luther King, Jr.; Ralph David Abernathy; S. S. Seay; Jesse Douglas, the Methodist minister of the First CME Church; and now, Carr. "I spend much of my time educating people about what happened back in the 1950s," she says. "Unless we tell them, the young people won't know about the struggles and the hardships we went through to get what we have today. We've come a long, long way, but we've also got a lot to do to keep the dream alive."

Standing behind the lectern, Carr tells about the rule of Jim Crow. She recalls a time when she and her son, Arlam Carr, Jr., were riding down Court Street together in a car. He looked across the expansive lawn at the handsome red-brick facade of Sidney Lanier High School. "Mama, that's such a pretty school," he told her. "One day I'll be a student there." She remembers shaking her head and saying, "Son, that's not possible. That's a white school."

"It wasn't that we were stupid and ignorant and didn't care," Carr tells her audience, a biracial group that was formed in the early 1980s after several incidents in which white police officers and black citizens sparked racial unrest. As a result, these leaders in the community decided to come together once a month to discuss their problems. "We were taught to obey the laws, and the laws back then were unfair to our race. So we swallowed, took our medicine, and went on about our business."

She speaks in a soft voice. "As I have said over and over, the Lord brought us Martin Luther King, Jr., to lead us. And he brought us the idea to combat evil through love, nonviolence, without retaliation. It was hard, but we did it. It's almost impossible to do it for 381 days, but we did.

"And after we got on the buses, we thought about other places: homes, jobs, schools."

When it came time to integrate the public school system in accordance with the Supreme Court ruling of *Brown v. Board of Education* that had been issued more than a year before the bus boycott had started, the NAACP and the MIA looked for a litigant who would sue to force integration. Carr told Fred Gray, "Suppose you use our child?" Gray subsequently filed *Carr v. Montgomery County Board of Education*. After a hearing, U.S. district judge Frank Johnson ruled that the defendants illegally operated a dual school system based on race. He ordered the system integrated. Because the judge ruled that only tenth, eleventh, and twelfth grades be integrated that year, young Carr, who was in the ninth grade, could not attend Sidney Lanier High School right away. However, the following year he got his wish. After graduating, he attended the University of Texas at El Paso, studied business, and later moved back to Montgomery, where he became a director-producer at WSFA-TV, the city's NBC affiliate.

Nowadays, Johnnie Rebecca Carr works as hard as ever to right what she sees as wrongs in her world. She exudes a quiet strength that she once saw in her mentor, E. D. Nixon. As president of the MIA, she spreads the word, speaking to groups gathered at the Rosa Parks Library & Museum at Troy State University at Montgomery, at the Southern Poverty Law Center, across the street from the Civil Rights Memorial, and at schools across central Alabama. Recently when a tour bus pulled up in front of her small framed house on Hall Street, she climbed aboard and told her story to the tourists from the Midwest. In 1997 she was invited to Berlin, Germany, with Reverend Robert Graetz. Together they served as the representatives of civil rights in America at the worldwide symposium.

"It was through the NAACP that we first came together to express our wants and our needs. And, of course, the NAACP came out of the black church, formed in the beginning to eliminate lynchings. That was the first organization that gave us strength as an entire group of people. And now the MIA continues to work to make Montgomery a better place. We've done a lot, but there's still much to be accomplished."

As she speaks of "God's plan to roll away the rock of injustice," the people of the One Montgomery Breakfast Club nod in agreement. As they stand and applaud, eleven floors below a city bus containing a black driver and a half dozen black riders—all of whom are sitting near the front—passes on I-85, named Martin Luther King Expressway by the Alabama Legislature. Next to the expressway stands an oversized billboard that announces, in big black letters, "I Am the Dream." Next to the words is the image of Martin Luther King, Jr., watching the people passing by.

For the people on the bus, the dream has become a reality. The atmosphere on the Montgomery public buses in the twenty-first century is calm. City buses today are sleek, modern, and polished to a spotless shine. The drivers, most of whom are black, are respectful of their riders. There are only a few white riders on buses today, but when they board they are greeted gracefully. As it had been fifty years ago, most riders are black women, and many of them work as domestic servants. They board the front of the bus and pay their fare with prepurchased cards. None of the riders remembers the tragic death of Thomas Edward Brooks.

"There is no feeling of tension on the buses these days," says Louella James, who has ridden the integrated buses for years. "For a while, there were few routes around the city. But today buses get us where we're going without any problems." Some of the smaller buses, which are not much larger than big SUV-style vans, deliver and pick up riders at prearranged locations. This Rides on Demand program is part of a wholly public transportation system that is operated by a division of the city's government.

James smiles and nods, greeting the driver, who asks about her children. She sits behind him and chats with a friend. In the summertime the buses are air-conditioned; in the winter they are heated. There is a fond remembrance of Rosa Parks and her heroic action in the past, but none of these women knew her as adults. One remembers seeing her from a distance when she was a teenager. "But we know who she is," one said. "We know what she stood for."

Acknowledgments

D<small>URING THE RESEARCH</small> and writing of *The Thunder of Angels* many people offered worthy ideas, suggestions, and facts. The authors would like to thank all of those who gave their timely and weighty advice.

Donnie Williams wishes to especially thank his brother Doug Williams for his valued assistance and encouragement throughout this long journey.

We could not have written this book without the help of numerous librarians and archivists, both professional and amateur. We appreciate the support of Dr. Ed Bridges, director of the Alabama Department of Archives and History, and the help of his generous and gracious staff, particularly Ricki Brunner, Norwood Kerr, and Ken Tilley.

Through the years, Wayne Greenhaw has rubbed shoulders and sought advice from a large number of journalists and historians. Not least among these have been Howell Raines, Diane McWhorter, Ray Jenkins, Jack Nelson, Joe Azbell, Tom Johnson, Bob Ingram, Willy Leventhal, Frank Sikora, Jack Bass, Tom Gardner, Mills Thornton, III, and William Bradford Huie.

Without Huie's long-term friendship and mentoring, Greenhaw would have never begun his journalistic book-writing career.

Both authors have been given much help by those whose courageous lives made *The Thunder* sound: Inez Jesse Baskin, E. D. Nixon, Rosa Parks, Dr. Martin Luther King, Jr., Fred Gray, Johnnie Rebecca Carr, Dr. J. E. Pierce, Robert Graetz, Clifford Durr, Virginia Durr, and Judge Frank M. Johnson, Jr.

As the book was being written, the authors felt twin spirits watching over them each step of the way. A marvelous British woman with a wry sense of truth and beauty, Cecil Roberts married into one of Birmingham's elite families, then guided journalists from afar through the wilderness of 1950s Alabama, setting a tone for civil rights reporting that spanned the continents. And Earl Pippin, a child of rural Pike County who was trained in the institutions of higher learning in Great Britain, and who developed a keen sense of intellectual insight on the streets of Montgomery as a lineman for the telephone company and as a labor union organizer, watched us every step of the way. The friendship and guidance of these two people are greatly missed.

As though by divine providence, a worker in the Montgomery Sheriff's Department found a box filled with photographs in the dark corner of a storage room of the old Montgomery County Courthouse on Washington Street. Back in the early 1960s the mug shots of the boycott defendants were stored away in what was then the new courthouse, and no one was particularly interested in the images of these people who were arrested for quietly fighting for their civil rights. The authors want to thank Reese McKinney, Jr., Judge of Probate; the Montgomery County Archives; and Lyn Frazer, Montgomery County archivist, for the use of these photographs.

Finally, our agent, Barbara Ellis, of Scribes Literary Agency, and our editors, Yuval Taylor and Lisa Reardon, of Lawrence Hill Books, helped enormously in shaping the final manuscript, and we appreciate their efforts very much.

Notes and Sources

NOTES

The authors were furnished numerous interviews with Edgar Daniel Nixon by various journalists, historians, and scholars. Bill Edwards interviewed Nixon in the 1970s. Tom Gardner and his then-wife, Jennifer Johnson, interviewed him extensively during July 1985. Mike Williams also interviewed Nixon in the mid-1980s. Both Gardner and Williams were reporters for the *Montgomery Advertiser* at the time of their interviews. Other interviews with Nixon, conducted by television journalist Norman Lumpkin, were made available to the authors by the Alabama Center for Higher Education, Statewide Oral History Project, Tuskegee Institute. Although we did not use direct quotes from any of these, they were valuable in that they allowed the authors to compare their own notes with others in order to ensure accuracy of dates, facts, and other items. Wayne Greenhaw interviewed Nixon many times from the spring of 1967 until shortly before Nixon's death on February 25, 1987.

Papers and letters of E. D. Nixon were made available by the Levi Watkins Library at Alabama State University.

Jack D. Shows, former Montgomery city detective and state attorney general's investigator, not only agreed to be interviewed, but also shared his personal papers and scrapbook.

The authors were given the opportunity to study the videotape of an all-day symposium on the Montgomery bus boycott on February 7, 1986, the thirteenth anniversary of the boycott. Not only did scholars present papers, but participants in the boycott, including E. D. Nixon, Fred Gray, Joe Azbell, Johnnie Rebecca Carr, and others, spoke to a group that assembled at the Alabama Department of Archives and History during the event, which was sponsored by the Alabama Humanities Foundation.

Finally, Johnnie Rebecca Carr gave freely of her time and energy. She is a remarkable ninety-four-year-old woman with an outstanding memory.

SOURCES

Chapter One

Author Interviews: Johnnie Rebecca Carr, Jane Ann Thompson Dubois, Charles Gray, Mattie Simpkins Johnson, Lucy Ragsdale Martin, Edgar Daniel Nixon.

Greenhaw, Wayne. *Montgomery: The River City*. Montgomery, Alabama: River City Publishing, 2003.

Leventhal, Willy S., editor; Randall Williams, general editor. *The Children Coming On . . . A Retrospective of the Montgomery Bus Boycott*. Montgomery: Black Belt Press, 1998.

Chapter Two

Author Interviews: Ray Jenkins, E. D. Nixon, Rosa Parks, James E. Pierce, Earl Pippin.

Baldwin, Lewis W., and Aprille V. Woodson. *Freedom Is Never Free: A Biographical Portrait of E. D. Nixon, Sr.* Nashville, Tennessee: Office of Minority Affairs, Tennessee State University, 1992.

Durr, Virginia Foster, and Hollinger F. Barnard, editor. *Outside the Magic Circle: The Autobiography of Virginia Foster Durr.* Tuscaloosa: University of Alabama Press, 1985.

Gray, Fred D. *Bus Ride to Freedom: The Life and Works of Fred Gray.* Montgomery: Black Belt Press, 1995.

Leventhal, Willy S., editor; Randall Williams,. *The Children Coming On . . . A Retrospective of the Montgomery Bus Boycott.* Montgomery: Black Belt Press, 1998.

Montgomery Advertiser. June 4, 1944; December 5, 1985.

Robinson, Jo Ann Gibson. *The Montgomery Bus Boycott and the Women Who Started It: The Memoir of Jo Ann Gibson Robinson.* Knoxville: University of Tennessee Press, 1987.

Terkel, Studs. *Hard Times.* New York: Antheneum Press, 2000.

Thornton, J. Mills, III. *Dividing Lines: Municipal Politics and the Struggle for Civil Rights in Montgomery, Birmingham, and Selma.* Tuscaloosa: University of Alabama Press, 2002.

Chapter Three

Author Interviews: Betty Azbell, Joe Azbell, E. D. Nixon.

Gray, Fred D. *Bus Ride to Freedom: The Life and Works of Fred Gray.* Montgomery: Black Belt Press, 1995.

Montgomery Advertiser. December 2, 5, 6, 1955.

Robinson, Jo Ann Gibson. *The Montgomery Bus Boycott and the Women Who Started It: The Memoir of Jo Ann Gibson Robinson.* Knoxville: University of Tennessee Press, 1987.

Chapter Four

Author Interviews: Joe Azbell, Michelle Lacy Grant, E. D. Nixon, Roscoe Williams.

Abernathy, Ralph David. *And the Walls Came Tumbling Down: An Autobiography.* New York: Harper & Row, 1989.

King, Coretta Scott. *My Life with Martin Luther King, Jr.* New York: Holt, Rinehart and Winston, 1969.

King, Martin Luther, Jr. *Stride Toward Freedom: A Leader of His People Tells the Montgomery Story.* New York: Harper & Brothers, 1958.

Leventhal, Willy S., editor; Randall Williams, general editor. *The Children Coming On . . . A Retrospective of the Montgomery Bus Boycott.* Montgomery: Black Belt Press, 1998.

Montgomery Advertiser, December 9, 1955; January 19, 1956.

Oates, Stephen B. *Let the Trumpet Sound: The Life of Martin Luther King, Jr.* New York: Harper & Row, 1982.

Chapter Five

Author Interviews: Joe Azbell, Leonard Toliver Green, Terry Leon Hall, Tommy Joe Long, E. D. Nixon, Jack Shows, Roscoe Williams.

Alabama Journal. January 28, 1956.

Alabama Magazine. February 1956.

King, Coretta Scott. *My Life with Martin Luther King, Jr.* New York: Holt, Rinehart and Winston, 1969.

Mobile Register. January 21, 1956.

Montgomery Advertiser, December 5, 1955; February 1, 1956.

Chapter Six

Commercial Appeal. Memphis, January 12, 1956.

Graetz, Robert S. *A White Preacher's Story: The Montgomery Bus Boycott.* Montgomery: Black Belt Press, 1998.

Jet, December 1955.

Montgomery Advertiser. January 11, 12, 14, 1956.

Chapter Seven

Author Interviews: Joe Azbell, Clifford Durr, Virginia Durr, Jack Shows.

Alabama Journal. February 8, 1956.

Gray, Fred D. *Bus Ride to Freedom: The Life and Works of Fred Gray.* Montgomery: Black Belt Press, 1995.

Montgomery Advertiser. February 2, 5, 8, 9, 17, 22, 1956.

Chapter Eight

Branch, Taylor. *Parting the Waters: America in the King Years, 1954–63.* New York: Simon & Schuster, 1986.

Jet, April 1956.

Mobile Register. April 8, 1956.

Montgomery Advertiser. February 23, March 20, March 27, April 8, April 10, April 11, April 12, 1956.

New York Times. March 24, 1956.

Chapter Nine

Author Interviews: Frank M. Johnson, Jr., E. D. Nixon.

Alabama Journal. May 9, 1956.

Browder v. Gayle. Official transcript. Montgomery Circuit Court, April 1956.

Bass, Jack. *Taming the Storm: The Life and Times of Judge Frank M. Johnson, Jr., and the South's Fight over Civil Rights.* New York: Doubleday, 1993.

Gray, Fred D. *Bus Ride to Freedom: The Life and Works of Fred Gray.* Montgomery: Black Belt Press, 1995.

Montgomery Advertiser. February 2, April 3, May 4, May 12, June 20, 1956; March 18, 1957.

Sikora, Frank. *The Judge: The Life & Opinions of Alabama's Frank M. Johnson, Jr.* Montgomery: Black Belt Press, 1992.

Chapter Ten

Author Interviews: L. T. Green, Terry Leon Hall, E. D. Nixon.

Alabama Journal. June 1, August 25, 1956.

Graetz, Robert S. *A White Preacher's Story: The Montgomery Bus Boycott.* Montgomery: Black Belt Press, 1998.

Gray, Fred D. *Bus Ride to Freedom: The Life and Works of Fred Gray.* Montgomery: Black Belt Press, 1995.

Montgomery Advertiser. May 25, July 9, August 8, August 9, August 23, August 26, 1956.

New York Post. June 15, 1956.

New York Times. June 19, 1956.

U.S. News & World Report. August 25, 1956.

Chapter Eleven

Author Interviews: Joe Azbell, E. D. Nixon.

Alabama Journal, November 14, December 3, December 20, 1956.

Associated Press, November 21, 1956.

Baskin, Inez Jesse. Personal notes.

Gray, Fred D. *Bus Ride to Freedom: The Life and Works of Fred Gray.* Montgomery: Black Belt Press, 1995.

Mobile Press. United Press International: November 13, 1956; Associated Press: November 14, 1956; Associated Press, November 20, 1956.

Mobile Register, November 15, 1956.

Montgomery Advertiser. October 27, October 28, November 14, November 15, November 16, November 20, November 21, November 22, November 23, November 24, November 25, December 4, December 21, December 22, 1956.

United Press International, November 19, 1956.

Epilogue

Author Interviews: Johnnie Rebecca Carr, Jack Shows.

Branch, Taylor. *Parting the Waters: America in the King Years, 1954–63.* New York: Simon & Schuster, 1988.

Brinkley, Douglas. *Rosa Parks.* New York: Viking Penquin, 2000.

Flynt, Wayne. *Alabama: The History of a Deep South State.* Tuscaloosa: University of Alabama Press, 1994.

McWhorter, Diane. *Carry Me Home: Birmingham, Alabama: The Climactic Battle of the Civil Rights Revolution.* New York: Simon & Schuster, 2001.

Mobile Register. November 19, 1956.

Montgomery Advertiser. December 24, December 27, January 11, January 14, January 17, January 21, January 24, January 25, 1957.

New York Times. April 14, 1957.

Bibliography

Abernathy, Ralph David. *And the Walls Came Tumbling Down: An Autobiography*. New York: Harper & Row, 1989.

Adams, Frank, with Myles Horton. *Unearthing Seeds of Fire: The Idea of Highlander*. Winston-Salem, North Carolina: Blair, 1975.

Adams, Henry H. *Harry Hopkins: A Biography*. New York: G. P. Putnam's Sons, 1977.

Anderson, Jervis. *Bayard Rustin: Troubles I've Seen*. New York: HarperCollins, 1997.

Anderson, Jervis. *A. Philip Randolph: A Biographical Portrait*. New York: Berkeley, 1986.

Ashmore, Harry S. *Hearts and Minds: The Anatomy of Racism from Roosevelt to Reagan*. New York: McGraw Hill, 1982.

Atkins, Leah Rawls, Wayne Flynt, William Warren Rogers, and Robert David Ward. *Alabama: The History of a Deep South State*. Tuscaloosa: University of Alabama Press, 1994.

Baldwin, Lewis V. and Aprille V. Woodson. *Freedom Is Never Free: A Biographical Portrait of E. D. Nixon, Sr.* Nashville, Tennessee: Office of Minority Affairs, Tennessee State University, 1992.

Barnard, William D. *Dixiecrats and Democrats: Alabama Politics, 1942–1950*. Tuscaloosa: University of Alabama Press, 1974.

Bartley, Numan V. *The Rise of Massive Resistance: Race and Politics in the South During the 1950s*. Baton Rouge: Louisiana State University, 1969.

Bass, Jack. *Taming the Storm: The Life and Times of Judge Frank M. Johnson, Jr., and the South's Fight over Civil Rights*. New York: Doubleday&Company, 1993.

Bass, Jack. *Unlikely Heroes*. New York: Simon & Schuster, 1981.

Black, Hugo L., and Elizabeth Black. *Mr. Justice and Mrs. Black*. New York: Random House, 1986.

Branch, Taylor. *Parting the Waters: America in the King Years 1954–63*, New York: Simon & Schuster, 1988.

Brinkley, Douglas. *Rosa Parks*. New York: Viking Penquin, 2000.

Carr, Johnnie Rebecca, as told to Randall Williams. *Johnnie: The Life of Johnnie Rebecca Carr*. Montgomery: New South Books, 2000.

Clark, E. Culpepper. *The Schoolhouse Door: Segregation's Last Stand at the University of Alabama*. Tuscaloosa: University of Alabama Press, 1993.

Dorman, Michael. *We Shall Overcome*. New York: Delacorte Press, 1964.

DuBois, W. E. B. *The Souls of Black Folk*. New York: Signet, New 1969.

Durr, Virginia Foster, Hollinger F. Barnard, ed. *Outside the Magic Circle: The Autobiography of Virginia Foster Durr*. Tuscaloosa: University of Alabama Press, 1985.

Durr, Virginia Foster, Patricia Sullivan, ed. *Freedom Writer: Letters from the Civil Rights Years*. New York; London: Routledge, 2003.

Egerton, John. *Speak Now Against the Day: The Generation Before the Civil Rights Movement in the South*. New York: Knopf, 1994.

Evans, Zelia S., ed. *Dexter Avenue Baptist Church: 1877–1977*. Unpublished treatise written for the congregation. Montgomery, 1978.

Forman, James. *The Making of Black Revolutionaries*. New York: Macmillan, 1972.

Flynt, Wayne. *Montgomery: An Illustrated History*. Woodland Hills, CA: Windsor Publications, Inc., 1980.

Gaillard, Frye. *Cradle of Freedom: Alabama and the Movement That Changed America*. Tuscaloosa: University of Alabama Press, 2004.

Garrow, David J. *The FBI and Martin Luther King, Jr.* New York: W. W. Norton, 1981.

Garrow, David J. *Bearing the Cross: Martin Luther King, Jr., and the Southern Christian Leadership Conference*. New York: William Morrow, 1986.

Graetz, Robert S. *A White Preacher's Story: The Montgomery Bus Boycott.* Montgomery: Black Belt Press, 1998.

Grafton, Carl, and Anne Permaloff. *Big Mules and Branchheads: James E. Folsom and Political Power in Alabama.* Athens: University of Georgia Press, 1985.

Gray, Fred D. *Bus Ride to Freedom: The Life and Works of Fred Gray.* Montgomery: Black Belt Press, 1995.

Greenhaw, Wayne. *Montgomery: The River City.* Montgomery, Alabama: River City Publishing, 2003.

Hackney, Sheldon. *Populism to Progressivism in Alabama.* Princeton, NJ: Princeton University Press, 1969.

Hamilton, Virginia Van der Veer. *Alabama.* New York: Norton, 1977.

Hamilton, Virginia Van der Veer. *Lister Hill: Statesman from the South.* Chapel Hill: University of North Carolina Press, 1987.

Hamilton, Virginia Van der Veer. *Hugo Black: The Alabama Years.* Tuscaloosa: University of Alabama Press, 1972.

King, Coretta Scott. *My Life with Martin Luther King, Jr.* New York: Holt, Rinehart and Winston, 1969.

King, Jr., Martin Luther. *Stride Toward Freedom: A Leader of His People Tells the Montgomery Story.* New York: Harper & Brothers, 1958.

King, Jr., Martin Luther. *Strength to Love.* New York: Harper & Row, 1964.

King, Jr., Martin Luther. *Why We Can't Wait.* New York: Harper & Row, 1963.

Krueger, Thomas A. *And Promises to Keep: The Southern Conference for Human Welfare, 1938–1948,* Nashville: Vanderbilt University Press, 1967.

Lash, Joseph P. *Eleanor and Franklin.* New York: W. W. Norton, 1971.

Leventhal, Willy S., ed.; Williams, Randall, general ed. *The Children Coming On . . . A Retrospective of the Montgomery Bus Boycott.* Montgomery: Black Belt Press, 1998.

McWhorter, Diane. *Carry Me Home: Birmingham, Alabama: The Climactic Battle of the Civil Rights Revolution.* New York: Simon & Schuster, 2001.

Oates, Stephen B. *Let the Trumpet Sound: The Life of Martin Luther King, Jr.* New York: Harper & Row, 1982.

Raines, Howell. *My Soul Is Rested.* New York: G. P. Putnam's Sons, 1977.

Reddick, Lawrence D. *Crusader Without Violence: A Biography of Martin Luther King, Jr.* New York: Harper and Brothers, 1959.

Reporting Civil Rights: Part One: American Journalism 1941–1963. New York: Library of America, 2003.

Robinson, Jo Ann Gibson. *The Montgomery Bus Boycott and the Women Who Started It: The Memoir of Jo Ann Gibson Robinson.* Knoxville: University of Tennessee Press, 1987.

Rowan, Carl T. *Go South to Sorrow.* New York: Random House, 1957.

Safire, William, ed. *Lend Me Your Ears: Great Speeches in History.* New York: W. W. Norton, 1992.

Salmond, John A. *A Southern Rebel: The Life and Times of Aubrey Willis Williams, 1890–1965.* Chapel Hill: University of North Carolina Press, 1983.

Salmond, John A. *The Conscience of a Lawyer: Clifford J. Durr and American Civil Liberties, 1899–1975.* Tuscaloosa: University of Alabama Press, 1990.

Sikora, Frank. *The Judge: The Life & Opinions of Alabama's Frank M. Johnson, Jr.* Montgomery: Black Belt Press, 1992.

Sims, George E. *The Little Man's Big Friend: James E. Folsom in Alabama Politics, 1946–1958.* Tuscaloosa: University of Alabama Press, 1985.

Thornton, J. Mills, III; *Dividing Lines: Municipal Politics and the Struggle for Civil Rights in Montgomery, Birmingham, and Selma.* Tuscaloosa: University of Alabama Press, 2002.

Tye, Larry. *Rising from the Rails: Pullman Porters and the Making of the Black Middle Class.* New York: Henry Holt & Company, 2004.

Watters, Pat. *Down to Now: Reflections on the Southern Civil Rights Movement.* New York: Random House, 1971.

Watters, Pat, and Reese Cleghorn. *Climbing Jacob's Ladder.* New York: Harcourt, Brace & World, 1967.

Westin, Alan F., and Barry Mahoney. *The Trial of Martin Luther King.* New York: Crowell, 1974.

Williams, Juan. *Eyes on the Prize: America's Civil Rights Years, 1954–65.* New York: Viking Press, 1987.

Woodward, C. Vann. *Origins of the New South 1877–1913.* Baton Rouge: Louisiana State University Press, 1951.

Woodward, C. Vann. *The Burden of Southern History.* New York: Vintage Books, 1960.

Index